Beginning
Statistics

An Introduction for Social Scientists

Ian Diamond and Julie Jefferies

SAGE Publications
London • Thousand Oaks • New Delhi

First published 2001. Reprinted 2001

SAGE Publications Ltd
6 Bonhill Street
London EC2A 4PU

SAGE Publications Inc
2455 Teller Road
Thousand Oaks, California 91320

SAGE Publications India Pvt Ltd
32, M-Block Market
Greater Kailash – I
New Delhi 110 048

British Library Cataloguing in Publication Data
A catalogue record for this book is available from the British Library

ISBN 0 7619 6061 9
ISBN 0 7619 6062 7 (pbk)

Library of Congress catalog card number 133958

Typeset by Keystroke, Jacaranda Lodge, Wolverhampton.
Printed in Great Britain by The Bath Press, Bath

To
Jane, Tom, Mark, Alexandra, Neil and Callum

CONTENTS

PERMISSIONS

The authors and publisher would also like to thank the following for permission to use copyright material.

The Data Archive/University of Essex for Tables 3.10 and 14.14 and Figure 3.26. Material from the General Household Survey is Crown Copyright, has been made available by the Office for National Statistics through the Data Archive, and has been used by permission; neither the ONS nor the Data Archive bear any responsibility for the analysis or interpretation of the data reported here.

Table 2.2 from *Living in Britain: Results from the 1996 General Household Survey*, Office for National Statistics Crown Copyright 1998.

Table 2.3 and 2.4 and Figures 5.5 and 5.6 from *1991 Census, Key Statistics for Urban and Rural Areas: The South East*, Office for National Statistics © Crown Copyright 1998.

Table 2.5 from 'Children looked After by Local Authorities, Year Ending 31 March 1996'. Crown Copyright is reproduced with the permission of the Controller of Her Majesty's Stationery Office.

Tables 2.7 and 14.1 reproduced with the permission of Butterworth-Heinemann from A. Heath, et al. *Understanding Political Change* (1991).

Table 3.1 reproduced with permission from Longman from David P. Conradt, *The German Polity*, 6th edition (1996).

Tables 3.2–3.9, 3.15, 3.16, 4.9, 4.10, 6.10, 13.1 and 13.5 extracted from 'Human Development Report 1997' UNDP and reproduced with permission from Oxford University Press Inc.

Table 3.17 from 'Employment Outlook, July 1997', OECD 1997 reproduced with permission from OECD Publications, Paris.

Table 3.18 from 'Europe's International Migrants 1994'. Crown Copyright is reproduced with the permission of the Controller of Her Majesty's Stationery Office.

Tables 4.3, 4.11, 10.1 and 10.2 reproduced with permission of Macmillan Ltd from D. Butler and D. Kavanagh, *The British General Election of 1992* (1992).

Table 4.7 from *Family Spending: A Report on the 1996–97 Family Expenditure Survey*, Office for National Statistics © Crown Copyright 1997.

Table 4.8 from 'Children Come First: The Government's Proposals on the Maintenance of Children, Volume 2'. Crown Copyright is reproduced with the permission of the Controller of Her Majesty's Stationery Office.

Table 4.13 from *New Earnings Survey 1997, Part D, Analyses by Occupation*, Office for National Statistics © Crown Copyright 1997.

Tables 5.2, 5.3 and 9.1 reproduced with the permission of The Alan Guttmacher Institute from J. Trussell and C. F. Westoff, Contraceptive practice and trends in coital frequency, Family Planning Perspectives, 1980, 12(5): 246–49.

Table 9.2 is reproduced with permission of Peters, Fraser & Dunlop from *Sexual Behaviour in Britain* by Kaye Wellings et al. (1994).

Table 9.3 adapted with kind permission H.G. Tittmar.

Table 12.4 from CIPFA Charges for Leisure Services Statistics 1997–98 reproduced with permission of CIPFA.

Table 14.15 reproduced with permission of the National Children's Bureau from D. Cliffe and D. Berridge, *Closing Children's Homes – An End to Residential Care* (1991).

Tables A1.1, A1.2 and A1.3 in Appendix 1 reprinted with permission of Addison Wesley Longman Ltd from R. A. Fisher and F. Yates, *Statistical Tables for Biological Agricultural and Medical Research* (1974).

Every effort has been made to trace all copyright holders. If any have been overlooked, or if any additional information can be given, the publishers will be pleased to make the necessary arrangements at the first opportunity.

ACKNOWLEDGEMENTS

The authors would like to thank all past and present members of the Department of Social Statistics, University of Southampton, for any contributions they have made directly and indirectly to the content of this book. In particular we would like to thank Steve Pearson, who has read through some of the final manuscript and Dave Holmes for his useful advice. A big thank you also goes to all the students we have taught, for their many comments, criticisms and suggestions about how to improve the teaching of quantitative methods.

INTRODUCTION

A good grasp of statistics is fundamental to study in any of the social sciences and it is *not* possible to become a social scientist without an understanding of statistics. Even if you think you will never need to calculate any statistics yourself, you will undoubtedly come across statistics in journal articles, books and newspapers and need to know how to interpret them.

The problem is that many people believe that statistics is a subject characterised by mysterious symbols and difficult calculations which they will never be able to understand. They also think it bears little resemblance to their chosen subject. As a result, many students try to avoid statistics as much as possible.

This is a mistake as the good news is that *anyone* can understand the basic ideas of statistics at a level commensurate with being a good social scientist. (Many people even find that they come to enjoy it, though they would never dare to admit such heresy in polite society!)

This book is aimed primarily at students studying the social sciences; those taking social science as a combined subject or those on a specific course in sociology, social policy, social work, politics, population sciences or similar disciplines. It can either accompany a course in quantitative methods or stand alone as a handy reference guide.

The emphasis is on practical presentation and analysis of data, rather than heavy statistics. The book introduces, for example, the right ways to present data, how to describe a set of data using appropriate summary statistics and how to infer what is going on in a population when all you have to go on is a sample. The book uses small datasets for learning purposes, although in real life datasets tend to be much larger and need to be analysed using a computer package. No specific packages are referred to in this book, giving you the freedom to use whichever package suits you best. Only a very basic knowledge of maths is assumed and this can be revised in Appendix 3 beforehand if necessary.

The best learning approach is to work steadily and methodically through the book, making sure that you really understand one section before moving on to the next. Throughout the text, new terms introduced are in **bold print** to help you to learn and revise. The old adage 'practice makes perfect' certainly applies to quantitative methods, so make use of the practice questions at the end of each chapter too.

Always remember that learning quantitative methods is *not* just about doing maths and calculations. It is about understanding concepts. Getting the correct answer to a calculation but not knowing what your answer means is very little use. So try to make sure that you know *why* you are doing a particular calculation and what the result will tell you.

Now, after that brief introduction, let's get down to the real thing!

1

ARE STATISTICS RELEVANT TO REAL LIFE?

Believe it or not, you can *already* think statistically – in fact, it is something you do all the time. If you don't believe this, think how many times you have decided to take a coat with you because you have predicted it will rain; how many times you have commented on the amount that students drink or noted the fact that you tend to do better in coursework than exams (or vice versa). In each case, you have acted on the basis of statistical concepts and have used data that you had stored in the human computer that is your brain. You just didn't realise it!

We all use statistical concepts intuitively in our daily lives. Learning statistics is simply a case of learning how to express yourself more accurately.

Statistics is basically about understanding and knowing how to use **data**. You may have data on any number of topics, from crime rates to reaction times, from prices in a coffee bar to the number of visitors to a beach each day during August.

There are two main kinds of statistics. **Descriptive statistics** are methods used to describe data and their characteristics. For example if you were investigating the number of visitors to a beach in August (nice job if you can get it!), you might draw a graph to see how the number of visitors varied each day, work out how many people visit on an average day and calculate the proportion of visitors who were male/female or children/adults. These would all be descriptive data.

Inferential statistics involves using what we know to make inferences (estimates or predictions) about what we don't know. For example, if we asked 200 people who they were going to vote for, on the day before a local election, we could try to predict which party would win the election. Or if we asked 50 injecting drug users whether they share injecting equipment such as needles with other users, we could try to estimate the proportion of all injecting drug users who share equipment.

We would never be able to say for sure who would definitely win the election or what proportion of injecting drug users share equipment, but we *are* able to predict the *likely* outcome or proportion. Statistics is all about weighing up the chances of something happening or being true.

Statistics *are* relevant to real life because without real life we wouldn't need statistics. If everybody always voted for the same party and all injecting drug users shared equipment, we wouldn't need to predict the outcome of an election or estimate the proportion of drug users sharing equipment because it would be obvious from asking one voter or one injecting drug user. Only in a world of clones would statistics about people be unnecessary! And life would be pretty boring if everybody were exactly the same.

In real life everybody is different and in social science statistics are frequently used to highlight the differences between groups of people or places. For example, we might want to investigate how smoking behaviour varies by socio-economic group or how unemployment varies by local authority. A knowledge of statistical methods is crucial for answering many research questions like these.

Modern society is in fact driven by statistics – think of school league tables, opinion polls or crime figures – and these figures frequently influence our behaviour. Even if you never go on to do research, a good grasp of statistics will help you to understand the figures that you read or hear about in the press and to avoid being misled by people who misuse statistics to their own advantage.

2

DATA AND TABLE MANNERS

DATA

Before starting to do exciting things with data, you need to know a few bits of jargon so that you know what to call things!

Suppose you have done a survey of students in a university Students' Union on a Friday afternoon (our experience is that it is the best place to find students on a Friday!), asking them which area of the town they live in and how much rent they have to pay each week. The two topics that you are interested in finding out about, area and rent, are called the **variables**. Each student that you ask is called a **case** and the responses that you get from each student are known as **observations** (even if you don't physically 'observe' them yourself). Data, then, are simply a collection of observations.

Whatever a set of data (dataset) may refer to, the cases are the individuals in the sample (these may be people, countries, cars and so on), while variables are the characteristics which make the cases different to each other (for example age, opinion about a topic, type of political system).

There are an infinite number of possible variables that we might be interested in and, in fact, variables themselves can be divided into several types.

Continuous variables include things like 'weights of new-born babies', 'distance travelled to work by those in full-time employment', or 'percentage of children living in lone parent families'. Such variables are measured in numbers and an observation may take any value on a continuous scale. For example, distance travelled to work could take a value of zero miles for people working at home, 1.6 miles, 4.8 miles, or any other value up to 100 miles or more for those commuting long distances. Similarly, any variable measured as a percentage can take a value of 0%, 100% or anything in between.

Discrete variables or **Categorical variables** are not measured on a continuous numerical scale. Examples of discrete variables are:

- sex: male/female
- religion: Christian/Buddhist/Hindu/other
- degree subject studied: politics/sociology/social work

and so on. Such variables have no numeric value. We may assign them a number, for example, Politics = 1, Sociology = 2, Social Work = 3 and so on, but the value of the numbers do not actually mean anything. Social Work is not three times greater than politics!

Most variables can be easily classified into continuous or discrete, although there are a few grey areas.

Whenever you collect or use some data, you should write down a clear **code book** to describe your variables. A code book gives information about each variable, such as name and type, along with the units of measurement or categories, as in the following example:

Variable name	Variable type	Units of measurement/codes
Sex	Categorical	1 = male
		2 = female
Weight	Continuous	Kilograms
Attendance	Continuous	Percentage of lectures attended in semester
Political affiliation	Categorical	1 = Conservative
		2 = Labour
		3 = Liberal Democrat
		4 = other
		5 = none

Now you are ready to display the data.

TABLES

Tables are one of the best ways of presenting a set of data.

You may be thinking, 'Anyone can draw a table – don't insult my intelligence!' It is true that anyone can throw some figures and a few lines on to a page, but to produce a *good* table requires a little more thought.

The aim of drawing a table is to transform a set of numbers into a format which is easy to understand.

Look at Table 2.1. What is wrong with this table? A few of the problems are listed as follows. You may be able to find more.

- The title is uninformative: who do the data refer to?
- The variables are not defined, so we do not know, for example, what age '1' refers to. Does it refer to the alcohol consumption of 1-year-olds?!
- We do not know what units the data are measured in: is it number of drinks per week or number of gallons per month or something completely different?
- The layout is not very helpful. For example, the columns of data are not aligned with the column headings, there are no lines (rules) in the table, and the decimal points are not lined up.
- The number of decimal places is not the same throughout the data.
- We are not told where the sample came from or how many people were included.

TABLE 2.1 Alcohol consumption

Age	M	F
1	20.3	9.5000
2	18	7.2
3	15.6	6
4	11.00	3.5

An improved version of the same table might look something like Table 2.2. This is far more informative and the patterns shown in the data are immediately clear. You can see that on average males drink more units each week than females of comparable ages and that younger people in Britain drink more units on average than older people.

TABLE 2.2 Mean weekly alcohol consumption in units[1] by sex and age, Britain, 1996

	Sex	
Age group	Male	Female
16–24	20.3	9.5
	(881)[2]	(969)
25–44	17.6	7.2
	(2628)	(3182)
45–64	15.6	5.9
	(2215)	(2509)
65 and over	11.0	3.5
	(1445)	(1836)

[1] One unit of alcohol is equal to, for example, one measure of spirits or half a pint of beer.
[2] Numbers in brackets refer to number of people on whom the means were based.

Source: Office for National Statistics, 1998a

Some guidelines for tables

Here are some points to remember when drawing tables. This is not an exhaustive list, just some things to bear in mind!

1 Always have a clear title: who/what, when and where do the data refer to? You will usually need a numbering system too, such as Table 1, Table 2 and so on.
2 Make sure that all columns and rows are named properly, for example 'Male' and 'Female', not 'M' and 'F' (although you may understand it, your readers may not).
3 Remember to state the units of measurement used, for example '%', '£000s'.
4 If further explanation is needed to clarify certain points, put notes below the table, as in Table 2.2.
5 Include the source of the data: did you find them in a book or journal, or did you collect them yourself?

6 Take care with layout and presentation: the table should be easy to understand. The use of lines within a table is a matter of preference, but do not put lines around every single value or the table may just look cluttered!
7 For the same type of data, use the same number of decimal points throughout. One or two decimal places should be enough: if you use more you must have a good reason! Line up decimal points vertically.
8 Include relevant totals and subtotals in the table and always check that they add up correctly. If you have been rounding up to two decimal places, for example, the totals may be slightly out, but do not worry too much about this.
9 If you have a lot of data, it may be difficult to include all the data without the table becoming very complicated and difficult to read. You could try joining some categories together (known as collapsing categories), but bear in mind that you will lose some precision in doing this. You should not collapse categories just because there are small numbers in the cells of the tables.

In general, tables must stand alone. This means that somebody should be able to understand a table without having to read the text before or after it. However, you should always refer to a table in the writing.

Percentage tables

Table 2.2 contains a set of means (mean weekly alcohol consumption). Many tables simply consist of the number of people in each category. If this is the case, it may be useful to turn the numbers into percentages, so that two or more groups with a different total number of people can be compared. This is fairly straightforward, but the following example illustrates a hidden pitfall.

Suppose you have been asked by an environmental charity to find out which methods of transport people use to get to work in two different urban areas. You find some data and now want to draw a percentage table.

One way of calculating the percentages is shown in Table 2.3. Here the percentages have been calculated separately for each area. Percentages which add up to 100% vertically like this are known as **column percentages**. From this table, the two areas can be easily compared. In Tunbridge Wells, a much higher proportion of workers travel by train than in Southampton. This is probably because Tunbridge Wells is closer to London and many people commute to the City from there. On the other hand, greater proportions of workers in Southampton travel by bus, car and pedal cycle than in Tunbridge Wells.

Alternatively the percentages could be calculated as in Table 2.4. These are **row percentages** which add up to 100% horizontally. Table 2.4 tells us, for example, that of workers travelling on foot, 33.76% live in Tunbridge Wells and 66.24% live in Southampton. This does not really help us to compare transport use in the two areas. The percentages are actually meaningless

TABLE 2.3 Employees and self-employed residents of Tunbridge Wells and Southampton using different methods of transport to work, 1991 (column %)[1]

Method of transport	Town/city of residence	
	Tunbridge Wells	Southampton
Rail	11.93	2.32
Bus	4.67	12.47
Car	54.96	62.75
Pedal cycle	1.72	4.22
Foot	17.40	10.78
None (work at home)	5.89	3.47
Other	3.43	3.99
Total %	100.00	100.00
(Number)	(2851)	(9027)

[1] Data come from 10% sample of Census returns.

Source: Office for National Statistics, 1998b

because the total number of people from Southampton in the table is much greater than the total number from Tunbridge Wells. Most of the row percentages are higher for Southampton purely for this reason, irrespective of transport use.

TABLE 2.4 Employees and self-employed workers using different forms of transport to work in Tunbridge Wells and Southampton, 1991 (row %)[1]

Method of transport	Town/city of residence		Total % (number)
	Tunbridge Wells	Southampton	
Rail	61.93	38.07	100.00 (549)
Bus	10.56	89.44	100.00 (1259)
Car	21.67	78.33	100.00 (7232)
Pedal cycle	11.40	88.60	100.00 (430)
Foot	33.76	66.24	100.00 (1469)
None (work at home)	34.93	65.07	100.00 (481)
Other	21.35	78.65	100.00 (458)

[1] Data come from 10% sample of Census returns.

Source: Office for National Statistics, 1998b

The moral of the story is always to think about which type of percentages you need when constructing a table. Will row or column percentages make the most sense? Which will be more useful for answering the research question? This principle also applies to tables of counts rather than percentages: always add up the totals in the direction which makes most sense. Once you have decided, always make it clear which way the percentages add up by including the 100% totals.

Always ensure that somebody reading the table could find out the original numbers if they wanted to. Do this either by putting the actual numbers in brackets (as in Table 2.2) so they can simply be read from the table, or by including row and/or column totals into the table (as in Table 2.3) so that somebody with a calculator could work out the actual number in each category. For example, from Table 2.3, 11.93% of Tunbridge Wells workers use rail transport, and 11.93% of 2851 is 340 people. If you do not do this, somebody reading the table will not know if the percentages are out of 1000 people or out of 10 people!

Table 2.5 is another example of a percentage table with column percentages. This enables placements for 5–9-year-olds in local authority care to be compared with similar placements for 10–15-year-olds.

TABLE 2.5 Children looked after by local authorities in different placement types: a comparison of two age groups on 31 March 1996 (column %)

	Age group	
Placement type	**5–9 years**	**10–15 years**
Foster placements	72[2]	65
Other community placements	20	9
Community homes	3	16
Other[1]	5	10
Total %	100	100
(Number)	(10 800)	(21 500)

[1] 'Other' includes voluntary homes and hostels, privately registered children's homes, schools and associated homes and hostels and other types of accommodation.
[2] Figures are rounded to the nearest percentage.

Source: Department of Health, 1997; Crown copyright, reproduced with the permission of the Controller of Her Majesty's Stationery Office

PRACTICE QUESTIONS

2.1 Table 2.6 shows the marital status composition of the British population in 1991 by sex. Construct an appropriate table to see whether there are any differences in marital status between males and females. What does the table show?

TABLE 2.6 Legal marital status of males and females (all ages) in Britain, 1991 (number of people)

Marital status	Sex	
	Males	**Females**
Single	11 900 684	10 678 865
Married	12 737 170	12 863 967
Widowed	799 572	3 227 866
Divorced	1 137 528	1 543 192

Source: Office of Population Censuses and Surveys and General Register Office Scotland, 1993

2.2 Table 2.7 shows voting patterns among salaried workers in the 1987 British election, according to whether the voters had been to university or not.

TABLE 2.7 Voting patterns of salaried workers in the 1987 British election, by whether university educated or not (number of people)

Education	Party voted for				Total
	Conservative	**Alliance**	**Labour**	**Other**	
University educated	80	80	45	2	207
Not university educated	387	161	84	13	645

Source: British Election Study 1987 cross-sectional survey, from Heath et al., 1991

(a) Construct an appropriate percentage table using these data. Calculate the percentages to the nearest whole number only.

(b) Answer the following questions to check your understanding:

(i) What percentage of the university educated workers voted Labour?

(ii) What percentage of the non-university educated workers voted Conservative?

(iii) What patterns in voting are apparent from the table?

3

PRETTY GRAPHS

Producing graphs enables you to learn a lot about a dataset at a glance. A graph should be easier for the average person to understand than a table: after all, everybody prefers to look at a pretty picture rather than wade through a table of numbers.

The only drawback is that you cannot always display as much data in a graph as in a table. Think about the audience you are writing for when deciding which format to use.

The correct type of graph to use depends on the type of data you have: do not use a particular type of graph just because it looks pretty! This chapter will examine graphs for discrete data, continuous data, time series data and time-to-an-event data.

GRAPHS FOR DISCRETE DATA

You should remember from the previous chapter that discrete variables are those based on categories. The data in Tables 3.1 and 3.2 are discrete because they are classified by categories such as 'health' and 'police' which do not take numeric values.

TABLE 3.1 Percentage of those living in the former East and West Germany reporting trust in various institutions, 1992

| | Origin of respondents | |
Trust in:	Former West Germany	Former East Germany
Police	84	53
Justice	67	54
Local administration	56	51
Parliament	60	46
Television	43	52

Source: INFAS (Institut für Angewandte Sozialforschung) Surveys, cited in Conradt, 1996; reproduced with the permission of Longman Publishers USA

Table 3.1 uses data from a survey of people living in the former East and West Germany. Respondents were asked whether or not they trusted various public institutions. Table 3.2 compares central government spending on various items in Denmark and the Netherlands in 1992–5. By drawing graphs it will be easier to compare, for example, which country spends more on health or to see whether there are any differences in trust between East and West Germans.

TABLE 3.2 Central government expenditure in Denmark and the Netherlands, 1992–5

	Country	
Expenditure on:	**Denmark**	**Netherlands**
Social security and welfare	39.9	37.2
Housing and community amenities	1.8	3.2
Health	1.1	14.3
Education	10.6	10.1
Other	46.6	35.2
Total	100.0	100.0

Source: UNDP, 1997; reproduced with the permission of Oxford University Press

Bar charts

The most straightforward type of graph to produce is a **bar chart**. Figure 3.1 shows the West German data from Table 3.1 presented as a bar chart. The chart clearly shows that of the five institutions, the police are the most trusted by West Germans and television is the least trusted. It is easier to see this at a glance from the graph than it was from the original table, so the graph has achieved its aim.

Similarly, Figure 3.2 presents the central government expenditure data for Denmark on a bar chart. Again it is easy to see that of the four named categories, social security and welfare makes up by far the largest proportion of central government expenditure, while only a small proportion is spent on

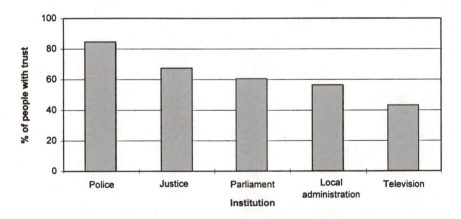

FIGURE 3.1 A BAR CHART SHOWING THE PERCENTAGE OF WEST GERMANS WITH TRUST IN VARIOUS INSTITUTIONS, 1992 (CITED IN CONRADT, 1996)

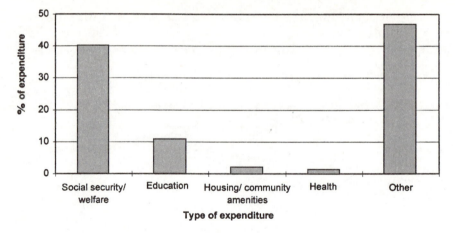

FIGURE 3.2 PERCENTAGE OF CENTRAL GOVERNMENT EXPENDITURE ON VARIOUS ITEMS IN DENMARK, 1992–5 (UNDP, 1997)

housing and community amenities or health. In addition, nearly half of Denmark's central government expenditure is on 'other' items not specifically classified in the table.

Note that the bars in a bar chart are always rectangular and are all the same width. The height of each bar is proportional to the number or percentage in each category. Because each bar represents a completely separate category, the bars must not touch each other: always leave a gap between categories.

Also notice the ordering of the bars. There is no hard and fast rule here, but a common practice is to order them from shortest to tallest or tallest to shortest, as in Figure 3.1. Sometimes you may want to order the bars like this, but leave a category such as 'none' or 'other' at the end. This has been done in Figure 3.2 where the bars are ordered from tallest to shortest, apart from the 'other' category. In some cases, the categories themselves may have a natural order: for example, social class or educational qualifications should be arranged in a logical order from highest to lowest or vice versa, irrespective of the height of the bars.

Multiple bar charts

The bar chart showing the percentage of West Germans trusting various institutions is accurate, but we really wanted to compare the feelings of West Germans with those of East Germans. This can be done on a multiple bar chart, as in Figure 3.3, where the bars for East and West Germans stand side by side. A key (legend) is important now, to identify which bar represents East Germans and which represents West Germans.

The multiple bar chart makes it easy to see that a greater percentage of West Germans put their trust in the police, justice system, parliament and local

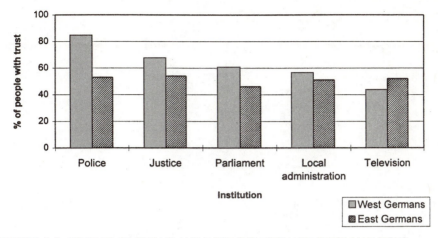

FIGURE 3.3 PERCENTAGE OF EAST AND WEST GERMANS WITH TRUST IN VARIOUS
INSTITUTIONS, 1992 (CITED IN CONRADT, 1996)

administration than do East Germans. The only institution trusted by a
greater percentage of East than West Germans is television.

Try to avoid putting more than three or four sets of bars on a multiple bar
chart, as the chart becomes cluttered and difficult to interpret.

Stacked bar charts

You may have noticed a subtle difference in the two datasets in Tables 3.1
and 3.2. In Table 3.1 the values for central government expenditure all add
up to 100% for each of the two countries. Therefore each category makes up
part of a whole. This is not the case in Table 3.2 where all the categories are
separate and have no numerical relationship to each other.

Bar charts and multiple bar charts are suitable for both types of data, as
they compare the size of each category with the size of other categories.
However, stacked bars and pie charts can only be used for data where the
categories make up part of a whole. They make it easier to see what proportion one category is of the whole.

To draw a stacked bar chart by hand, the **cumulative percentages** must be
calculated. The following example shows the calculation of cumulative percentages for Denmark. All it involves is some simple addition, starting with
the first percentage and then adding each subsequent percentage to the total.
You should end up with 100% as the final cumulative percentage; if not,
something has gone wrong!

	%	Calculation	Cumulative %
Social security and welfare	39.9	39.9	39.9
Housing and community amenities	1.8	39.9 + 1.8	41.7
Health	1.1	41.7 + 1.1	42.8
Education	10.6	42.8 + 10.6	53.4
Other	46.6	53.4 + 46.6	100.0

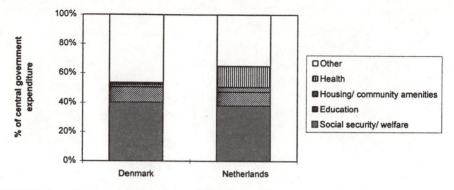

FIGURE 3.4 CENTRAL GOVERNMENT EXPENDITURE IN DENMARK AND THE NETHERLANDS, 1992–5 (UNDP, 1997)

The data are then ready to be presented on a graph like Figure 3.4. The categories should be ordered as appropriate as before. Either the labels can be included in a key (legend) as in Figure 3.4, or each section can be labelled at the side of one of the bars, providing it is clear for both bars which part is which. Always use the same colour or shading for the same category in different bars.

Having the two columns side by side makes it easy to identify any differences. In Figure 3.4, you can see that the proportion of central government expenditure on social security/welfare and education is very similar in Denmark and the Netherlands. However the Netherlands central government spends a much greater proportion of its budget on health than does the Danish central government. This could be because in Denmark more health care is paid for privately. The last sentence is purely a speculation made after observing the data; take care to distinguish between factual observations about a graph and your own suggestions for any patterns or trends that you can see.

Pie charts

Pie charts must only be used when the categories of data make up part of a whole, otherwise the chart will be meaningless. The data must be in the form of either percentages or proportions, so if they are not, the first step is to convert them into one of those forms.

A pie chart presents the categories of data as parts of a circle or 'slices of a pie'. A circle contains 360 degrees (360°), so to convert a proportion to degrees, simply multiply it by 360. To convert a percentage to degrees, first divide by 100 to convert it to a proportion and then multiply by 360. The following tabulation shows how the percentages for Denmark are converted into degrees. If the calculation has been done correctly the slices should add up to 360°, give or take a degree for rounding. The figures have only been calculated

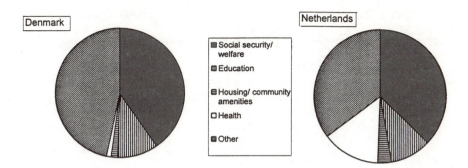

FIGURE 3.5 CENTRAL GOVERNMENT EXPENDITURE ON VARIOUS ITEMS IN DENMARK AND THE NETHERLANDS, 1992–5 (UNDP, 1997)

to the nearest degree because it is difficult to measure much more accurately than this with a protractor.

	%	Proportion (% ÷ 100)	Degrees (proportion × 360)
Social security and welfare	39.9	0.399	144
Housing and community amenities	1.8	0.018	6
Health	1.1	0.011	4
Education	10.6	0.106	38
Other	46.6	0.466	168
Total			360

Then the pie chart can be drawn as in Figure 3.5. It is usual to start measuring your angles from a vertical line at the top of the circle, but some people start from a horizontal line on the right.

Include a key to show what the different colours/shadings in each 'slice' represent. If you are drawing several pie charts on the same subject (such as expenditure in several different countries), always put the categories in the same order on each pie chart: this avoids confusion. Sometimes the circles may be drawn in different sizes in proportion to the size of the total, for example, the total amount of government spending or the total number of people in the sample.

Like the stacked bar chart in Figure 3.4, the pie charts in Figure 3.5 clearly show that a much greater proportion of central government money is spent on health in the Netherlands than in Denmark. Whether you use stacked bars or pie charts comes down to personal preference but try to use the type which shows the data in question more clearly.

RULES FOR GOOD GRAPHS

Before moving on to look at other types of graph, let us just summarise some of the ground rules for producing an excellent graph of any type.

1 *Always use the correct type of graph for your data.* Ask yourself whether the data are discrete or continuous, or whether you have data showing change over time. Then use an appropriate graph type. Do not choose your favourite type of graph and fit the data into it!

2 *Label the graph clearly.* All graphs should have a clear title explaining what or who the data refer to and when and where they refer to. For example, 'Infant mortality rates in Malawi, 1975–94' is far more informative than 'A graph of IM rates'. Both the X (horizontal) and Y (vertical) axes of the graph should also have titles, not forgetting the units of measurement.

3 *The graph itself should be neat and clear.* Apart from obvious scruffiness, avoid cluttering up a graph with too many bars or lines. Always use the same colours or shadings for the same categories when you have more than one pie chart or stacked bar. Include a key (legend) where appropriate.

4 *Include the source.* You will normally know where the data came from (perhaps a book or a survey). Put a note below the graph to this effect; for example 'Source: British Household Panel Study, 1994'. Or include the source in the title as we have done here.

Using a computer

Once you have learnt the basic steps, it is relatively easy to produce professional looking graphs on a spreadsheet or statistical package.

Do not be deceived! *It is also very easy to produce a completely meaningless graph on a computer.* Take as much care with a computer graph as you would with a hand-drawn one. Just because a graph looks neat and impressive in print does not necessarily mean that you have chosen the correct type of graph for the data or labelled the graph properly.

GRAPHS FOR CONTINUOUS DATA

On seeing this number floating aimlessly in mid-air, you would naturally wonder what it is. Out of context, the number 69 could mean any number of things.

In fact, 69 is the percentage of births attended by trained health personnel (such as midwives or doctors) in Sudan in the early 1990s (UNDP, 1997). This is interesting, but it simply leads to more questions, such as:

TABLE 3.3 Percentage of births attended by trained health personnel in 21 African countries, 1990–6

45	45	38	15	31	42	15
31	46	46	44	21	24	26
51	69	55	25	19	14	25

Source: UNDP, 1997; reproduced with the permission of Oxford University Press

TABLE 3.4 An array of the percentage of births attended by trained health personnel in 21 African countries, 1990–6

14	15	15	19	21	24	25
25	26	31	31	38	42	44
45	45	46	46	51	55	69

Source: UNDP, 1997

1 How many African countries have a higher percentage of births attended by trained health personnel than Sudan? How many countries have a lower percentage?
2 Is there a big variation between countries or do they all have a similar percentage of births attended by trained health personnel?

These are questions which ask about the **distribution** of the percentage of births attended by trained health personnel in African countries.

Table 3.3 gives some raw data for some African countries. It is not very clear: it's just a jumble of numbers! With more data it would get even murkier! What can we do about it?

One way of making the data easier to look at is to use an **array**. This just means putting the data in numerical order, as in Table 3.4. Having ordered the data it is possible to see that Sudan actually has the highest percentage of births attended by trained personnel among the 21 African countries included. Sudan is doing relatively very well with respect to maternal care at childbirth.

Alternatively you could use a **complete frequency distribution**. As Table 3.5 shows, this involves listing every value and the 'frequency' or number of times it occurs. This helps us to see which values occur more than once, but otherwise is not much more useful than an array. If there were more data in the table it would become too large and unmanageable.

The solution is to **group** the data. The table then becomes an **abridged frequency table**, as in Table 3.6. This table takes up much less space and tells us much more about the distribution of the data. For example, we now know that in four countries, only between 10% and 19% of births are attended by trained health personnel. The interval with the most countries in is the 40–49% group with six countries. Sudan is the only country in the data with over 60% of births attended.

TABLE 3.5 A complete frequency distribution of the percentage of births attended by trained health personnel in 21 African countries, 1990–6

% births attended by trained health personnel	Frequency (number of countries)	% births attended by trained health personnel	Frequency (number of countries)
14	1	38	1
15	2	42	1
19	1	44	1
21	1	45	2
24	1	46	2
25	2	51	1
26	1	55	1
31	2	69	1
Total			21

Source: UNDP, 1997

TABLE 3.6 An abridged frequency table of the percentage of births attended by trained health personnel in 21 African countries, 1990–6

% births attended by trained health personnel	Frequency (number of countries)
10–19	4
20–29	5
30–39	3
40–49	6
50–59	2
60–69	1
Total	21

Source: UNDP, 1997

STEPS FOR CREATING AN ABRIDGED FREQUENCY TABLE

Step 1: *find the range of the distribution and determine the width of each class interval*

The percentages in the example range from 14 to 69. Therefore it might be appropriate to start at 10 and go up to about 70 (nice round numbers!).

The width of each class interval should be chosen bearing in mind the range and the size of the dataset. You do not want too many or too few observations in a class. Using class intervals of 10–39 and 40–69 will only give you two classes and there will be so many observations in each class that the distribution will be hidden. On the other hand, using class intervals of 10–12, 13–15, 16–18 and so on will give you 20 classes, which is equally unhelpful.

There is no right or wrong width as such, but all classes must be the same width and the width chosen should be *sensible*! Ideally you might want five to ten classes if you have a reasonable number of observations. Table 3.6 has six class intervals of width 10.

Step 2: *list the class intervals starting at the bottom*
Make sure that the numbers do not overlap, in other words use 10–19, 20–29,
. . ., not 10–20, 20–30, ... Do not use obscure numbers for class boundaries.
The classes 0–15.6, 15.7–31.2, . . . will only confuse people!

Step 3: *find the frequency in each class*
You might want to go through the data, crossing off each observation and
putting a tally mark in the appropriate class. When all the observations have
been crossed off, add up the tally marks to find the total number or frequency
in each class. Always add up the frequencies for each class to check that they
add up correctly to the total number of observations.

Now we have completed a frequency distribution, but it still doesn't show us
the *percentage* of countries in each category. For example, we might want to
know what percentage of countries have fewer than 40% of births attended by
a trained person. For this we must work out the percentages and cumulative
percentages.
   The calculations are fairly straightforward. The percentages are worked out
in the usual way (see Appendix 3 for extra help with percentages). For
example, the percentage of countries with between 10% and 19% of births
attended is calculated as follows (to two decimal places):

$$Percentage \ = \frac{4}{12} \times 100 = 19.05\%$$

Once the percentage in each group has been calculated, always add up the
percentages to make sure that they add up to 100% in total, as in Table 3.7.
(Answers of 100.01 or 99.99 are perfectly acceptable due to rounding!)

**TABLE 3.7 Percentages and cumulative percentages for the percentage
of births attended by trained health personnel in 21 African
countries, 1990–6**

% births attended by trained health personnel	Frequency (number of countries)	% of countries	Cumulative %
10–19	4	19.05	19.05
20–29	5	23.81	42.86
30–39	3	14.29	57.15
40–49	6	28.57	85.72
50–59	2	9.52	95.24
60–69	1	4.76	100.00
Total	21	100.00	

Source: UNDP, 1997

To calculate the cumulative percentages, simply add up the percentages as you go down the table. The top cumulative percentage (for the 10–19 group) will be the same as the first percentage, 19.05%. The cumulative percentage for the 20–29 group is 19.05 + 23.81 = 42.86. For the 30–39 group, the cumulative percentage will be 42.86 + 14.29 = 57.15. So each time, the percentage of the group is added to the previous cumulative percentage. The final cumulative percentage should equal 100%.

The cumulative percentage is the percentage of scores which lie below the upper limit of a particular interval. So, for example, 42.86% of the countries have 29% or fewer births attended by a health professional (because 29 is the top of this group).

Going back to our original question, what percentage of the countries have fewer than 40% of births attended by trained health personnel? The answer is 57.15% of the countries (57.15% have 39% or fewer births attended).

Note that it is also possible to work out the **cumulative frequency** for each group, by adding up the frequencies going down the table instead of the percentages. You could also work out the proportion of countries in each group; this is known as the **relative frequency**. Which of these methods you use depends on the questions you want to answer. If you had wanted to know the *number* of countries with fewer than 40% of births attended by trained health personnel, the cumulative frequency would be more useful than the cumulative percentage.

Stem and leaf plots

A frequency distribution can be made more visually appealing by turning it into a **stem and leaf plot**. Table 3.8 shows the percentage of males and females who were literate in 37 African countries in 1994.

TABLE 3.8 Percentage of males and females literate in 37 African countries in 1994

Males									
89	78	72	81	79	63	55	74	90	75
74	85	89	80	66	84	49	47	66	79
48	67	56	73	42	72	67	61	51	56
48	48	45	37	29	21	44			
Females									
57	50	44	81	58	37	28	52	79	51
50	68	67	61	44	69	28	23	34	54
26	44	31	49	21	40	41	33	23	22
20	21	24	20	9	6	17			

Source: UNDP, 1997; reproduced with the permission of Oxford University Press

What can we discover about female literacy in Africa from these data? In their current state, not a lot! A jumble of numbers is not very useful, so to make them easier to interpret, an array or frequency table could be drawn up. Alternatively the data could be presented as a stem and leaf plot, as in Figure 3.6.

The column to the left of the line is known as the **stem**, while the other numbers to the right of the line are the **leaves**. The stem represents the 'tens' and the leaves the 'digits'. For example, the row beginning with '6' has the digits '1', '7', '8' and '9'. Therefore we know there are observations of 61, 67, 68 and 69 among the data.

```
0 | 6 9
1 | 7
2 | 0 0 1 1 2 3 3 4 6 8 8
3 | 1 3 7 4
4 | 0 1 4 4 4 9
5 | 0 0 1 2 4 7 8
6 | 1 7 8 9
7 | 9
8 | 1
```

FIGURE 3.6 A STEM AND LEAF PLOT SHOWING THE PERCENTAGE OF FEMALES LITERATE IN 37 AFRICAN COUNTRIES, 1994 (UNDP, 1997)

STEPS FOR DRAWING A STEM AND LEAF PLOT
Step 1
Mentally separate each digit into a stem and a leaf, for example 17 = stem 1, leaf 7. Note that stems can have as many digits as you like, but leaves can only have one digit. For larger numbers, such as 176, the stem would be 17 and the leaf 6.

Step 2
List the stems, increasing as you move downwards. If you feel that you want intervals narrower than tens, another possibility is to divide the stems into two, where for example the stem '0' is for the leaves 0 to 4 and '0*' is for the leaves 5 to 9. Figure 3.7 shows part of the data in the example presented in this way.

Step 3
Add the leaves to the diagram, in numerical order, spacing the numbers evenly. Figure 3.8 shows how *not* to draw a stem and leaf plot. It is important to space the numbers evenly so that the number of observations in each row can be easily compared.

```
2    | 0  0  1  1  2  3  3  4
2*   | 6  8  8
3    | 1  3  4
3*   | 7
```

FIGURE 3.7 PART OF THE STEM AND LEAF PLOT IN FIGURE 3.6 WITH STEMS DIVIDED INTO TWO

```
0 | 1 1  5 7 2
1 | 1  3  9 9
2 | 2  2  5  7  3
3 | 4 9 5 4 2
4 | 1 1 6    7 5
```

FIGURE 3.8 HOW *NOT* TO DRAW A STEM AND LEAF PLOT

INTERPRETING A STEM AND LEAF PLOT

Look first at the shape of a stem and leaf plot. Are the data concentrated around the middle of the distribution (a **normal distribution**) or is the distribution **skewed** with most of the data concentrated at one end of the plot? In Figure 3.6, most of the data lie in the middle of the plot with fewer countries having very high or very low values. The only exception are the 11 countries with 20 to 29% literacy – perhaps more countries than we would expect in this row.

Also think about where the 'average' value might lie: where is the middle of the distribution? In Figure 3.6 we might guess that the average value is in the 40s. Finally, check whether there are any outliers (points all by themselves at one end of the range). In this example there are no outliers to worry about, but if there were any, it might be a good idea to check that the values have been inputted correctly.

What does Figure 3.6 tell you about female literacy in Africa in 1994?

BACK-TO-BACK STEM AND LEAF PLOTS

So far we have only examined the data for females. It would be interesting to compare female literacy with male literacy in the 37 countries to see whether there are any gender differences. In order to compare two different distributions, two stem and leaf plots can be drawn next to each other, sharing the same stem. This is known as a **back-to-back stem and leaf plot**. Figure 3.9 presents the data for both males and females. It is now very easy to compare the shapes of the two different distributions.

What does the plot tell us about gender differences in literacy in Africa in

	Males		0	6 9	Females

Males   Females

				0	6 9
			1	7
		9 1	2	0 0 1 1 2 3 3 4 6 8 8
		7	3	1 3 7 4
9 8 8 8 7 5 4 2			4	0 1 4 4 4 9
	6 6 5 1		5	0 0 1 2 4 7 8
	7 7 6 6 3 1		6	1 7 8 9
9 9 8 5 4 4 3 2 2			7	9
	9 9 5 4 1 0		8	1
		0	9	

FIGURE 3.9 A BACK-TO-BACK STEM AND LEAF PLOT SHOWING THE PERCENTAGE OF MALES AND FEMALES LITERATE IN 37 AFRICAN COUNTRIES, 1994 (UNDP, 1997)

1994? Straight away we can see that male literacy tends to be higher than female literacy because there are many more countries with literacy above 70% for males than there are for females. Correspondingly there are no countries with male literacy below 20% while there are three countries with female literacy below 20%. The average male literacy rate is likely to be higher than the average female literacy rate.

ADVANTAGES AND DISADVANTAGES OF STEM AND LEAF PLOTS

The unique advantage of a stem and leaf plot is that it displays all the data. By looking at the plot you know the exact values of all the observations in the dataset, so no accuracy is lost. Back-to-back stem and leaf plots are also particularly good for comparing two distributions side by side.

However, with a very large sample, producing a stem and leaf plot would be very time-consuming and there would simply be too many data to look at all at once. With a large sample, a **histogram** is a better choice for data presentation.

Histograms

Histograms display only the number (or percentage) of observations that fall into each interval, not the actual data in the way that a stem and leaf plot does. In order to plot the data for male literacy on to a histogram, you must first construct an abridged frequency table. Bear in mind that the number of intervals in the table will correspond to the number of bars on the graph. Table 3.9 shows an abridged frequency table for male literacy with intervals of width 10.

TABLE 3.9 An abridged frequency table showing the percentage of males literate in 37 African countries in 1994

% of males literate	Frequency (number of countries)
0–9	0
10–19	0
20–29	2
30–39	1
40–49	8
50–59	4
60–69	6
70–79	9
80–89	6
90–99	1
Total	37

Source: UNDP, 1997; reproduced with the permission of Oxford University Press

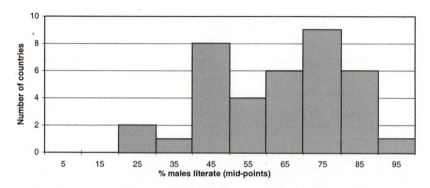

FIGURE 3.10 A HISTOGRAM OF THE PERCENTAGE OF MALES LITERATE IN 37 AFRICAN COUNTRIES, 1994 (UNDP, 1997)

The histogram can then be constructed as in Figure 3.10. It will be exactly the same shape as the male distribution in the stem and leaf plot in Figure 3.9.

Note that because the data are continuous rather than in discrete categories, the bars of a histogram must touch each other. The height of each bar represents the frequency (number of countries) in that interval and the width of each bar must be proportional to the width of the interval on the continuous scale. In this case, all the intervals are the same width, so the bars are also the same width.

The way in which the horizontal axis is labelled can vary. The mid-point of the interval can be used in the middle of the bar, as in Figure 3.10, or the bottom of the interval (0, 10, 20, . . .) can be used at the bottom left of each bar. Alternatively, you can label the bars '0–9', '10–19' and so on.

This previous example uses the *number* of countries on the Y axis, but histograms can also use percentages. This is particularly useful if you are

TABLE 3.10 Numbers and percentages of British women aged 40 or above at interview by number of children ever born

Number of children ever born	Number of women	% of women
0	354	12.5
1	414	14.6
2	1130	39.9
3	567	20.0
4	246	8.7
5	66	2.3
6	33	1.2
7	11	0.4
8	6	0.2
9	1	0.0
10	1	0.0
Total	2829	99.8[1]

[1] Percentages do not add up to exactly 100% due to rounding.

Source: General Household Survey 1995–6.

comparing two or more distributions with different numbers of observations because the graphs can still be drawn on the same scale.

The data in Table 3.10 have been converted from frequencies into percentages. The figures were obtained from General Household Survey data for 2829 British women aged 40 or above at interview in 1995–6. The women were asked how many children they had ever given birth to, with the responses ranging from zero to ten. Note that 'number of children' is one of those awkward variables which is difficult to classify as either continuous or discrete. The scale from 0 to 10 is clearly ordered and meaningful, but on the other hand, it is not possible to have 2.4 or 3.1 children, so the scale is not truly continuous. For now, we will treat the variable as continuous.

The data can then be plotted on to a histogram, as in Figure 3.11.

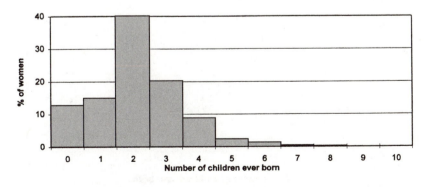

FIGURE 3.11 NUMBER OF CHILDREN EVER BORN TO A SAMPLE OF 2829 BRITISH WOMEN AGED 40 OR ABOVE AT INTERVIEW (GENERAL HOUSEHOLD SURVEY 1995–6)

What is the most common family size among these women? The histogram clearly shows that around 40% of the women had given birth to two children and that this is by far the most common number of children. A greater percentage of the women had had three children than only one child or no children. Only a very small percentage of women had had more than five children.

In light of this, we might want to combine the very small percentages of women with five or more children into one larger category. If the number of women with five, six, seven, eight, nine and ten children are added together and converted into a percentage, the result is 4.2% of women who have had between five and ten children (($118 \div 2829$) $\times$ 100). The new histogram could then be plotted as in Figure 3.12.

Can you see anything wrong with the histogram in Figure 3.12? Remember that the width of a bar should match the width of the interval. The interval 5–10 has a width of six children (it includes six different possible numbers of children), while the other bars only have a width of one child. One solution would be to label the *X* axis from 0 to 10 as before and then make the bar for the 5–10 group six bars wide. However if you do this, you *must* adjust the height of the bar.

The total size of each bar in a histogram is proportionate to its total area, not just its height. Therefore in order to make the 5–10 bar six times wider, we must also make it six times shorter! What we are really doing is averaging out the percentage over the six groups. If 4.2% of the women have 5–10 children, then the height of the bar for this group will be 4.2% $\div$ 6 = 0.7%. Figure 3.13 shows the correctly drawn histogram.

Note that this averaging process involves making the assumption that the percentage of women with each number of children is uniformly distributed throughout the large interval of 5–10 children (in other words the percentage

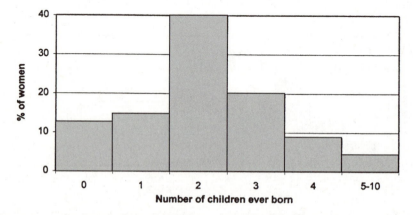

FIGURE 3.12 AN INCORRECTLY DRAWN HISTOGRAM OF NUMBER OF CHILDREN EVER BORN TO A SAMPLE OF 2829 BRITISH WOMEN AGED 40 OR ABOVE AT INTERVIEW (GENERAL HOUSEHOLD SURVEY 1995–6)

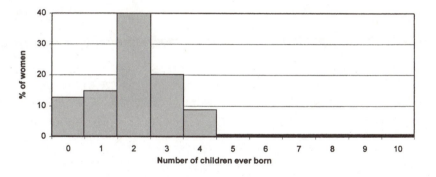

FIGURE 3.13 A CORRECTLY DRAWN HISTOGRAM OF NUMBER OF CHILDREN EVER BORN
TO A SAMPLE OF 2829 BRITISH WOMEN AGED 40 OR ABOVE AT INTERVIEW
(GENERAL HOUSEHOLD SURVEY 1995–6)

of women with five children is the same as the percentage with six, seven, eight, nine or ten children). This assumption may not always be sensible. In this example we actually know how many women have each number of children and know that the percentages are not equal. Figure 3.11 is still the best histogram because no information is lost. However, sometimes the data will be grouped when you obtain them, so you have no choice but to make this assumption and adjust the width and height of the bars accordingly. You should always make it clear when bars are for averaged values, either by including a note to that effect, as in Figure 3.13, or by not dividing the wider bars with vertical lines.

EXAMPLE: USING HISTOGRAMS TO COMPARE DISTRIBUTIONS

In 1787–8, the famous *Federalist* papers were published in the US to try to persuade the citizens of New York to ratify the constitution. Political historians have spent much time trying to determine the authorship of the 85 papers. They agree about the authorship of 73 of the papers, but the remaining 12 papers could have been written by either of two famous political writers, Hamilton and Madison. The political content of the papers does not provide convincing evidence either way as both authors used similar arguments and both changed their political views later in life.

Using histograms it is possible to throw some light on the question. Different authors tend to have different writing styles and to use non-contextual words such as 'by', 'to' and 'from' to different extents. By examining the frequency of usage of such words in known works by Hamilton and Madison and comparing this to the frequency of usage in the 12 disputed papers, it may be possible to obtain more evidence about the authorship of the disputed papers.

Mosteller and Wallace (1964) used this approach to solve the dispute. They calculated use rates per 1000 words for various words in Hamilton's papers, Madison's papers and the 12 disputed papers. The results for each word were then plotted on histograms and the rates for the disputed papers compared with the rates in the papers of known authorship. Figures 3.14 and 3.15 show their results for the words 'by' and 'to'. Note that the histograms have all been drawn to the same scale and use percentages to make comparisons easier. If you are drawing two or more graphs which you want to compare to each other, always try to present them in the same format and on the same page like this.

The evidence points strongly to one author. Who do you think wrote the 12 disputed papers?

Line plots

Line plots are useful for small datasets. They are not generally used for final presentation, but can be drawn up quickly to give you an idea of the distribution of your data.

Suppose a lecturer has taught a group of students for a course. She has just marked all the exam papers and coursework, and wants to quickly get a feel for how the students performed in each.

TABLE 3.11 Results for 30 students from an exam (%)

35	40	42	43	44	45
45	46	49	50	50	50
51	52	53	53	54	55
55	58	58	58	58	59
60	60	61	64	64	65

Source: authors' data

The ordered results from the exam itself are shown in Table 3.11. Various methods could be used to present these data, including a grouped frequency table, a stem and leaf plot or a histogram. However the lecturer does not want to spend a lot of time presenting the results, so a line plot would be suitable for simply exploring the data.

On a line plot, each data value is represented as a blob on a scaled horizontal line. Data of the same value or too close together to be distinguishable are placed in even stacks, as shown in Figure 3.16.

It is easy to see from the line plot how the students performed in the exam. Most of the marks are in the 40s and 50s with a few marks in the 60s plus one

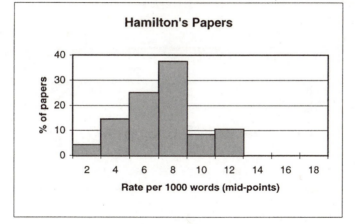

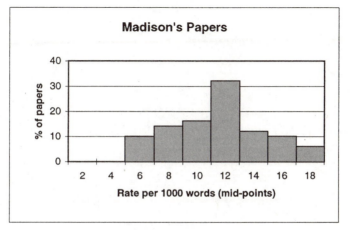

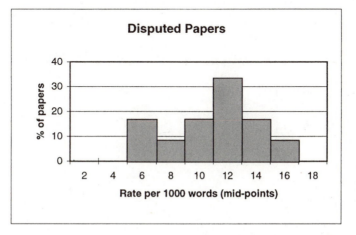

FIGURE 3.14 USAGE RATES OF THE WORD 'BY' IN PAPERS BY HAMILTON AND MADISON AND THE 12 DISPUTED FEDERALIST PAPERS (DATA FROM MOSTELLER AND WALLACE, 1964)

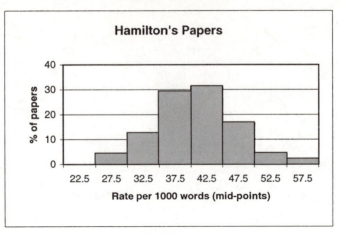

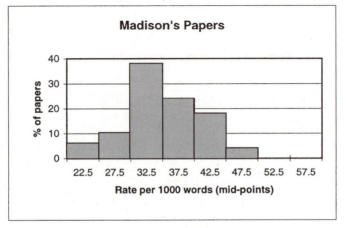

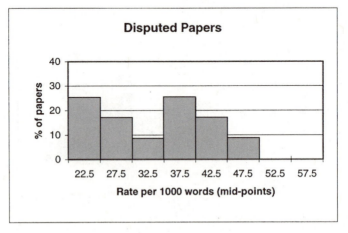

FIGURE 3.15 USAGE RATES OF THE WORD 'TO' IN PAPERS BY HAMILTON AND MADISON AND THE 12 DISPUTED FEDERALIST PAPERS (DATA FROM MOSTELLER AND WALLACE, 1964)

FIGURE 3.16 A LINE PLOT SHOWING THE EXAM RESULTS OF 30 STUDENTS (AUTHORS' DATA)

mark in the 30s. The students have not done outstandingly well in the exam. Let us see whether they did better in the coursework.

TABLE 3.12 Results for 30 students from coursework (%)

48	49	50	51	54	55
59	60	60	60	61	61
62	63	64	65	65	66
67	67	67	67	70	70
71	71	74	77	78	80

Source: authors' data

Table 3.12 shows the students' coursework marks. If the lecturer wants to compare the distribution of exam marks with that of coursework marks, she can draw a **parallel line plot**, as in Figure 3.17. The two scales should be identical on a parallel line plot to enable a straight comparison.

What conclusion might the lecturer draw from Figure 3.17 about the relative performance of her students in the exam and the coursework?

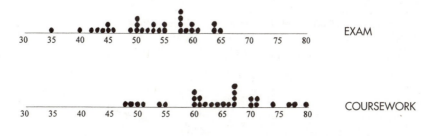

FIGURE 3.17 A PARALLEL LINE PLOT SHOWING THE EXAM AND COURSEWORK RESULTS OF 30 STUDENTS (AUTHORS' DATA)

GRAPHS FOR TIME SERIES DATA

A set of data which shows changes in a variable over time is known as a **time series**. For such data, it is best to use a **line graph**. Numbers, percentages or proportions can all be used on a line graph. On any graph, the horizontal axis is known as the **X axis** and the vertical axis as the **Y axis**. On a line graph, time should always be measured on the X axis.

Table 3.13 shows changes in the percentage of British women aged 16–49 using five different methods of contraception. The data come from then General Household Surveys of 1986, 1989, 1991, 1993 and 1995; questions about contraceptive use are not included in the survey every year.

Figures 3.18 and 3.19 show changes over time in condom and IUD use. What do the graphs tell you about the trends in the use of the two methods? Can you see any problems with these two graphs?

Figure 3.18 appears to show that the percentage of women using condoms has increased greatly over the period 1986 to 1995, while Figure 3.19 suggests that IUD use has declined dramatically during the same period. One might speculate that condom use has probably increased due to the health promotion campaigns linked to HIV prevention.

However, look at the Y axis scales on the two graphs: they do not start at zero. This does not make the graphs inaccurate, but it does make them misleading. The vertical scales are deliberately designed so that the increases and decreases appear as large as possible: this clever trick is often used in advertising. For a graph which does not mislead, you should preferably start

TABLE 3.13 Percentage of British women aged 16–49 using five methods of contraception, 1986–95[1]

Method	1986	1989	Year 1991	1993	1995
Pill	23	22	23	25	25
IUD (intra-uterine device)	7	5	5	5	4
Condom	13	15	16	17	18
Other non-surgical	8	7	6	6	7
Male/female sterilisation	23	23	25	24	24

[1] Percentages do not add up to 100% for each year because some women used more than one method and others were not using any method.

Source: Office for National Statistics, 1997a

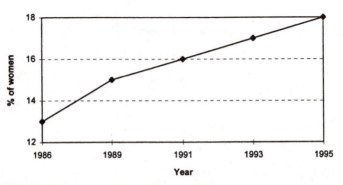

FIGURE 3.18 PERCENTAGE OF BRITISH WOMEN AGED 16–49 USING CONDOMS, 1986–95 (GENERAL HOUSEHOLD SURVEY)

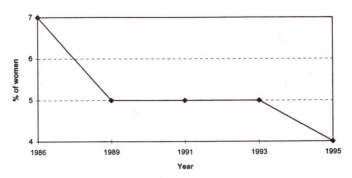

FIGURE 3.19 PERCENTAGE OF BRITISH WOMEN AGED 16–49 USING AN IUD, 1986–95
(GENERAL HOUSEHOLD SURVEY)

at zero on the *Y* axis or, if this is not appropriate, at least make it clear to the
reader that it does not start at zero by including a break at the bottom of the
axis.

There is another less obvious problem with the two graphs. The *X* axis
measures years on a continuous scale, but in this case the axis jumps between
years with unequal intervals. The first interval from 1986 to 1989 is a three-
year interval, while the subsequent intervals are only two years. This causes
a distortion in the line: for example, in Figure 3.19 there is an apparently steep
decline in IUD use between 1986 and 1989. If the interval was made wider as
it should be, the slope of the line would be less steep and the drop would
appear less dramatic. When drawing a line graph, always mark the years on
the *X* axis with equal intervals before drawing the points and line; it does not
matter if lack of data means that you do not have a point for each year marked
on the *X* axis.

*A good line graph should show the trend clearly at a glance, without exaggerating or
minimising it.*

Figures 3.20 and 3.21 show the trends in the percentage of women using
condoms or an IUD in a less misleading way. Note that each *Y* axis scale starts

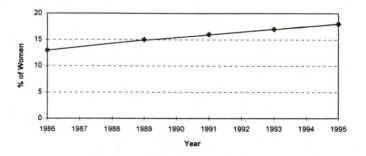

FIGURE 3.20 PERCENTAGE OF BRITISH WOMEN AGED 16–49 USING CONDOMS,
1986–95 (GENERAL HOUSEHOLD SURVEY)

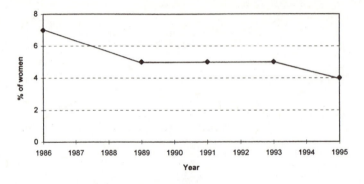

FIGURE 3.21 PERCENTAGE OF BRITISH WOMEN AGED 16–49 USING AN IUD, 1986–95 (GENERAL HOUSEHOLD SURVEY)

at zero and that the Y axis scale is continuous, so the actual points are not evenly spaced. The graphs still show an increase in the percentage of women using condoms and a decrease in the percentage using an IUD, but the changes are no longer exaggerated.

If we wanted to compare the trend in condom use with the trend in IUD use, there is one extra amendment that should be made to the graphs. The Y axis scales are currently different, with Figure 3.20 having a longer scale (0–20) than Figure 3.21 (0–8). Therefore changes in IUD use still appear larger than they should when compared to changes in condom use.

When comparing two or more line graphs, the X and Y axis scales should be identical. An alternative is to put all the lines on one graph, as in Figure 3.22 which shows changes in the percentages of women using five different methods of contraception. It is generally better to use colour to distinguish the different lines from each other, but if this is not possible, different marker styles or line styles can be used on a black and white graph. If the lines are all on top of each other, you may need to adjust the scale or use separate graphs.

Figure 3.22 shows that the pill and male/female sterilisation were the most common methods used over the whole period, followed by condoms. The percentages for most methods fluctuate year on year. The only method showing a steady change is the condom, which became more widely used between 1986 and 1995.

TIME-TO-AN-EVENT DATA

Often in the social sciences we have data which measure the length of time which occurs before a particular event takes place. Many interesting research questions use data like these. Some examples are:

- How soon after their first birth do women have a second child?
- How quickly do workers find a new job after being made redundant?

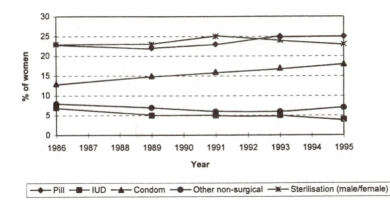

FIGURE 3.22 PERCENTAGE OF BRITISH WOMEN AGED 16–49 USING DIFFERENT METHODS OF CONTRACEPTION, 1986–95 (GENERAL HOUSEHOLD SURVEY)

- At what age do young people have their first sexual experiences?
- How long do children in foster care stay in one family before leaving or being moved?

Note that with such data, time is measured from a starting date to the date of an event. The starting date may be obvious in some cases, for example date of redundancy or date of entering a foster family, but in other cases there is no clear starting date and a fixed time such as birth or age 16 is used as the start point.

We are usually interested in the **cumulative proportion** of people who have experienced the event by each age or after each number of months or years. To present such data graphically we can use a **cumulative frequency histogram** or **cumulative frequency polygon**. Both graphs types use the same type of data and can use either frequencies or percentages.

EXAMPLE: TIME TO FIRST SNOG

A study by Roger Ingham and colleagues (unpublished) took a sample of 42 young British men and asked them at what age they had their first snog (defined as consensual kissing with a sexual meaning). Their responses, ranging from age 7 to age 20, are shown in Table 3.14. The data could be graphed as cumulative frequencies, but in this case they have been turned into cumulative percentages.

TABLE 3.14 Age at first snog among 42 young British men:[1] frequencies, cumulative frequencies and cumulative percentages

Age at first snog	Frequency (number of men)	Cumulative frequency	Cumulative %
7	1	1	2.38
8	0	1	2.38
9	1	2	4.76
10	0	2	4.76
11	3	5	11.90
12	6	11	26.19
13	5	16	38.10
14	6	22	52.38
15	12	34	80.95
16	2	36	85.71
17	4	40	95.24
18	1	41	97.62
19	0	41	97.62
20	1	42	100.00
21	0	42	100.00
Total	–42		

[1] Sample consists of 42 men with multiple sexual partners in the previous 12 months, interviewed in 1995–6.

Source: Roger Ingham et al., unpublished

A cumulative frequency histogram plots the cumulative frequencies or percentages using bars in the same way as an ordinary histogram. The histogram should always go upwards from left to right, as in Figure 3.23. The graph shows that the percentage having had a first snog increases steadily with age and there is a particularly large jump between ages 14 and 15. It can be seen that 50% of the men had experienced their first snog by age 14.

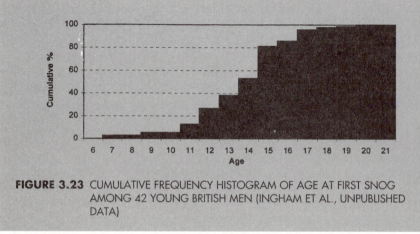

FIGURE 3.23 CUMULATIVE FREQUENCY HISTOGRAM OF AGE AT FIRST SNOG AMONG 42 YOUNG BRITISH MEN (INGHAM ET AL., UNPUBLISHED DATA)

A cumulative frequency polygon plots the same points as the histogram, but joins them with a line rather than using bars. Figure 3.24 shows the data presented in this way. Polygons tend to be used more frequently than histograms because they are clearer and more than one line can be put on the same graph. In Figure 3.25, the age at first snog is compared with the age at first sexual intercourse for the sample of young men. As we would expect, first intercourse tends to occur at an older age than first snog. The percentage having had intercourse is very low up until age 13, after which it rises steeply and consistently to age 20 when the entire sample have experienced intercourse.

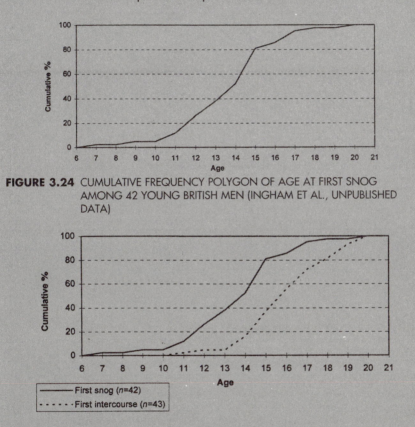

FIGURE 3.24 CUMULATIVE FREQUENCY POLYGON OF AGE AT FIRST SNOG AMONG 42 YOUNG BRITISH MEN (INGHAM ET AL., UNPUBLISHED DATA)

FIGURE 3.25 AGE AT FIRST SNOG AND FIRST INTERCOURSE AMONG 43 YOUNG BRITISH MEN (INGHAM ET AL., UNPUBLISHED DATA)

Note that in this example, all respondents experienced the event, so at the greatest age the cumulative percentage reached 100%. This is not always the case. Figure 3.26 is an example of a cumulative frequency polygon with several lines and in which many sample members do not experience the event. The sample consists of British women who have been separated or widowed from their first marriage. The graph shows the cumulative percentage of the women who have a birth after their marriage breaks down. Each line represents the childbearing of women of a particular age at marital breakdown.

Figure 3.26 shows that a much higher percentage of younger women go on to have a birth than older women. After, for example, four years, over 50% of those aged 15–19 at marital breakdown had since given birth, compared with less than 30% of those aged 25–29 at breakdown and less than 10% of those aged 35–39 at breakdown. What explanations can you think of for this?

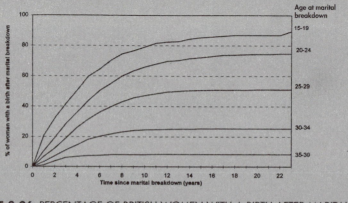

FIGURE 3.26 PERCENTAGE OF BRITISH WOMEN WITH A BIRTH AFTER MARITAL BREAKDOWN BY TIME SINCE MARITAL BREAKDOWN AND AGE AT MARITAL BREAKDOWN (JEFFERIES, UNPUBLISHED, DATA FROM GENERAL HOUSEHOLD SURVEY 1990–5)

Summary – two rules for good graphs

A good graph has two main features:

1 *It is the correct type of graph to use for presenting the particular type of data.* Before drawing the graph, remember to check whether the data are discrete or continuous, or whether they measure a change over time or time to an event. Only then can you decide which type of graph to use. Many students get confused between bar charts and histograms. Remember that a bar chart is for presenting discrete data and a histogram is for continuous data.
2 *The graph is clear and well labelled.* All graphs should have a clear title, X and Y axis labels, a key (legend) if necessary and the source of data if known. Always check that the graph is clear and conveys the relevant information to the reader.

PRACTICE QUESTIONS

3.1 Table 3.15 shows the percentage of 1-year-olds fully immunised against measles in 30 of the poorest African countries in 1995.

TABLE 3.15 Percentage of 1-year-olds fully immunised against measles in 30 of the poorest African countries in 1995

46	46	73	40	69	57
72	65	82	53	36	60
32	74	79	80	70	82
26	87	40	69	45	50
43	49	55	18	50	46

Source: UNICEF, 1997, in UNDP, 1997; reproduced with the permission of Oxford University Press

(a) Construct an abridged frequency table of these data.
(b) Present the data from the frequency table on an appropriate graph and comment on the distribution of the data.

3.2 Table 3.16 gives data for the percentage of males and females who smoke in 23 industrialised countries (1986–94 figures). Construct a back-to-back stem and leaf plot of the data. What does it show you about gender differences in smoking in industrialised countries?

3.3 Present the datasets in (a) Table 3.17, (b) Table 3.18 and (c) Table 3.19 using an appropriate graphical method. You could try this by hand or using a computer package.

TABLE 3.16 Percentage of men and women who smoke in 23 industrialised countries, 1986–94[1]

| Country | % adults who smoke | |
	Males	Females
Canada	31	28
France	49	26
Norway	42	32
USA	30	24
Iceland	39	32
Netherlands	41	33
Japan	66	14
Finland	35	17
New Zealand	35	29
Sweden	26	30
Spain	58	27
Austria	33	22
Belgium	35	21
Australia	37	30
UK	36	32
Switzerland	46	29
Denmark	49	38
Greece	54	13
Italy	46	18
Portugal	37	10
Hungary	50	25
Poland	63	29
Romania	48	13

[1] For a small number of countries, data refer to years prior to 1986.

Source: UN, 1994, in UNDP, 1997; reproduced with the permission of Oxford University Press

TABLE 3.17 Percentage of women's employment which is part-time, in four countries, 1996

Country	% of total women's employment that is part-time
France	22.10
Norway	46.30
UK	38.90
USA	19.10

Source: OECD, 1997; reproduced with the permission of OECD

TABLE 3.18 Number of asylum seekers entering the UK and France, 1985–92 (thousands)

Year	Country UK	France
1985	5.4	28.8
1986	4.8	26.3
1987	5.2	27.6
1988	5.7	34.3
1989	16.5	61.4
1990	30.0	54.7
1991	57.7	50.0
1992	24.6	27.5

Source: Salt et al., 1994; Crown copyright, reproduced with the permission of the Controller of Her Majesty's Stationery Office

TABLE 3.19 Known first destinations of first-degree social science graduates in the UK, by sex, 1993–4 (number of graduates)

First destination	Sex Male	Female
Employment	2644	2403
Further study or training	2484	2544
Returned overseas	601	578
Not available for employment	373	410
Unemployed	547	382
Total	6649	6317

Source: UCAS, 1995; reproduced with the permission of HESA

4

AVERAGES AND PERCENTILES

In this and the following chapter, we will look at ways of describing the characteristics of a set of continuous data. We have already started to investigate the distribution of data by drawing graphs such as histograms; now we will learn how to describe the distribution of a set of data statistically, so that we can *summarise* the features of a distribution. This is all known as descriptive statistics.

This chapter looks first at various types of average. The 'average' income or 'average' waiting time for an operation are concepts which most people understand. But what exactly do they tell us?

Secondly, the chapter explains how a distribution can be divided up into different parts, so that we can say something, perhaps, about the top 5% of the distribution or the bottom 10%. For example, 'In the UK, the poorest 10% of households have a gross income of £85 per week or lower' (Office for National Statistics, 1997c).

Using these different measures enables us to condense a huge amount of data into just one or two numbers which can tell us something about the distribution.

AVERAGES

Averages are often useful for answering questions. For example:

- What would a student sharing a house with friends expect to pay in rent each week?
- What do most social workers earn?
- At what age do people usually get married for the first time?

An average value would be a good response to any of these questions. However, there are a number of different kinds of average and we need to choose an appropriate one. Three are the **mean**, the **median** and the **mode**. We will use all three to answer the first question.

Table 4.1 shows the rents paid by a group of 15 second-year students living in shared houses. Of course, in practice we would like a larger sample to answer the question, but the sample has been kept deliberately small to illustrate the methods.

TABLE 4.1 Weekly rent paid by 15 second-year students living in shared houses, 1998 (£)

45	35	51	45	49
51	40	42	46	36
37	42	47	49	42

Source: authors' data

The mean

The mean is the most commonly known measure of the average.

There are two steps for calculating a mean. First, add together all the numbers:

$$45 + 35 + 51 + 45 + 49 + 51 + 40 + 42 + 46 + 36 + 37 + 42 + 47 + 49 + 42 = 657$$

Secondly, divide this total by the number of observations (15 in this example):

$$657 \div 15 = 43.8$$

The mean rent paid by the students is £43.80.

In statistical jargon, the formula for a mean is written:

$$\bar{x} = \frac{\Sigma x}{n}$$

To explain, the mean is usually called $\bar{x}$ and the observations are called x_1, x_2, x_3 and so on. The symbol Σ is the Greek capital letter 'sigma' and it means 'sum of', so Σx is the sum of all the values of x (the rents for each student). The letter n is simply the number of observations (students) in the sample. Note that sometimes y is used instead of x.

So the formula just describes what we did to calculate the mean: we added together all the values and divided by the number of observations. Don't be put off by the jargon: it is just a much quicker way of writing things than using words. (See Appendix 4 for a brief guide to mathematical notation.)

The mode

The mode is the number which comes up most frequently. In this dataset, two students pay rents of £45, two pay rents of £49 and two pay rents of £51, but three students pay rents of £42. So the modal rent is £42.

If there are two numbers which come up the most frequently, the distribution is **bimodal**; in other words it has two modes.

The median

Another way of finding an average is to find the middle observation in a set of data. The middle observation is known as the median. Half of the observations will lie above the median and half below.

The first step is to order the data:

35 36 37 40 42 42 42 45 45 46 47 49 49 51 51

In the example, there are 15 observations. Assuming that the data have been ordered, the middle observation will be the 8th observation, because there are seven observations either side of it:

35 36 37 40 42 42 42 45 45 46 47 49 49 51 51
↑
8th

The 8th observation will be the median, so the median rent paid by the students is £45.

However, 15 is an odd number. It was easy to find the middle number because there were seven observations on each side of it. What about even numbers?

Suppose you find a 16th student to add to your sample. She pays a weekly rent of £40. The new ordered dataset would look like this:

35 36 37 40 40 42 42 42 45 45 46 47 49 49 51 51
↑ ↑
8th 9th

Now there are two observations in the middle! In such cases, we usually take the median to be halfway between the middle two, in this case the 8.5th observation. Add together the 8th and 9th observations and divide by two to get the median:

$$\text{Median} = \frac{42 + 45}{2} = 43.5$$

For any dataset, whether the number of observations is odd or even, the formula for the median can be calculated as:

$$\text{Median} = \frac{n+1}{2} \text{th observation}$$

EXAMPLE: AVERAGE HEIGHT OF A FOOTBALL TEAM

The heights of players in Ian's football team are shown in Table 4.2. What is the average height of the players?

TABLE 4.2 Heights of all 11 players in Ian's football team (cm)

190	185	182	208	186	187
189	179	183	191	179	

Source: authors' data

The mean height is calculated:

$$\text{Mean} = \frac{190+185+182+208+186+187+189+179+183+191+179}{11}$$

$$= \frac{2059}{11} = 187.18\text{cm}$$

The mode will be 179 cm because there are two players of this height. This is clearly not a very good measure of the average, because 179 cm is actually the shortest height in the team.

To find the median, the data must be ordered:

179 179 182 183 185 186 187 189 190 191 208

With 11 observations, the median will be the $(11 + 1) \div 2 = $ 6th observation. The 6th or middle observation in these data is 186 cm.

You may notice that the mean is larger than the median. This is probably because there is an outlier in the data: the player who is 208 cm tall, far taller than the rest of the team. This outlier increases the value of the mean, but does not affect the median.

Summary

$$\text{Median} = \frac{n+1}{2} \text{ th observation}$$

$$\text{Mean} = \frac{\Sigma x}{n}$$

Mode = number which ocurs most frequently

Averages for grouped data

So far we have only considered ungrouped data. Sometimes you will only have access to data which have been grouped and will need to calculate an average. Table 4.3 shows the ages of Conservative parliamentary candidates elected in the 1992 British general election. The data have been grouped into 10 year intervals.

TABLE 4.3 Ages[1] of elected Conservative Party candidates in the 1992 British general election

Age of candidate	Frequency
30–39	47
40–49	129
50–59	112
60–69	46
70–79	2
Total	336

[1] Ages are at 1 January 1992.

Source: Butler and Kavanagh, 1992. Reproduced with the permission of Macmillan Ltd.

What was the average age of elected Conservative candidates? Let's try all three approaches.

THE MODE

The modal age of the candidates is 40–49. We say this because the largest number of candidates (129) lie in this interval.

However '40–49' is not very specific! This is a major flaw with the mode. For this reason modes are rarely used with grouped data.

THE MEAN

To calculate the mean we need to know what each of the ages is. For example we need the answer to the following question:

- Question: what are the ages of the candidates in the interval 50–59?
- Answer: we don't know! They could be any age between 50 and 59!

Therefore we must make an *assumption*. We must assume that ages are evenly distributed within each interval. Therefore the mean age in an interval will be the *mid-point* of that interval.

What is the mid-point of the interval 50–59? This interval actually goes from 50 years and 0 days to 59 years and 364 days; in other words it goes from 50 to 59.99 recurring. For practical purposes, we can say that the top of the interval is 60. Therefore the mid-point between 50 and 60 is 55. A common mistake is to forget that the interval includes the bit above 59.0 and to use 54.5 as the mid-point.

STEPS FOR CALCULATING A MEAN FOR GROUPED DATA
Step 1
List the mid-points of each category (as in column C in the working to follow).

$$\text{Midpoint} = \left(\frac{\text{top of interval} - \text{bottom of interval}}{2} \right) + \text{bottom of interval}$$

This is easier than it sounds! For example, the mid-point for 30–39 will be:

$$\left(\frac{40 - 30}{2} \right) + 30 = 5 + 30 = 35$$

Remember that 40 (39.99) is the top of the interval, not 39.

Step 2
For each category, multiply the mid-point by the number in that category (see column D in the working).

Step 3
Add together all the numbers you have just obtained in step 2 and divide this total by the total number of observations (336 in this case).

And there you have a mean!
    To understand what has just been done, follow it on the working below:

A Age	B Number of candidates	C Mid-point of interval	D Number × mid-point
30–39	47	35	1 645
40–49	129	45	5 805
50–59	112	55	6 160
60–69	46	65	2 990
70–79	2	75	150
Total	336		16 750

Mean = 16 750 ÷ 336 = 49.85

Therefore the mean age of elected Conservative parliamentary candidates in 1992 was 49. (Age is a special case, where we usually round down to the previous birthday.)

THE MEDIAN
To find the median of a set of grouped data, we must first work out which

observation the median is as before. In this example there are 336 observations in total.

$$\text{Median} = \frac{n+1}{2} = \frac{336+1}{2} = 168.5\text{th observation}$$

The median lies halfway between the 168th and the 169th observation. But how can we find out what observations 168 and 169 are?

To do this, we need to calculate the cumulative frequency distribution, by adding the frequencies together going down the table as shown. The cumulative frequencies show which observations lie in or below each group: for example, 288 observations lie in the 50–59 group or below.

Age group	Frequency	Cumulative frequency	
30–39	47	47	
40–49	129	176	← median in here
50–59	112	288	
60–69	46	334	
70–79	2	336	

Observations 168 and 169 lie in the group 40–49, because they lie between 47 (the highest observation in the 30–39 group) and 176 (the highest observation in the 40–49 group). *But* – whereabouts in the group do they lie?

Let's draw a diagram to help! The top of the line in Figure 4.1 shows the top (50) and bottom (40) of the age interval. The bottom of the line shows the highest observation in the interval (176) and the highest in the interval below (47). We mark 168.5 on the bottom of the line and want to work out what age it corresponds to on the top of the line.

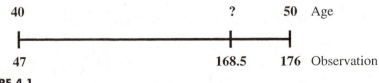

40	**?**	**50** Age
47	168.5	176 Observation

FIGURE 4.1

Now there are three distances to mark on the diagram. The distance between 40 and 50 on the top of the line is 50 – 40 = 10 (this is the width of the interval). The total distance between 47 and 176 on the bottom of the line is 176 – 47 = 129 (this is the frequency in the class). Finally, the distance between the lowest observation 47 and the median 168.5 is worked out as 168.5 – 47 = 121.5. These distances are shown in Figure 4.2. Note that you need to divide the full distance up into 130 parts (one more than the frequency) so as to spread the data uniformly along the continuum.

Therefore we can say that the median is 121.5 ÷ 130 of the way along the interval:

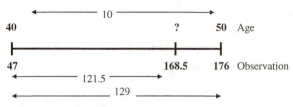

Note: you will need to divide the continuum into one more part than the number of observations (i.e. 130).

FIGURE 4.2

$$\frac{121.5}{130} = 0.94$$

The width of the interval is 10, that is 50 − 40, so we want to move 0.94 of the way along the 10:

$$0.94 \times 10 = 9.4$$

Now add this to 40, the bottom of the interval:

$$40 + 9.4 = 49.4$$

And there we have it! The median age of elected Conservative parliamentary candidates was 49 years. (Always remember to put a proper conclusion like this at the end of your workings.)

The equation we have just calculated in stages was:

$$\text{Median} = 40 + \left(\frac{121.5}{130} \times 10\right) = 49.5$$

This could be turned into an equation we could use to find any median:

Median = Bottom of interval	+	distance from bottom of interval to median	Position of median × width of interval
		total number of observations in interval + 1	

(Remember to divide and multiply before doing the addition.)

Using the different averages

Here are two examples to set you thinking.

EXAMPLE: LEGS

Table 4.4 gives some hypothetical data for the percentage of people in a country who have no legs, only one leg or two legs. What is the 'average' number of legs of people in this country?

TABLE 4.4 Number of legs of people in a country

Number of legs	% of people
0	0.01
1	0.05
2	99.94

The mean and the median of these data are as follows:

$$\text{Mean} = 1.99$$
$$\text{Median} = 2.00$$

The mean implies that 99.94% of the population have more than the 'average' number of legs!

In this case, the median, two legs, is a more sensible average, because nearly everybody has two legs.

EXAMPLE: SWIMMING RATS

There is an apocryphal story from a department in the late 1970s (when Ian was doing his PhD) that one of the lecturers wanted to see whether there was any difference in a rat's brain function if it were swimming in opaque as opposed to clear liquid. As a good opaque liquid he chose milk. The lecturer wanted to see how long it would take for a rat to swim through milk or water (Figure 4.3), so he timed five rats over a fixed distance in each liquid. Table 4.5 shows how the data might have looked. The mean and median times in milk and water have been calculated in Table 4.6.

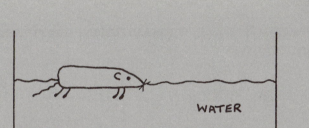

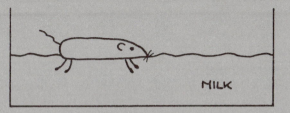

FIGURE 4.3

TABLE 4.5 Time for rats to swim through milk and water (seconds)

Liquid	Rat number				
	1	**2**	**3**	**4**	**5**
Water	10	12	13	15	11
Milk	12	14	17	126	13

Source: authors' data

TABLE 4.6 Average times for rats to swim through milk and water (seconds)

Liquid	Average	
	Median	**Mean**
Water	12	12.2
Milk	14	36.4

Source: authors' data

Points to ponder:

- What do these results suggest about the relative ease of swimming in milk and water for a rat?
- Why are the mean and median so different? Which is a better measure in this situation?
- What happened to rat 4 (Figure 4.4)?!

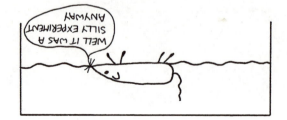

FIGURE 4.4

THE SHAPE OF A DISTRIBUTION

If data are distributed in a symmetrical pattern, the mean and median will be about the same. If data are skewed, the values of the mean and median will be different because the mean is affected by the extreme values.

A histogram lets us see whether a set of data is normally distributed or skewed. The shape of a set of data can also be drawn as a sketch graph, as shown in Figure 4.5.

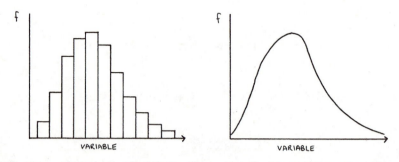

FIGURE 4.5 A HISTOGRAM AND SKETCH GRAPH SHOWING THE DISTRIBUTION OF A DATASET

If data are distributed in a 'bell-shaped' pattern, as in Figure 4.6, we say that they follow a normal distribution. The normal distribution is the most important statistical distribution. Most of the observations are concentrated around the middle, with some values on either side. Data on heights or weights usually follow a normal distribution, because most people are around

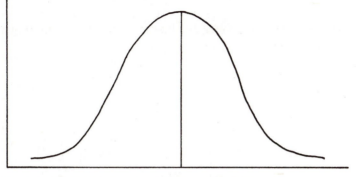

FIGURE 4.6 DATASET FOLLOWING A NORMAL DISTRIBUTION

the average height, for example, but there are a few particularly short and particularly tall individuals in the population. When the data are symmetrical like this, the mean and median are equal.

If a set of data are positively skewed, as in Figure 4.7, the data are concentrated at the lower end of the range. There are more observations where the variable takes a low value. The age of higher education students is a positively skewed variable because most are concentrated in the 18–24 age range but there are some mature students who are older than this.

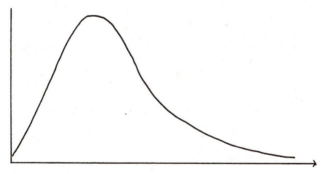

FIGURE 4.7 A POSITIVELY SKEWED DATASET

Where data are positively skewed, the mean will be greater than the median. The value of the mean is pulled upwards by the few very high values, whereas these do not affect the median.

For example, the median number of sexual partners ever among British men is 4, while the mean is 9.9 (Wellings et al., 1994). The mean is much higher than the median due to a small number of men with a very large number of partners.

If a set of data is negatively skewed, the data are concentrated at the higher end of the range, in other words there are more observations where the variable takes a high value. For example, the age at death of adults would be negatively skewed because more adults die at older ages than at younger ages. Figure 4.8 shows the shape of a negatively skewed distribution.

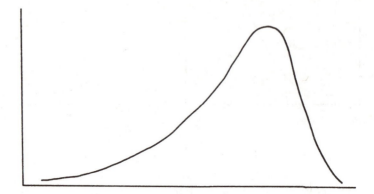

FIGURE 4.8 A NEGATIVELY SKEWED DATASET

Where data are negatively skewed, the mean will be lower than the median. The value of the mean is pulled downwards by the few very small observations.

HANDY HINT
With positively and negatively skewed distributions, it can sometimes be difficult to remember which is which. If you look at the diagrams sideways (rotate clockwise!), the positive skew looks like the letter P!

Guidelines for choosing a measure of the average

Here are some points to bear in mind when deciding whether to use a mean, a median or a mode in a particular situation:

1 Modes are not used very often, though they can be useful in certain circumstances. Avoid them in general!
2 The median is more intelligible to the general public because it is the 'middle' observation.
3 The mean uses all the data, but the median does not. Therefore the mean is influenced more by unusual or extreme data (as in the rat example). If the data are particularly subject to error, use the median.
4 The mean is more useful when the distribution is symmetrical or normal. The median is more useful when the distribution is positively or negatively skewed, because outliers do not affect the median.
5 The mean is best for minimising **sampling variability**. If we take repeated

samples from a population, each sample will give us a slightly different mean and median. However the means will vary less than the medians. (For example, if we took 10 different samples of 20 students and calculated the average weight for each of the 10 groups, the mean weights would differ less between the 10 groups than the median weights.)

PERCENTILES

In the previous chapter we looked at cumulative percentages. These can be taken a step further with the idea of **percentiles**. What is a percentile? Percentiles divide a set of data into hundredths (100 equal parts).

> A percentile is the value at or below which a specified
> percentage of the scores in the distribution fall.

As an example, let's think about the 60th percentile. Here, 60% of the observations in a distribution will lie at or below the 60th percentile. Conversely, 40% of the observations will lie at or above the 60th percentile. So the 60th percentile is like the dividing value between the bottom 60% and the top 40%.

Suppose we had a set of exam marks and we knew that the 30th percentile was a mark of 52. This means that 30% of people who sat the exam got a mark of 52 or lower.

QUESTIONS: PERCENTILES AND INCOME DISTRIBUTIONS

One common use of percentiles is for describing income distributions. Table 4.7 shows some percentiles for gross household income in the UK in 1996–7. The 10th percentile is £85. This means that the bottom 10% of households have a weekly income of £85 or less. However, the 90th percentile tells us that 90% of households have a weekly income of £793 or less, and so from this we can work out that the top 10% of households have a weekly income of £793 or more.

Check that you can answer these questions. The answers are given at the end of the chapter.

(a) What percentage of households have a weekly income of £175 or less?
(b) What percentage of households have a weekly income of £394 or more?
(c) What is the cut-off income for the bottom 70% of households?
(d) What is the median weekly household income?

TABLE 4.7 Percentiles for gross weekly household income in the UK, 1996–7

Percentile	Gross weekly household income (£)
10th	85
20th	127
30th	175
40th	239
50th	313
60th	394
70th	485
80th	602
90th	793

Source: Office for National Statistics, 1997c

You may have had to think about the last question. Remember that the median is the middle of the distribution. The median is therefore the same as the 50th percentile.

Percentiles (or **centiles**) come up in many other contexts. You may have seen centile charts showing the heights and weights of babies. These enable health professionals to see whether a baby is particularly large or small compared to the average.

Table 4.8 shows how percentiles have been used to describe the distribution of times taken between divorce petitions and the court's decision about child maintenance in two different court systems. In the magistrates courts, 50% of cases are dealt with in 48 days or fewer, while in county courts, 50% of cases are dealt with in 131 days or fewer. This suggests that divorce cases are processed much more quickly in magistrates courts. However, both distributions are positively skewed because there are a small number of cases which take a very long time to process. For example, in the magistrates courts, 5% of cases take 312 days or more.

TABLE 4.8 Processing times between divorce petitions and court decisions about child maintenance in magistrates courts and county courts, England, 1990 (days)

Percentile	Type of court	
	Magistrates court	County court
50th (median)	48	131
75th	70	186
95th	312	310

Source: Department of Social Security 1990; Crown copyright, reproduced with the permission of the Controller of Her Majesty's Stationery Office

Calculating percentiles

How can we find out ourselves what the percentiles of a distribution are?

UNGROUPED DATA

With ungrouped data, the formula is as follows:

$$\text{Value of a percentile} = \frac{\text{percentile}}{100} \times (n+1)\text{th observation}$$

where n is the total number of observations.

For example, the 30th percentile in a distribution with 200 observations will be:

$$\frac{30}{100} \times (200+1) = 60.3\text{rd observation}$$

In other words, the 30th percentile will lie 0.3 of the way between the 60th and 61st observations.

You will not often need to calculate percentiles like this and it is rather meaningless to calculate them for a very small dataset.

GROUPED DATA

If the data are grouped, all we need to do is to calculate the cumulative frequencies and then see which group the different percentiles will lie in.

Suppose you are given the data in Table 4.9, a frequency table referring to female life expectancy at birth in 149 countries in 1994. In the third column, the frequencies have been turned into cumulative frequencies.

TABLE 4.9 Female life expectancy in 149 countries of the world, 1994

Female life expectancy	Frequency	Cumulative frequency
35–39	1	1
40–44	4	5
45–49	9	14
50–54	16	30
55–59	11	41
60–64	6	47
65–69	17	64
70–74	34	98
75–79	37	135
80–84	14	149
Total	149	

Source: UNDP, 1997; reproduced with the permission of Oxford University Press

Suppose we want to know roughly where the 40th percentile lies. We can use the previous formula to find out which observation is the 40th:

$$40\text{th percentile} = \frac{40}{100} \times (149 + 1) = 60\text{th observation}$$

Which group will the 60th observation lie in? There are 47 observations in the group 60–64 or below, while the lowest 64 observations lie in the group 65–69 or below. Therefore the 60th observation must lie in the 65–69 group. So the 40th percentile lies in the group with a life expectancy of between 65 and 69 years.

We could calculate the exact values of any percentile by assuming that the observations are evenly spread within each group and interpolating as for the median. You will probably not need to do this except for the 25th, 50th and 75th percentiles which are dealt with separately. The important thing is to understand what percentiles mean when you read statements or tables which contain them.

Special percentiles

We have already noted that the 50th percentile is the same as the median. The median or 50th percentile is probably the most used percentile as it gives an estimate of the middle of a distribution.

You may also come across deciles (which divide a distribution into ten equal parts), quintiles (which divide a distribution into five equal parts) and quartiles (which divide a distribution into four equal parts).

The most common percentiles are:

> 25th percentile = **lower quartile**
> 50th percentile = **median**
> 75th percentile = **upper quartile**

Figure 4.9 shows how the upper quartile, median and lower quartile divide a distribution into four equal parts.

THE LOWER QUARTILE

The lower quartile is the 25th percentile, so 25% of observations will lie at or below the lower quartile (LQ) and 75% at or above it.

The formula for the lower quartile is:

$$\text{Lower quartile} = \frac{n + 1}{4} \text{ th observation} \qquad \text{or LQ} = 0.25 \times (n + 1) \text{ th observation}$$

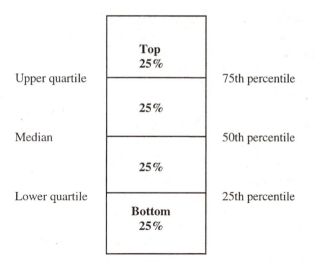

FIGURE 4.9 THE QUARTILES OF A DISTRIBUTION

where n is the total number of observations. This gives exactly the same result as the formula for the 25th percentile as follows, so either can be used:

$$\text{Lower quartile} = \text{25th percentile} = \frac{25}{100} \times (n-1)\text{th observation}$$

Let's go back to the data from the beginning of the chapter about the weekly rent paid by 16 students (the original set in Table 4.1, plus the extra student paying £40). The ordered data were as follows:

35 36 37 40 40 42 42 42 45 45 46 47 49 49 51 51

The lower quartile will be:

$$LQ = \frac{16+1}{4} = 4.25\text{th observation}$$

35 36 37 40 40 42 42 42 45 45 46 47 49 49 51 51
　　　↑ ↑
　 4th 5th

The lower quartile will be 0.25 (one-quarter) of the way between the 4th observation and the 5th observation. In fact, in this case, the 4th and 5th observations are both the same, £40, so there is no calculation to be done. The lower quartile for rents is £40. This means that 25% of students are paying £40 per week or less in rent.

THE UPPER QUARTILE

The upper quartile (UQ) is the 75th percentile, so 75% of observations will lie at or below it and 25% at or above it.

The formula for the upper quartile is:

$$\text{Upper quartile} = \frac{3 \times (n + 1)}{4} \text{ th observation} \quad \text{or} \quad UQ = 0.75 \times (n + 1)\text{th observation}$$

Again, it does not matter which formula you use as they give the same result.

Using the same data, the upper quartile for rents will be:

$$UQ = \frac{3 \times (16 + 1)}{4} = 12.75\text{th observation}$$

35 36 37 40 40 42 42 42 45 45 46 47 49 49 51 51
                                           ↑ ↑
                                        12th 13th

The upper quartile is 0.75 (three-quarters) of the way between 47 and 49. You may be able to work out in your head that the result is 48.5. If not, the way to work it out is to interpolate, as we did when calculating the median. Figure 4.10 shows how.

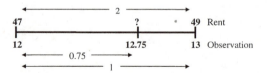

FIGURE 4.10

So: $$\text{Upper quartile} = 47 + \left(\frac{0.75}{1} \times 2\right) = 47 + 15 = 48.5$$

The upper quartile is £48.50, which means that 75% of the students pay £48.50 per week or less in rent.

ANSWERS: PERCENTILES AND INCOME DISTRIBUTIONS

(a) 30% of households.
(b) 40% of households. (60% receive £394 or less).

(c) 70% of households receive less than £485 per week.
(d) The median or middle observation is the 50th percentile. Therefore the median weekly household income is £313.

PRACTICE QUESTIONS

4.1 Table 4.10 shows book publishing rates in 15 industrialised countries in the early 1990s.

TABLE 4.10 **Book publishing rates in 15 industrialised countries, 1992–4**

Country	Book titles published per 100 000 people
Canada	76
USA	20
France	78
Iceland	537
Netherlands	222
Sweden	158
Spain	112
Austria	100
Australia	61
UK	164
Switzerland	217
Denmark	230
Germany	87
Italy	57
Portugal	68

Source: UNDP, 1997; reproduced with the permission of Oxford University Press

(a) Calculate the mean and the median book publishing rates in the 15 countries.
(b) There is an outlier in the data. Which country does this represent?
(c) Remove the outlier from the data and calculate the mean and median book publishing rates again. Which measure of the average changes more with the removal of the outlier?

4.2 The data in Table 4.11 are similar to the example in the text (Table 4.3), but show the age of *defeated* Conservative Party candidates in the 1992 British general election. Calculate the mean age and median age of the defeated candidates. How do these differ from the mean and median ages of elected candidates found in the earlier example?

TABLE 4.11 Ages[1] of defeated Conservative Party candidates in the 1992 British general election

Age of candidate	Frequency
20–29	40
30–39	114
40–49	93
50–59	43
60–69	8
Total	298

[1] Ages are at 1 January 1992.

Source: Butler and Kavanagh, 1992.

4.3 Table 4.12 gives data from a sample of 560 hypothetical people who were asked their income. Calculate the mean and median for these data. Which is greater, and what does this tell you about the distribution of the data?

TABLE 4.12 Annual income of 560 people

Annual income (£000s)	Frequency
0–4.99	20
5–9.99	200
10–19.99	250
20–29.99	50
30–49.99	30
50–69.99	10
Total	560

4.4 Table 4.13 gives some percentiles for the gross weekly earnings of full-time male managers and administrators in different industries. Answer the following questions from the table.

(a) What income separates the bottom 25% and top 75% of managers and administrators in the education industry?

(b) What income do 10% of managers and administrators in construction earn equal to or less than?

(c) What income do 25% of financial intermediaries earn equal to or more than?

(d) What are the highest and lowest incomes of the middle 50% of managers and administrators in the hotel and restaurant trade?

(e) From the data, in which industry are managers and administrators paid the most? And in which the least?

TABLE 4.13 Selected percentiles for gross weekly earnings of full-time male managers and administrators in four industries (£)

Industry	10th percentile	Lower quartile	Median	Upper quartile	90th percentile
Construction	287.9	364.3	460.0	595.0	767.8
Hotels and restaurants	191.9	250.0	342.8	456.0	637.7
Education	307.2	386.6	489.3	602.6	783.9
Financial intermediation	382.1	500.8	675.7	950.1	1439.5

Source: Office for National Statistics, 1997d

4.5 Table 4.14 shows data from a survey of women with babies in rural southern India. The women were asked how many times during the night they fed their baby. Calculate the median, the lower quartile and the upper quartile for this distribution.

TABLE 4.14 Average number of times 179 women from rural southern India feed their baby during the night, 1997–8

Average number of times feed baby during night	Frequency
0	86
1	0
2	11
3	24
4	34
5	13
6	7
7	1
8	1
9	0
10	1
11	0
12	1
Total	179

Source: S.Ganapathy, 1998 (unpublished)

5

SPREADS

Will an average alone be enough to describe the distribution of some data?

No! The two distributions in Figure 5.1 have the same mean, the same mode and the same median. However 'distribution 1' is short and fat while 'distribution 2' is taller and thinner. In other words the two distributions have different spreads.

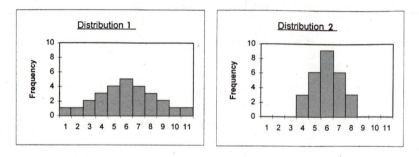

FIGURE 5.1

Don't worry – you haven't just stepped into a sandwich making lesson. The **spread** is another indicator of a distribution (like the average). A measure of spread summarises how variable a distribution is.

Look at Figure 5.2. How has the age at marriage changed between the 1960s and the 1990s? We cannot tell from the diagrams whether the mean age at marriage has changed, because there are no numbers on the X axis. However,

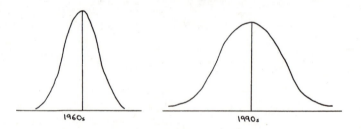

FIGURE 5.2 DISTRIBUTION OF AGE AT MARRIAGE FOR BRITISH WOMEN

assuming that the scale is the same on both diagrams, it would appear that the age at marriage has become more variable in the 1990s, because the distribution is wider (more spread out). In other words, a larger proportion of women are marrying much earlier and later than the average than they were in the 1960s.

MEASURES OF SPREAD

How can we measure how 'spread out' a distribution is? We have already used percentiles and quartiles to discover more about the shape of a distribution. But it is often useful to be able to summarise how spread out a distribution is by using just one number (rather than several percentiles or both the upper and lower quartiles).

Three possible measures which can be used are:

- the **range**
- the **interquartile range**
- the **standard deviation** and the **variance**.

The three measures will be calculated on the dataset in Table 5.1 in order to see how they work.

TABLE 5.1 Birthweights of 12 babies born in rural southern India in 1997–8 (g)

2500	4000	3500	3000	3100	3000
4000	2500	3500	3000	2800	3000

Source: S. Ganapathy, 1998 (unpublished)

EXAMPLE: BIRTHWEIGHTS IN INDIA

A researcher asked mothers in rural southern India how much their youngest child weighed at birth. Unfortunately the majority of the women had not had their baby weighed at birth and so she only obtained 12 birthweights from a large sample of women. The weights of these 12 babies, in grams, are shown in Table 5.1. What is the average birthweight among those who responded? Do you think that the sample is representative of the weights of Indian babies?

You should be able to work out the answer to the first question. The mean birthweight is 3158.33 grams and the median is 3000 grams (check these yourself for practice). As for the representativeness of the sample, it is a rather small sample. It is possible that only women who gave birth in a hospital had their baby weighed and such women may be better off than the majority who gave birth at home. You may also have noticed that the data are not very precise: they seem to have been rounded to the nearest 100 grams. In real life, it is often hard to get the data that we need to answer our research questions.

In order to get a real feel for the data we need to know how variable the birthweights in the sample are. To answer this question, we will calculate the range, interquartile range and standard deviation for the data. In each case we will first introduce the measure.

The range

The range is easy to calculate using the following formula:

Range = largest observation − smallest observation

For the birthweight data the range will be calculated as:

Range = 4000 − 2500 = 1500 grams

The range measures the total width of the dataset. It is easy to calculate and makes intuitive sense to the public. However it is very sensitive to extreme values. For example, if a hypothetical baby with a birthweight of 4500 g were added to the dataset, the range would increase to 2000 g just because of this one baby.

Interquartile range (IQR)

The interquartile range is usually used as a measure of spread if the data are skewed or the median is being used as a measure of the average.

The formula for the interquartile range (also known as the interquartile deviation or mid-spread) is as follows:

Interquartile range = upper quartile − lower quartile

Therefore, to find the interquartile range, the upper and lower quartiles must be found. To revise this topic see Chapter 3.

For the birthweight data, the 12 observations must first be ranked:

2500 2500 2800 3000 3000 3000 3000 3100 3500 3500 4000 4000

Then the upper and lower quartiles can be found:

$$UQ = \frac{3}{4}(n+1) = 9.75\text{th observation}$$

The 9th observation is 3500 and so is the 10th observation! This makes life easy; the upper quartile or 9.75th observation will be 3500 grams.

$$LQ = \frac{n+1}{4} = 3.25\text{th observation}$$

The 3rd observation is 2800 grams and the 4th observation is 3000 grams, so the 3.25th observation will be:

LQ = 2800 + (0.25 × (3000 − 2800)) = 2850 grams

Draw a diagram to help you with these calculations if necessary.

Now the interquartile range (IQR) can be calculated:

IQR = UQ − LQ = 3500 − 2850 = 650 grams

This means that the middle 50% of observations (birthweights) have a range of 650 grams.

The standard deviation

The standard deviation (SD) is usually used when the data are not too skewed or when the mean is being used as a measure of the average.

The standard deviation measures the 'average' amount by which all the values deviate from the mean; in other words, it tells us something about the size of the **residuals**. A residual is the difference between a particular observation and the mean. More accurately speaking, the standard deviation is the square root of the sum of the squared residuals! The larger is the standard deviation, the greater is the spread of the data.

The standard deviation (SD) is calculated using this equation:

$$SD = \sqrt{\left[\frac{\Sigma(Y_i - \bar{Y})^2}{n-1} \right]}$$

where Y_i are the observations (i indicates *all* the values of Y rather than just one) and $\bar{Y}$ is the mean.

In words rather than jargon, the steps that must be taken to work out this formula are as follows:

1 Calculate the residual $(Y - \bar{Y})$ for each observation, that is, the observation minus the mean.
2 Square each residual.
3 Add together all your squared residuals (Σ means 'sum of').
4 Divide your answer by $n - 1$, where n is the total number of observations.
5 Finally, square root the whole thing.

EXAMPLE: STANDARD DEVIATION OF BIRTHWEIGHTS

The best way to do a calculation like this is to draw up a worksheet with a column for the observations, a column containing the mean and two columns for the first two steps of the calculation. The following shows how a worksheet would look for the calculation of the standard deviation for the birthweight data. Note that the Y_i values are the values for the 12 different babies. The mean has also been calculated beforehand.

Observation Y_i	Mean $\bar{Y}$	Residual $Y_i-\bar{Y}$	Residual squared $(Y_i-\bar{Y})^2$
2500	3158.33	−658.33	433 398.39
4000	3158.33	841.67	708 408.39
3500	3158.33	341.67	116 738.39
3000	3158.33	−158.33	25 068.39
3100	3158.33	−58.33	3 402.39
3000	3158.33	−158.33	25 068.39
4000	3158.33	841.67	708 408.39
2500	3158.33	−658.33	433 398.39
3500	3158.33	341.67	116 738.39
3000	3158.33	−158.33	25 068.39
2800	3158.33	−358.33	128 400.39
3000	3158.33	−158.33	25 068.39
Total: $\Sigma (Y_i-\bar{Y})^2$			2 749 166.67

There are 12 observations, so $n - 1 = 11$. We now have all the numbers to put into the formula:

$$\text{SD} = \sqrt{\left[\frac{2\,749\,166.67}{11}\right]} = 499.92$$

The standard deviation of the birthweights in the sample is 499.92 grams (or approximately 500 grams). We will see in a later chapter what inferences we can make as a result of knowing this.

EXAMPLE: STANDARD DEVIATION OF FOOTBALLERS' HEIGHTS

With practice, you will remember how to calculate a standard deviation by hand. Here is another worked example to help you get the hang of it. We will use the data on the heights of Ian's football team from Table 4.2.

Observation Y_i	Mean $\bar{Y}$	Residual $Y_i - \bar{Y}$	Residual squared $(Y_i - \bar{Y})^2$
190	187.18	2.82	7.95
185	187.18	−2.18	4.75
182	187.18	−5.18	26.83
208	187.18	20.82	433.47
186	187.18	−1.18	1.39
187	187.18	−0.18	0.03
189	187.18	1.82	3.31
179	187.18	−8.18	66.91
183	187.18	−4.18	17.47
191	187.18	3.82	14.59
179	187.18	−8.18	66.91
Total: $\Sigma (Y_i - \bar{Y})^2$			643.61

$$ SD = \sqrt{\left[\frac{\Sigma\left(Y_i - \bar{Y}\right)^2}{n-1} \right]} = \sqrt{\left[\frac{643.61}{11-1} \right]} = 8.02 $$

The standard deviation of the heights of Ian's football team is 8.02 cm.

FURTHER POINTS ABOUT THE STANDARD DEVIATION

Working out the standard deviation by hand is time-consuming but it does help you to understand what it really means in terms of being the square root of the sum of the squared residuals. In practice, datasets tend to be much larger and so the standard deviation is often found using a calculator or computer package. (Calculators often have two formulae for the standard deviation, so make sure you use the one dividing by $n-1$ and not just n; using $n-1$ gives you the standard deviation of a sample whereas using n gives the standard deviation for a population, and in real life data usually come from a sample.)

What does the standard deviation actually tell us? A larger standard deviation means that the data are very spread out, while a smaller standard deviation tells us that the data are quite concentrated around the mean. When comparing two distributions with similar potential ranges, the one with a larger standard deviation has a wider spread than the other.

Suppose the marks for an exam in International Relations had a standard deviation of 6.4%, while the marks for a course on Gender in Society had a standard deviation of 19.1%. This means that the marks for Gender in Society were much more variable than the marks for International Relations. More students taking Gender in Society received marks much higher or lower than the mean than the students who took International Relations, where the marks were generally closer to the mean.

Another feature of the standard deviation is that it uses *all* the observations, just like the mean. Moving one observation further away from the mean will increase the standard deviation, while moving the observation closer to the mean will reduce the standard deviation.

THE VARIANCE

The variance is simply the standard deviation squared. Omitting the last stage of the standard deviation formula where the value is square rooted will give the variance instead of the standard deviation.

In the example with the birthweights, the standard deviation was 499.92 g, but the variance found before square rooting was 249 924.24 g.

The variance is used far less frequently than the standard deviation as a measure of spread. The reason for this is that the standard deviation is in the same units as the data and so is more easily interpretable. It is important to understand what the variance means if you see it used in a report.

THE STANDARD DEVIATION FOR GROUPED DATA

In the previous chapter we calculated the mean for grouped data. What happens if you need to calculate a standard deviation for data that are grouped?

The method is similar to that for calculating the mean. Find the mid-point of each group and subtract the mean from the mid-point to obtain the residuals. Square each residual as usual and then, in an extra column, multiply it by the frequency (number in the group). Then add this column up and use it in the equation.

As a formula, this could be written:

$$SD = \sqrt{\left\{ \frac{\sum\left[(\text{mid-point} - \text{mean})^2 \times \text{frequency}\right]}{n-1} \right\}}$$

Choosing between measures of spread

RANGE
This is not a very good measure, although it is easy to understand.

STANDARD DEVIATION (OR VARIANCE)
The standard deviation should be used with a mean as a measure of spread relative to the mean.

It makes use of all the observations, which is a good thing if the data are not skewed. However if the data are skewed the standard deviation will be affected by outliers. Therefore it is best to use the standard deviation as a measure of spread when the data are not skewed.

The standard deviation is also preferable in terms of **sampling variability**. If we take lots of samples from a population, the mean value and standard deviation of each sample will be slightly different due to chance. But the means and standard deviations of the different samples will vary less than the medians and IQRs of the different samples, so the mean and standard deviation are preferable.

INTERQUARTILE RANGE
The interquartile range should be used as a measure of spread when the median is used as the measure of the average. The interquartile range does not use all the observations in the dataset (it only considers the middle 50%) and so it is not affected by outliers. This means that it is more reliable as a measure of spread than the standard deviation when there are outliers or the data are skewed.

It is however less reliable in terms of sampling variability than the standard deviation, as explained above.

PRESENTING THE SPREAD OF A DISTRIBUTION GRAPHICALLY

Some of the graphical methods discussed in Chapter 3 show the shape of a distribution. These include histograms and stem and leaf plots. However there are also methods of presenting the standard deviation or interquartile range of a distribution using tables and box plots.

Tables of means and standard deviations

The National Fertility Studies in the USA in 1965, 1970 and 1975 collected data on the frequency of intercourse among married women. Some of the data collected are shown in Table 5.2. There appears to be a decline in the frequency of intercourse with age, but the trend over time is less clear.

TABLE 5.2 Mean frequency of intercourse for married women aged 30 or below in four weeks before interview, USA, 1965–75

Age	Year of Interview		
	1965	**1970**	**1975**
<19	12.5	11.6	12.1
19, 20	9.6	9.8	12.1
21, 22	9.3	8.3	10.3
23, 24	7.8	9.7	9.8
25, 26	7.6	9.4	8.9
27, 28	7.5	8.9	9.1
29, 30	6.7	8.6	8.7

Source: Trussell and Westoff, 1980

If we consider the age group 19–20, it appears that the mean frequency of intercourse increased slightly between 1965 and 1970, from 9.6 times to 9.8 times in the four-week period. The mean frequency of intercourse then rose to 12.1 times by the 1975 survey.

But suppose we took another sample for each of the three years: would we expect to get exactly the same means? No! Each sample we take from a population will give a slightly different answer (this is known as **sampling variability** and we will discuss it more in Chapter 8).

The trouble here is that 9.6 and 9.8 are so close together that if different samples of women had been taken there might not be an increase between 1965 and 1970 at all!

To get a better idea of what is really going on, we can include a measure of variation with each mean. To make means more meaningful (!), include the standard deviation and the number in the sample for each mean in a table. The standard deviation can then tell us how variable the distribution in the sample is and the number in the sample gives an idea of how good the sample mean may be as an estimate of the population mean. Overall this can give us some idea of how much the means of different samples will vary.

Table 5.3 gives some sensible standard deviations and sample sizes for these data. The standard deviations show that there could be quite large variations in the means of different samples. So it may not be safe to say that the frequency of sex has increased between 1965 and 1970 because a slightly different sample could have led to a different conclusion.

TABLE 5.3 Means and standard deviations for frequency of intercourse for married women aged 19–20 in four weeks before interview, USA, 1965–75

	Year of interview		
	1965	**1970**	**1975**
Mean	9.6	9.8	12.1
Standard deviation	1.1	1.3	1.2
n	19	249	219

Source: means from Trussell and Westoff, 1980; other data hypothetical

We will come back to this example in Chapter 9, where we will find out how to be confident about whether the frequency of sex increased or not.

Note that we have been assuming a normal distribution here. You may like to think about whether it is safe to do so in this instance.

Box plots

Box plots are used to present the median and interquartile range of a distribution, along with any outliers.

Suppose you ask 20 students how many units of alcohol they consumed in the week after exams and obtained the results in Table 5.4.

TABLE 5.4 Number of units of alcohol consumed by 20 hypothetical students in the week after exams

6	13	15	8	9	0	40	20	12	27
4	27	10	21	39	50	3	25	17	10

To draw a box plot, we will need to calculate the median, lower quartile and upper quartile plus some other measures.

STEPS FOR DRAWING A BOX PLOT

Step 1: *order the data*

0 3 4 8 9 10 10 12 13 15 16 17 20 21 25 27 27 39 40 50

Step 2: *calculate the median, lower quartile and upper quartile*
Try this yourself for revision: the answers are given later on.

(a) Median =
(b) LQ =
(c) UQ =

Step 3: *calculate the interquartile range*

(d) IQR = UQ − LQ =

Step 4: *calculate the lower and upper fences*
The following are the formulae:

> **Lower fence** = lower quartile − (1.5 × interquartile range)
> **Upper fence** = upper quartile + (1.5 × interquartile range)

(e) Lower fence =
(f) Upper fence =

Step 5: *find the first observations inside the fences*

(g) First observation above lower fence =
(h) First observation below upper fence =

Step 6: *list the outliers*
Outliers are observations which lie outside the two fences, in other words observations greater than the upper fence or smaller than the lower fence.

(i) Outliers =

Step 7: *range*
Look at the range of the data so you know what to put on the Y axis of your graph.

Step 8: *draw a box plot*

Figure 5.3 shows how to plot all your answers onto a graph.

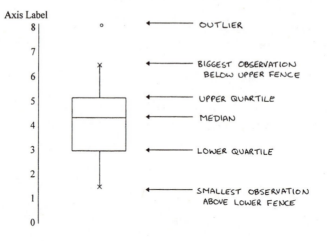

FIGURE 5.3 DRAWING A BOX PLOT

The answers for the calculations are:

(a) Median = 15.5
(b) LQ = 9.25
(c) UQ = 26.5

(d) IQR = 17.25
(e) Lower fence = –8.00
(f) Upper fence = 43.75
(g) First observation above lower fence = 0
(h) First observation below upper fence = 40
(i) Outlier = 50 (50 is greater than the upper fence, 43.75).

Figure 5.4 shows these results on a box plot.

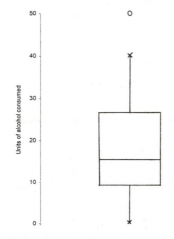

FIGURE 5.4 A BOX PLOT SHOWING UNITS OF ALCOHOL CONSUMED BY 20 STUDENTS IN
THE WEEK AFTER EXAMS

INTERPRETING BOX PLOTS
How should a box plot be interpreted? There are two important points to
consider:

• Is it symmetric (in the vertical sense)? A symmetric box plot implies a
  normal distribution. If the distribution is skewed, the box plot will not be
  symmetric.
• Are there outliers? Can they be explained?

The box plot in Figure 5.4 shows that the median number of units drunk in the
week after exams was around 15. The box is not symmetrical; in fact it is
positively skewed. We can tell this because the part of the box itself below
the median represents a quarter of the students and the part of the box above
the median represents another quarter of the students. The quarter below the
median drank between 9.25 and 15.5 units in the week and the quarter
above the median drank between 15.5 and 26.5 units – a wider range. Thus the
quarter of students below the median are more concentrated (that part of
the box is smaller) than the quarter above where the box is larger.

There is one outlier – the student who drunk 50 units during the week. Were they having a great party or drowning their sorrows?

Figure 5.5 is another example of a box plot. This has been drawn slightly differently but can be interpreted in the same way. It shows the percentage of families which are lone parent families in the different districts of Greater London.

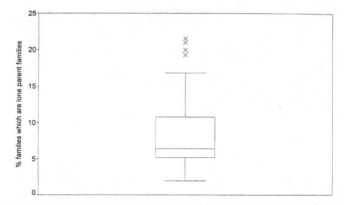

FIGURE 5.5 PERCENTAGE OF FAMILIES WHICH ARE LONE PARENT FAMILIES IN THE 64 DISTRICTS OF GREATER LONDON (OFFICE FOR NATIONAL STATISTICS, 1998B)

We can see that the median percentage of lone parents in a district is around 6.5%. The box plot is again positively skewed: all the observations below the median are concentrated between around 2% and 6.5%, while the observations above the median are far more spread out. There are four outliers, all with a particularly high percentage of lone parent families. These districts are Lambeth, Hackney, Southwark and Islington. Sometimes outliers like this are named on the box plot itself.

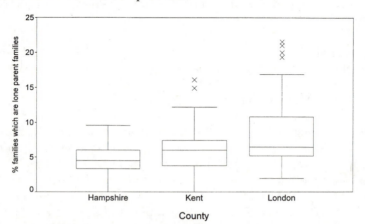

FIGURE 5.6 PERCENTAGE OF FAMILIES WHICH ARE LONE PARENT FAMILIES IN URBAN AREAS OF HAMPSHIRE, KENT AND GREATER LONDON (OFFICE FOR NATIONAL STATISTICS, 1998B)

Several box plots can be presented on the same graph in order to compare different groups or areas. Figure 5.6 compares the percentage of families which are lone parent families in Greater London districts with the percentages in urban areas of Hampshire and Kent. Notice that the median percentages in Greater London and Kent are very similar, but the box plots show how the two distributions are in fact quite different.

PRACTICE QUESTIONS

5.1 Table 5.5 gives the marks awarded to 10 students for two pieces of assessed coursework.

TABLE 5.5 Marks awarded to 10 students in two assessments

Student number	Assessment 1	Assessment 2
1	53	55
2	61	77
3	54	57
4	59	70
5	59	61
6	48	50
7	53	41
8	49	60
9	60	17
10	60	55

Source: authors' data

(a) Calculate the mean mark for assessment 1 and assessment 2. Did the students improve between the two assessments on average?
(b) Calculate the standard deviation of the marks for each assessment. In which assessment was performance more variable?

5.2 Suppose that a group of 20 women were asked how many sexual partners they had had in the last 12 months. The hypothetical results are shown in Table 5.6.

TABLE 5.6 Number of sexual partners in the last 12 months among a group of 20 women (hypothetical data)

1	0	3	1	2	12	0	0	1	3
2	1	2	0	16	1	1	1	3	2

(a) Find the median, upper quartile and lower quartile of the data and hence the interquartile range.

(b) Why is the interquartile range a better measure of spread than the standard deviation for these data?

5.3 The manager of a petrol station is hoping to reduce the time taken by customers queuing to pay for their petrol. To obtain some initial data on waiting times, he pays somebody to measure how long a sample of customers have to wait in a queue before being served. The data are shown in Table 5.7. Draw a box plot of the waiting times and comment on it.

TABLE 5.7 Waiting times before being served in a petrol station shop (hypothetical data) (seconds)

0	22	33	65	10
8	0	122	32	55
41	60	35	44	15
61	0	18	29	0
5	37	11	23	12
13	31	0	26	14

6

TRANSFORMING DATA

Are data sacrosanct or can we do things with them?

We can do things with them, within reason! When you look at some data, you should ask yourself:

- What are the possible errors in the data?
- Can the data be improved?

How might you want to improve some data?

1 You might want to make meaningful comparisons between distributions in different scales. For example, was it hotter in Miami (105 °F) or Nice (29 °C) on a certain day? The data could be altered to make them easier to compare, for example by converting both scales into degrees Celsius.
2 You might want to highlight differences in the data rather than the data themselves, for example, to look at whether observations are above or below the mean, rather than considering the actual numbers.
3 If there are lots of cases with missing or inconsistent data (for example, age at first marriage comes before age at divorce), it is often worth removing these cases from the dataset.

These procedures do not constitute 'fiddling' the data! They just make it easier to use and understand!

Here we will look at:

- Adding or subtracting a constant to the data or multiplying or dividing the data by a constant. This is known as **scaling**.
- **Standardising** the data.

SCALING

Adding or subtracting a constant

Consider a group of women who are training for the London marathon. Their weights before they started training are shown in Table 6.1.

TABLE 6.1 Weights of five women before training for the London marathon (kg)

55	59	63	66	67

The mean weight of the women was:

$$\text{Mean} = \frac{310}{5} = 62 \text{ kg}$$

The standard deviation of their weights is calculated as follows:

X	$\bar{X}$	$X - \bar{X}$	$(X - \bar{X})^2$
55	62	−7	49
59	62	−3	9
63	62	1	1
66	62	4	16
67	62	5	25
Total			100

$$\text{Standard deviation} = \sqrt{\left(\frac{100}{5-1}\right)} = \sqrt{25} = 5 \text{ kg}$$

So the mean weight of the women was 62 kg with a standard deviation of 5 kg.

Now suppose that the women had been running five times a week and had each lost 5 kg. Their new weights are shown in Table 6.2. We have, in effect, subtracted a constant (fixed) number (5 kg) from each weight.

TABLE 6.2 Weights of five women after each had lost 5 kg (kg)

50	54	58	61	62

What are the mean weight and SD now?

$$\text{Mean} = \frac{285}{5} = 57 \text{ kg}$$

X	$\bar{X}$	$X - \bar{X}$	$(X - \bar{X})^2$
50	57	−7	49
54	57	−3	9
58	57	1	1
61	57	4	16
62	57	5	25
Total			100

$$\text{Standard deviation} = \sqrt{\left(\frac{100}{5-1}\right)} = \sqrt{(25)} = 5 \text{ kg}$$

What do you notice? The mean has decreased by 5 kg and the standard deviation has stayed the same!

Why has the standard deviation not changed? If you look at the workings, you will see that the residuals $X - \bar{X}$ have not changed at all. Each observation is still the same distance away from the mean as before. So the shape of the distribution has not changed at all.

These facts always hold true. The rule can be summarised as follows:

Adding or subtracting by a constant:

- changes the mean by the value of the constant
  - does not change the standard deviation.

Multiplying or dividing by a constant

Suppose instead that the hard training had the effect of reducing each runner's weight by 10%. To find the new weights, the old weights must be multiplied by 0.9 to make them 10% lower. The new weights are shown in Table 6.3 and the mean and standard deviation are found as follows:

TABLE 6.3 Weights of five women after a 10% weight loss (kg)

49.5	53.1	56.7	59.4	60.3

$$\text{Mean} = \frac{279}{5} = 55.8 \text{ kg}$$

$$\text{Standard deviation} = \sqrt{\left(\frac{81}{4}\right)} = 4.5 \text{ kg}$$

In fact, the mean of 55.8 kg is equal to the original mean multiplied by 0.9, as the following workings show. The standard deviation of 4.5 kg is equal to the original standard deviation multiplied by 0.9.

Mean: $62 \times 0.9 = 55.8$ kg
Standard deviation: $5 \times 0.9 = 4.5$ kg

Here you can see that a different rule applies to multiplying or dividing by a constant than that for adding or subtracting a constant:

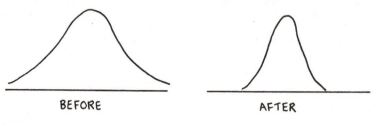

> Multiplying or dividing by a constant:
>
> - changes the mean by an amount equal to multiplying
>   or dividing by the constant
> - does the same to the standard deviation.

A 'multiplicative' effect like this shrinks or expands the range of the distribution. In Figure 6.1, was the constant used 1, more than 1, or less than 1?

BEFORE   AFTER

FIGURE 6.1

The constant used was less than 1, because the range has decreased. Multiplying by a constant of more than 1 will increase the range, while multiplying by a constant of less than 1 will decrease the range.

Knowing the two rules about scaling can save a lot of time. Instead of having to work out the new mean and standard deviation of a set of data that has been changed by a constant, you can simply apply the rules.

STANDARDISING DATA

Sometimes you may want to compare data from more than one distribution. To do this you need to standardise the data so that they are easily comparable. This can be done by calculating Z-**scores**. A variable where the observations have been converted into Z-scores is known as a **standardised variable**.

Suppose that two friends are arguing about who did better in their optional subject exam. Claire obtained 65 in her Politics exam, while Zoe obtained 60 for Economics. Which student did better?

We could simply say that Claire did better, because she got the higher mark. But what if most students did quite well in Politics while a lot of students did badly in Economics, and so Zoe actually performed relatively well? To answer the question properly, we need to know how the other students doing those subjects performed.

On investigation, you manage to find out that for Politics the average (mean) mark was 60, with a standard deviation of 5, while for the Economics course the mean mark was 50, with a standard deviation of 6. Now we have enough information to calculate a Z-score.

A Z-score is calculated using the equation:

$$Z_i = \frac{X_i - \bar{X}}{SD}$$

where X_i is the individual mark, $\bar{X}$ is the mean mark for the whole class and SD is the standard deviation for the whole class. In words rather than jargon, the same formula can be written as:

$$Z = \frac{observation - mean}{standard\ deviation}$$

The Z-score for Claire will be:

$$Z = \frac{65 - 60}{5} = 1.00$$

The Z-score for Zoe will be:

$$Z = \frac{60 - 50}{6} = 1.67$$

Zoe has the higher Z-score and so she in fact did better than Claire relative to the other students in the class. The results tell us that Zoe's score is 1.67 standard deviations above the mean result for Economics, while Claire's result was only 1 standard deviation above the mean Politics mark.

In fact both the students did well, because they scored above the average and hence had a positive Z-score. Suppose a third friend, Jo, obtained a mark of 47 in the Economics exam. Jo's Z-score would have been:

$$Z = \frac{47 - 50}{6} = -0.5$$

Jo had a negative Z-score, which meant that her Economics mark was below average for the class. In fact, her mark was exactly 0.5 standard deviations below the average. This makes sense if you think about it; the standard deviation is 6, so 0.5 of a standard deviation is 3. Jo's mark of 47 is 3 marks below the mean, 50.

By now, you have probably worked out the rules for interpreting Z-scores, as highlighted in the box.

> A Z-score measures the number of standard deviations an
> observation is away from the mean.
> A positive Z-score shows that the observation is greater than the
> mean (above average).
> A negative Z-score shows that the observation is lower than
> the mean (below average).
> The Z-score will be zero if the observation equals the mean.

Most Z-scores will lie in the range from $Z = -2$ to $Z = 2$. Values more than two standard deviations from the mean tend to be extreme values (outliers).

Note that we are assuming here that the results for both exams were roughly *normally distributed*, in other words a histogram of the results would be bell-shaped and not skewed. This is why it is safe to use the mean and standard deviation as measures of the average and spread.

The mean and standard deviation of a standardised variable

A standardised variable has certain properties.

Let's go back to the runners (before they were fortunate enough to lose weight!) and investigate some properties of Z-scores. The mean weight of the runners was 62 kg with a standard deviation of 5 kg. The Z-scores would be calculated like this:

X	$Z = \dfrac{X_i - \bar{X}}{SD}$
55	−1.4
59	−0.6
63	0.2
66	0.8
67	1.0

Try adding up all the Z-scores. What do you get?

The answer is zero! So if we wanted to calculate the mean Z-score, it would be $0 \div 5 = 0$! The mean of a set of Z-scores is always zero, so you can check that you have calculated your Z-scores correctly by seeing if they add up to zero.

To calculate the standard deviation of the Z-scores, we would have to subtract the mean (mean Z-score = 0) from each Z-score and then square it:

Z	$(Z_i - \bar{Z})^2$
−1.4	1.96
−0.6	0.36
0.2	0.04
0.8	0.64
1.0	1.00
	4.00

$$SD = \sqrt{\left[\frac{\Sigma(Z_i - \bar{Z})^2}{n-1}\right]} = \sqrt{\left[\frac{4.00}{4}\right]} = \sqrt{1} = 1$$

Therefore the standard deviation of the Z-scores is 1.

You won't need to do this calculation, but what we have discovered is a rule which applies to any dataset (whatever its shape) once you have standardised it:

> The mean of a standardised variable is zero.
> The standard deviation of a standardised variable is one.

This is useful when calculating a set of Z-scores, because you can check that your answers are right by finding the mean and standard deviation of them.

Z-scores are extremely useful, especially when you want to amalgamate scores on different scales (as in the first example and the example below) in order to rank people or countries in numerical order.

Calculating a Z-score index

Table 6.4 shows the distribution of marks on some introductory first-year courses taken by students in the first semester. All students take four subjects and we want to compare two students, student A and student B. Why would it not be fair to just find the average score of each student?

TABLE 6.4 Distribution of marks on six first-year courses

Course	Mean mark (%)	Standard deviation
Quantitative methods	65	2
Politics	55	5
Sociology	54	4
Psychology	49	3
Economics	51	6
Demography	53	4

The results would be biased in favour of those who did quantitative methods and other subjects with high mean scores. We want a score for each course which indicates the relative position of an individual on that course. Therefore we should standardise the data and calculate Z-scores.

Table 6.5 shows the actual marks obtained by the two students.

TABLE 6.5 Marks obtained by two students in first semester

Course	Marks for student A (%)	Marks for student B (%)
Quantitative methods	67	–
Politics	53	52
Sociology	56	54
Psychology	43	–
Economics	–	57
Demography	–	57

Who did better overall? It is not possible to tell at a glance, so a strategy is needed! The best strategy is to calculate a Z-score for each mark and then combine them.

For example, Student A got 67 for Quantitative Methods. The mean score for that course was 65 with a standard deviation of 2. The Z-score will be:

$$Z = \frac{67 - 65}{2} = 1.00$$

What does this tell us? It tells us that student A's mark for Quantitative Methods was exactly one standard deviation above the average mark for that course. In other words the student did pretty well!

Try the rest yourself and see if you come up with the answers shown within the mean calculations to follow. Note that a Z-score of 0 means that a student got the average mark. A Z-score of 1 means that they were one standard deviation above the average; a Z-score of –2 means they were two standard deviations below the average; and so on.

Now we need to find the mean Z-score for each student by adding up their Z-scores and dividing by four (the number of exams taken).

$$\text{Student A:} \quad \text{mean Z-score} = \frac{1.0 + (-0.4) + 0.5 + (-2.0)}{4} = -0.225$$

$$\text{Student B:} \quad \text{mean Z-score} = \frac{0.0 + 0.6 + 1.0 + 1.0}{4} = 0.65$$

Therefore we can conclude that student B did better then average on the chosen courses (because the mean Z-score is positive) and student A came below average when we put all the courses together (because the mean Z-score is negative). Student B performed better overall in the exams than student A.

EXAMPLE: DEPRIVATION IN SOUTHAMPTON

A common use of a Z-score index is to compare different regions. This example uses data from the 1991 Census to compare how relatively well off or deprived different wards in Southampton were in 1991. Social deprivation is measured here using three variables: the percentage of households who do not own a car; percentage of residents with a limiting long-term illness; and the percentage of households not in owner-occupied accommodation. The data are shown in Table 6.6. The variables have been named NOCAR, ILL and NOTOWN for short. A high value for any of the three variables could indicate that a ward is socially deprived, whereas a low value would suggest that a ward is more affluent. One reason for using Z-scores is that the raw percentages on the three variables would have very different ranges. One with generally large values would swamp the index compared with one with generally small values. By standardising each we compare like with like.

TABLE 6.6 Three variables measuring social deprivation for 15 Southampton wards, 1991

Ward	Deprivation measure		
	% of households with residents with no car (NOCAR)	% of residents with limiting long-term illness (ILL)	% of households not in owner-occupied accommodation (NOTOWN)
Bargate	56.9	16.1	65.4
Bassett	25.4	11.3	29.9
Bitterne	37.5	12.6	52.3
Bitterne Park	31.6	11.8	35.3
Coxford	32.5	10.7	44.9
Freemantle	36.5	13.1	32.4
Harefield	32.6	12.5	32.9
Millbrook	38.5	13.2	42.5
Peartree	32.2	12.6	27.4
Portswood	33.3	12.9	36.6
Redbridge	39.3	13.2	52.2
St Lukes	40.2	15.3	43.8
Shirley	32.6	12.9	29.4
Sholing	28.1	11.3	23.9
Woolston	34.4	12.5	40.4

Source: 1991 Census Hampshire, Ward and Civil Parish Monitor, OPCS, Crown Copyright 1993

To find out which wards are relatively more deprived or more affluent, the three variables can be combined in a Z-score index. With a large number of observations like this, it may be better to carry out the calculations on a computer spreadsheet.

First, the mean and standard deviation for each variable must be found. These are shown in Table 6.7.

TABLE 6.7 Mean and standard deviation of the three deprivation variables for Southampton wards

Ward	Deprivation measure		
	% of households with residents with no car (NOCAR)	% of residents with limiting long-term illness (ILL)	% of households not in owner-occupied accommodation (NOTOWN)
Mean	35.44	12.80	39.29
Standard deviation	7.19	1.41	11.20

Source: Data from 1991 Census Hampshire, Ward and Civil Parish Monitor, OPCS, Crown Copyright 1993

Secondly, Z-scores are calculated. For example, the Z-score for NOCAR for the Bargate district is worked out as follows:

$$Z = \frac{\text{observation} - \text{mean}}{\text{SD}} = \frac{56.9 - 35.44}{7.19} = 2.98$$

This is a very high Z-score and indicates that the Bargate ward is extremely deprived in terms of car ownership; in other words the percentage of people living in households with no car is particularly high (over three standard deviations above the average).

The Z-scores for all three variables are shown in Table 6.8. They have been calculated to two decimal places. When calculating Z-scores, check that the values of the Z-scores look sensible: they should mainly lie between −2 and +2. The Z-score for Bargate in the example is unusual, but if we check the raw data, we see that the ward does indeed have an extremely high percentage of people in households with no car (57%).

The final column in Table 6.8 shows the Z-score index, where the three Z-scores for each variable have been added together and the total divided by three (because there are three variables). This gives us a mean Z-score or index value for each ward.

For example, in the Bargate ward, the mean Z-score is calculated as follows:

$$\text{Index value} = \frac{2.98 + 2.34 + 2.33}{3} = 2.55$$

Note that you may be thinking correctly that the mean of a set of Z-scores equals zero. This applies to the Z-scores from one distribution, but here we are

TABLE 6.8 Z-scores and Z-score index for deprivation in Southampton wards

Ward	Z-scores NOCAR	ILL	NOTOWN	Deprivation index
Bargate	2.98	2.34	2.33	2.55
Bassett	−1.40	−1.06	−0.84	−1.10
Bitterne	0.29	−0.14	1.16	0.44
Bitterne Park	−0.53	−0.71	−0.36	−0.53
Coxford	−0.41	−1.49	0.50	−0.47
Freemantle	0.15	0.21	−0.62	−0.09
Harefield	−0.39	−0.21	−0.57	−0.39
Millbrook	0.43	0.28	0.29	0.33
Peartree	−0.45	−0.14	−1.06	−0.55
Portswood	−0.30	0.07	−0.24	−0.16
Redbridge	0.54	0.28	1.15	0.66
St Lukes	0.66	1.77	0.40	0.94
Shirley	−0.39	0.07	−0.88	−0.40
Sholing	−1.02	−1.06	−1.37	−1.15
Woolston	−0.14	−0.21	0.10	−0.08

Source: Data from 1991 Census Hampshire, Ward and Civil Parish Monitor, OPCS, Crown Copyright 1993

combining the scores for several distributions (the three different variables) and so the mean Z-score for each ward will not equal zero.

What do these values tell us? For all three variables, a high Z-score indicates deprivation, while a low score indicates relative affluence. So a ward with a positive index value will be relatively deprived and a ward with a negative index value relatively affluent. Bargate is then by far the most deprived ward, with an index value of 2.55, far higher than any other ward. This is what we might expect from an inner city ward. The next most deprived ward is St Lukes with a score of 0.94. Looking at the negative index values, the most affluent ward appears to be Sholing with a score of –1.15.

FURTHER NOTES ON CREATING A Z-SCORE INDEX
In the deprivation index calculated for Southampton wards each variable had equal weight. However if you think that unemployment, for example, is a particularly important indicator of deprivation, then you could give it extra weight by doubling the Z-score for that variable in each area. You would then need to divide the sum of the Z-scores by four instead of three to make the index, because in effect you are using four Z-scores (two ordinary Z-scores and one which has been doubled).

We were also fortunate with the deprivation index calculations because, for all three variables, a high value indicated deprivation. Suppose that instead of long-term illness, the variable used was male employment. A high value of male employment indicates affluence rather than deprivation. To overcome this problem, after calculating the Z-scores in the usual way, the signs can simply be changed. In other words, all the positive Z-scores for that variable become negative and all the negative Z-scores become positive. A high Z-score for male employment now indicates deprivation rather than affluence, so all the variables are working in the same direction. For an example of this, try practice question 6.2.

PRACTICE QUESTIONS

6.1 As a connoisseur of chocolate cakes, which you save to eat while doing statistics exercises, you want to investigate the prices of large chocolate cakes in the shops around the town. On your hunt, you manage to sniff out the prices of 15 brands of chocolate cake. Their prices are shown in Table 6.9.

TABLE 6.9 Prices of 15 brands of large chocolate cakes (p)

78	199	199	139	175	125	169	152
99	200	149	180	160	119	219	

(a) What is the mean price of a chocolate cake (to the nearest penny) and what is the standard deviation of the prices?

(b) Suppose that, due to general inflation, all the shops put up their cake prices by 20p. What is the new mean price and the new standard deviation? (You should not need to do all the calculations again.)

(c) On top of this, the government decides to put VAT on chocolate cakes (crisis!), so all the prices increase by 17.5%. What will the mean and standard deviation be now?

6.2 You have been asked by a human rights group to give some idea of how Asian countries compare in terms of female empowerment. You find comparable data on three topics: the percentage of earned income which is earned by women; the percentage of seats in parliament held by women; and the maternal mortality rate (rate of death during childbirth). The data for eight Asian countries are shown in Table 6.10.

Calculate a female empowerment index for the eight countries using Z-scores. In which countries are conditions most favourable for women? In which are conditions least favourable?

If you are panicking at this point, here are some hints to help you along the way!

(a) Calculate the mean score for each variable.

(b) Calculate the standard deviation for each variable.

TABLE 6.10 Measures of female empowerment in eight Asian countries

Country	% total income earned by women[1]	% seats in parliament held by women[1]	Maternal mortality rate (per 100 000 live births)[2]
Philippines	31	8.5	280
India	26	7.3	570
Thailand	37	6.6	200
Malaysia	30	10.30	80
Indonesia	33	12.60	650
China	38	21.0	95
Bangladesh	23	9.1	850
Pakistan	21	3.4	340

[1] Data refer to latest available year.
[2] 1990 data.

Source: UNDP, 1997; reproduced with the permission of Oxford University Press

(c) Calculate the Z-scores. Check that you have calculated them correctly by adding up the Z-scores for each variable: the total should be zero!

(d) Think about what the variables mean. If the share of earned income and the percentage of seats in parliament held by women are high, this is a good thing for women. However if the maternal mortality rate is high, this is a bad thing for women. Therefore reverse the signs of the Z-scores for maternal mortality so that pluses become minuses and minuses become pluses. Now a positive Z-score for maternal mortality means that mortality is low. A positive Z-score for all three variables now indicates a good outcome for women.

(e) Find the mean Z-score for each country.

(f) Interpret your answers. What does a high index value or a low index value indicate?

7

THE NORMAL DISTRIBUTION

We have already met the normal curve briefly. It looks rather like one of the rolling hills found in the Lake District (Figure 7.1). Whether you think that mountain climbing is 'normal' behaviour or not (Julie does!), the normal (or Gaussian) distribution is extremely useful, because many variables in the social sciences are distributed in this way or approximately so.

FIGURE 7.1

Some features of the normal curve shown in Figure 7.2 are:

- The mean lies in the middle and the curve is symmetrical about the mean. The mean is equal to the median.
- Most of the observations are close to the mean, so the frequency is high around the mean. There are fewer observations that are much greater or much smaller than the mean.
- The curve never actually touches the X axis on either side: it just gets closer and closer.

A normal curve can be defined uniquely by its mean and standard deviation. Therefore if we are given the mean and SD we can construct a normal curve exactly.

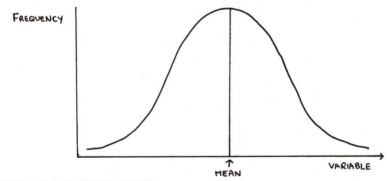

FIGURE 7.2 THE NORMAL CURVE

Normal curves are all the same basic shape, but can be tall and thin or short and fat. Both the curves in Figure 7.3 are normal and have the same mean, but we know that the dotted curve has a larger standard deviation (greater spread) because it is wider at the base.

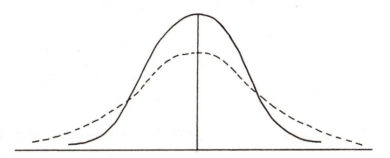

FIGURE 7.3

Because the basic shape is fixed, the proportion of the area under the curve falling between various points can be calculated. For example, if the variable in question was height and we knew the mean and standard deviation of heights in the population, we could work out what proportion of people were over 200 cm tall or between 160 cm and 180 cm tall.

AREAS UNDER THE NORMAL CURVE

We call the total area under the curve 1.0, as in Figure 7.4, so any proportion of the curve will be a number between 0 and 1.

Half of the area lies above the mean and half below the mean, so we can say that the proportion of the area greater than the mean is 0.5. The proportion below the mean is also 0.5. This is shown in Figure 7.5. We can also say that the **probability** of an observation being greater than the mean is 0.5, because half of the observations lie above the mean.

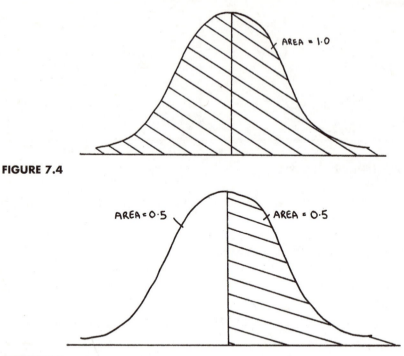

FIGURE 7.4

FIGURE 7.5

Other areas below the curve can be described in terms of standard deviations away from the mean. These areas are the same whether a normal curve is tall and thin or short and fat. Some important areas are shown in Figure 7.6. This shows, for example, that:

- 0.682 of the area lies between $\bar{X} - SD$ and $\bar{X} + SD$. This means that 68.2% of observations lie within one standard deviation either side of the mean.
- 0.954 of the area lies between $\bar{X} - 2SD$ and $\bar{X} + 2SD$. This means that 95.4% of observations lie within two standard deviations either side of the mean.

(Remember: to convert a proportion to a percentage, simply multiply by 100.)

QUESTIONS: AREAS UNDER THE NORMAL CURVE

See if you can answer these questions now (you will need a calculator). You will probably find it helpful to sketch a quick diagram each time, shading in the area that you are trying to find the size of.

(a) What proportion of the total area will lie between the mean and one standard deviation above the mean?

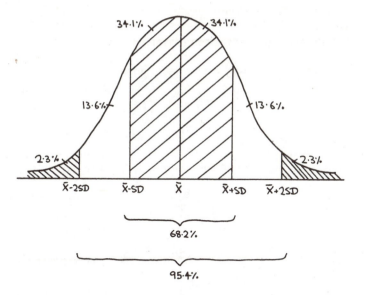

FIGURE 7.6 SOME AREAS UNDER THE NORMAL CURVE

(b) What proportion of the total area will lie between the mean and one standard deviation to the left of the mean?
(c) What proportion of the total area will lie to the left of one SD below the mean?
(d) What proportion of the total area will lie outside the region between $\bar{X} - 2SD$ and $\bar{X} + 2SD$?

The answers are given at the end of the chapter. These ideas may be confusing to start with, but it is all logic. Remember that the curve is symmetrical, so any area you have worked out to the right of the mean will be the same size as the opposite area on the left-hand side of the mean.

What use is all this? Let's look at two examples.

EXAMPLE: GRADUATE SALARIES

Suppose you have been told that full-time salaries for new graduates follow a normal distribution with a mean of £15 000 and an SD of £1500. What can we discover about graduate salaries by looking at the normal curve?

We know that 95.4% of observations in a normal distribution lie between two standard deviations either side of the mean. So let's calculate the salaries two standard deviations either side of the mean:

$$2SD = 2 \times 1500 = 3000$$
$$\bar{X} + 2\ SD = 15\ 000 + 3000 = 18\ 000$$
$$\bar{X} - 2\ SD = 15\ 000 - 3000 = 12\ 000$$

Figure 7.7 shows this on a diagram. We now know therefore that 95.4% of graduate salaries lie between £12 000 and £18 000. Only 4.6% of employed graduates earn less than £12 000 or more than £18 000.

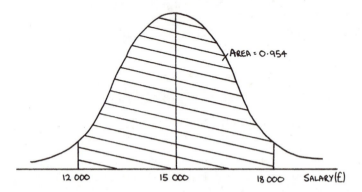

FIGURE 7.7 GRADUATE SALARIES

EXAMPLE: LENGTH OF STAY

The manager of a short-term nursing home for the elderly keeps records on how long residents stay at the nursing home before moving into long-term care or hospital or returning home. She tells you that the mean length of stay is 38 days with a standard deviation of 12 days and that the distribution of the data is normal.

We know that 68.2% of the area lies within one standard deviation.

$$\bar{X} + SD = 38 + 12 = 50 \text{ days}$$

$$\bar{X} - SD = 38 - 12 = 26 \text{ days}$$

Therefore we can say that 68.2% of the residents stay between 26 and 50 days at the home. This is shown in Figure 7.8.

What is the probability of a resident staying for more than 62 days?

We have that 62 days is the mean (38) plus two standard deviations (2 × 12

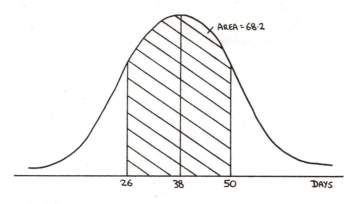

FIGURE 7.8 LENGTH OF STAY

= 24). We know that the area above $\bar{X}$ + 2SD is 0.023. Therefore only 2.3% of residents stay for more than 62 days.

Z-SCORES AND THE NORMAL DISTRIBUTION

We already know that when we standardise a variable by turning the values into Z-scores, the mean of the Z-scores is 0 and the SD is 1 (see Chapter 6). The distribution of a standardised variable is known as the 'standard normal distribution' and is pictured in Figure 7.9.

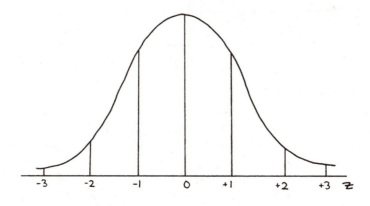

FIGURE 7.9 THE STANDARD NORMAL DISTRIBUTION

Remember that a Z-score of +1 indicates that you are one standard deviation above the mean. So the area between the mean and Z = +1 will be 0.341; this is the same as saying the area between $\bar{X}$ and $\bar{X}$ + SD is 0.341.

Unfortunately, Z-scores do not always take nice round values like +1. To find the area between the mean and any Z-score, we must use **normal tables**. A set of normal tables can be found in Appendix 1 (Table A1.1).

Normal tables give the proportion of the area of the curve between the mean and a certain positive value of Z, as shown in Figure 7.10. This is the same as the proportion between the mean and the same negative value of Z.

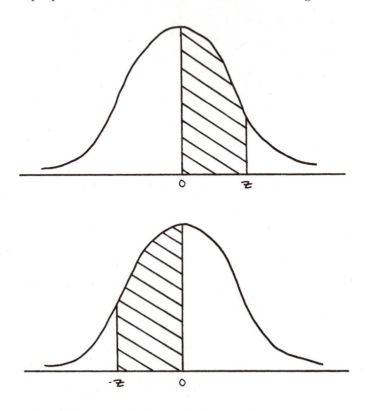

FIGURE 7.10 AREA BETWEEN THE MEAN AND A Z-SCORE

Have a look at the tables. The first column gives the Z-score to one decimal place. The top row gives the second decimal place of the Z-score you want to look up.

So suppose you wanted to look up a Z-score of 1.05. Look down the first column till you reach 1.0, then travel across the 1.0 row till you get to the column with 0.05 at the top. You should then be able to read off the area figure for a Z-score of 1.05, which is 0.3531.

This means that the proportion of the area that lies between the mean and $Z = 1.05$ (1.05 standard deviations above the mean) is 0.3531. This is shown in Figure 7.11. Sketching a quick diagram is always a good idea when finding an area like this.

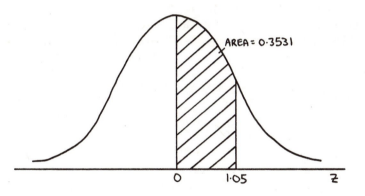

FIGURE 7.11

QUESTIONS: AREAS BETWEEN MEAN AND Z-SCORE

Try these examples to check that you can do this. The answers are at the end
of the chapter.

(e) What is the proportion between the mean and $Z = 2.00$?
(f)   What is the proportion between the mean and $Z = 0.59$?
(g) What is the proportion between the mean and $Z = 1.66$?
(h) What is the proportion between the mean and $Z = -0.03$?

Now, can you work out how to calculate the area to the *right* of $Z = 2.00$?
Again, always draw a diagram first. Figure 7.12 is an example. Your diagram
does not need to be perfect: you just need to be sure that you shade in the
correct area. So:

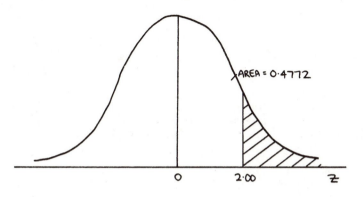

FIGURE 7.12

- The area between the mean and $Z = 2.00$ is 0.4772.
- The whole area to the right of the mean is 0.5 (half).
- Therefore the area to the right of $Z = 2.00$ must be $0.5 - 0.4772 = 0.0228$.

QUESTIONS: AREAS OUTSIDE Z-SCORES

Try the following questions for practice. Again, the answers are at the end of the chapter.

(i)   What is the area to the right of $Z = 1.00$?
(j)   What is the area to the right of $Z = 2.33$?
(k) What is the area to the left of $Z = -0.86$?
(l)   What is the area to the left of $Z = -1.17$?

The following two examples show how calculating the areas below the normal curve can be useful in different situations.

EXAMPLE 1: QUANTITATIVE METHODS RESULTS

Suppose you get really excited doing all these practice questions and end up scoring 80% in your Quantitative Methods exam. It sounds pretty brilliant. But what if everyone else found it really exciting too and did better than you? You go off and discover that the mean mark for the class was 74 with a standard distribution of 4. You have to assume that the marks are normally distributed. What is your Z-score?

$$Z = \frac{\text{your mark} - \text{mean mark}}{\text{standard deviation}} = \frac{80 - 74}{4} = 1.5$$

With a Z-score of 1.5, you should be very happy! You scored 1.5 standard deviations above the average. But you are still curious to know how many of your friends you beat! What we need to know is the proportion of marks that come below $Z = 1.5$.

In notation, we want to know $P(Z < 1.5)$, the **probability** that Z is less than 1.5. The area below $Z = 1.5$ is shaded in Figure 7.13. Note that this includes not only the area between the mean and $Z = 1.5$, but also the whole area below the mean.

From the normal tables, the area between the mean and $Z = 1.5$ is 0.4332. To this we must add the area below the mean, which is half of the observations or 0.5.

$$0.4332 + 0.5 = 0.9332$$

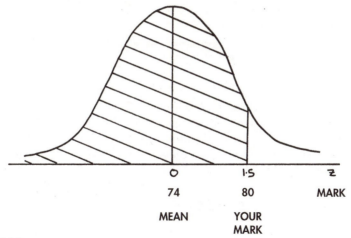

FIGURE 7.13

This means that 93.32% of the class got a lower mark than you (less than 80). So you should go and party!

EXAMPLE: MOTORWAY DRIVING

Suppose a researcher wanted to investigate the speed of driving on motorways. She took a sample of cars driving down her local motorway one morning and measured how fast they were travelling. She found that the speed of the cars in her sample followed a normal distribution with a mean of 75 mph and a standard deviation of 8 mph. What proportion of cars were breaking the legal speed limit of 70 mph?

---

1 Draw a diagram. We want to know the proportion of cars going at *over* 70 mph, so we need to find the shaded area shown in Figure 7.14.

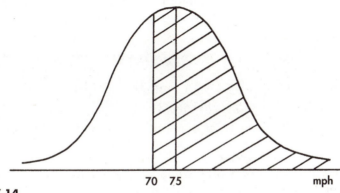

FIGURE 7.14

2 Calculate the Z-score:

$$Z = \frac{70 - 75}{8} = -0.625$$

3 Find the area. We need to find the area between the mean ($Z = 0$) and $Z = -0.625$. On Table A1.1 we can look up the values for 0.62 or 0.63, so to find the value for 0.625 we must **interpolate** between the two (as we did when calculating medians and percentiles). The value for $Z = 0.625$ will be halfway between 0.2324 and 0.2357, so we can calculate it like this:

$$\text{Area} = \frac{0.2324 + 0.2357}{2} = 0.2341$$

We must now add on 0.5 for the area to the right of the mean.

$$\text{Total area} = 0.5 + 0.2341 = 0.7341$$

4 Draw a conclusion. We have found that 73.41% of car drivers in the sample that morning were breaking the speed limit.

QUESTIONS: SPEEDING MOTORISTS

Now see if *you* can find:

(m) The proportion of motorists who were doing 90 mph or more and risking being stopped by the police.
(n) The proportion of cars being driven at speeds below 65 mph.

The answers are at the end of the chapter.

From your own experience, do you think that the researcher's sample was a representative sample of motorway driving speeds?

EXAMPLE: MOTORWAY DRIVING IN REVERSE!

Using the figures from the previous example, we might want to ask a question such as: at less than what speed were 60% of drivers travelling?

First of all we could put what we know onto a diagram, as in Figure 7.15. Here 60% of the area is equal to a proportion of 0.6. The shaded area consists of 0.5 below the mean and 0.1 above the mean (which adds up to 0.6). We are interested in the 60% travelling at less than the speed marked ? mph.

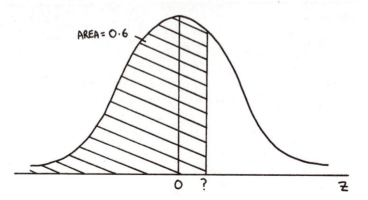

AREA = 0.6

0   ?

Z

FIGURE 7.15

In the previous examples, we worked out the Z-score and then looked up the area on the table. Now we must work backwards. We know the area, 0.1, and want to find the corresponding Z-score. In other words, what is the Z-score which corresponds to an area of 0.1 above the mean?

This time, look up the area 0.1 in the *middle* of the normal tables. The closest value to 0.1 is 0.0987, which will do as an approximation. If you then look along the row and up the column, you will see that this corresponds to a Z-score of 0.25.

Now that we have a Z-score, we can put what we know into the usual equation for Z (we know the answer, but not the value of '?').

$$Z = \frac{\text{observation} - \text{mean}}{\text{standard deviation}}$$

$$0.25 = \frac{? - 75}{8}$$

With a bit of rearranging it is now possible to find '?':

$$0.25 \times 8 = ? - 75$$
$$(0.25 \times 8) + 75 = ?$$
$$77 = ?$$

Therefore we can say that 60% of cars were travelling at a speed of less than 77 mph.

EXAMPLE: THE FASTEST DRIVERS

You want to know what speed the fastest 20% of cars are travelling above.

Figure 7.16 shows the top 20% or 0.2 of the area on a diagram. We cannot find this area from the tables; instead we must find the area between the mean and '?' which is 0.5 – 0.2 = 0.3 .

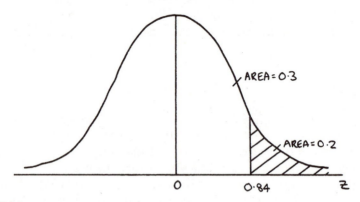

FIGURE 7.16

If you look up the area 0.3 in the middle of the normal tables, you will find that the closest value is the area 0.2995. This corresponds to a Z-score of 0.84.

To what speed does a Z-score of 0.84 correspond? To find out, everything we know must be put into the equation for Z as before:

$$Z = \frac{\text{observation} - \text{mean}}{\text{standard deviation}}$$

$$0.84 = \frac{? - 75}{8}$$

$$0.84 \times 8 = ? - 75$$

$$(0.84 \times 8) + 75 = ?$$

$$81.72 = ?$$

Therefore the top 20% of cars were travelling at over 81.72 mph.

QUESTION: INTERQUARTILE RANGE FOR DRIVING SPEEDS

Can you think how you would calculate the Interquartile range (IQR) for driving speeds in the sample?

The IQR is the difference between the upper quartile (75th percentile) and the lower quartile (25th percentile), so you would want to find the Z-scores corresponding to the area of 0.25 above the mean and 0.25 below the mean, as in Figure 7.17. The Z-scores would then be converted to actual speeds as in the examples above, and finally the speed that represents the lower quartile subtracted from the speed which equals the upper quartile to get the IQR.

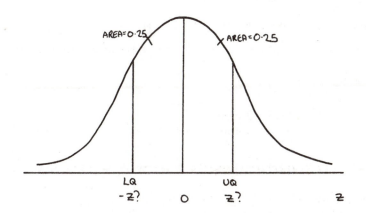

FIGURE 7.17 THE INTERQUARTILE RANGE ON A NORMAL CURVE

Try this yourself: the answer is with the others at the end of the chapter.

ANSWERS: AREAS UNDER THE NORMAL CURVE

(a) 0.341.
(b) 0.341. The curve is symmetrical, so the answers to (a) and (b) are the same.
(c) 0.159 (0.136 + 0.023).
(d) 0.046 (0.023 + 0.023).

ANSWERS: AREAS BETWEEN MEAN AND Z-SCORE

(e) 0.4772.
(f) 0.2224.
(g) 0.4515.
(h) 0.0120. This is the same as the area between the mean and $Z = 0.03$ due to symmetry.

ANSWERS: AREAS OUTSIDE Z-SCORES

(i)   0.1587 (0.5 – 0.3413).
(j)   0.0099 (0.5 – 0.4901).
(k)   0.1949 (0.5 – 0.3501).
(l)   0.1210 (0.5 – 0.3790).

ANSWERS: SPEEDING MOTORISTS

(m) $Z = \dfrac{90 - 75}{8} = -1.88$

Area = 0.5 – 0.4699 = 0.0301

Therefore 3.01% of motorists were going at more than 90 mph.

(n) $Z = \dfrac{65 - 75}{8} = -1.25$

Area = 0.5 – 0.3944 = 0.1056
Therefore 10.56% of motorists were travelling at less than 65 mph.

ANSWERS: INTERQUARTILE RANGE FOR DRIVING SPEEDS

The Z-score for the area 0.25 above the mean is 0.67 (closest). The Z-score for 0.25 below the mean will be –0.67.

Upper quartile: $0.67 = \dfrac{? - 75}{8}$, so ? = 80.36 mph

Lower quartile: $-0.67 = \dfrac{? - 75}{8}$, so ? = 69.64 mph

Interquartile range = 80.36 – 69.64 = 10.72 mph

PRACTICE QUESTIONS

7.1 Intelligence quotients (IQs) are known to be approximately normally distributed with a mean of 100 and standard deviation of 15.

(a) What two values will the middle 68.2% of the population's IQs lie between?
(b) What proportion of the population will have an IQ below 80?
(c) What proportion of the population will have an IQ below 110?

(d) What proportion of the population will have an IQ between 95 and 115?

(e) What proportion of the population will have an IQ between 70 and 85?

(f) What IQ value (to one decimal place) will the top 10% of the population have an IQ greater than? (Find the closest value of Z in the table.)

7.2 The time it takes students to walk from a hall of residence to the university campus is normally distributed with a mean of 19 minutes and a standard deviation of 3 minutes.

(a) What proportion of students take less than 22 minutes to reach the campus?

(b) What proportion of students take more than 15 minutes to reach the campus?

(c) What proportion of students take less than 17 minutes to reach the campus?

(d) If all students leave 20 minutes before a lecture is due to start, what proportion of them will be late?

(e) What proportion of students take between 21 and 25 minutes to reach the campus?

7.3 In a first year sociology course, the exam marks were normally distributed with a mean of 58% and a standard deviation of 10%.

(a) Students who get less than 35% are deemed to have failed. What proportion of students failed the exam?

(b) If an 'A' grade is awarded to all students achieving 70% or higher, what proportion of students got an 'A'?

(c) The best 40% of students achieved better than what mark?

8

FROM SAMPLES TO POPULATIONS

In social science, we frequently want to find something out about a particular group of people. For example, we may want to find out which party people are planning to vote for the day before an election, or what proportion of adults believe that cannabis should be legalised.

We could ask everybody in the country these questions. However it would be rather impractical; the cost would be immense! The good news is that we don't need to, as properly drawn, representative samples vary in a systematic way and make good estimates of the things in the population we are trying to find out about. Using a sample to estimate values of a population saves vast amounts of time and money.

EXAMPLES: POPULATIONS AND SAMPLES FOR RESEARCH QUESTIONS

1 What is the average income of full-time workers in Great Britain?
   Population: all full-time workers in Great Britain.
   Sample: 1000 full-time workers selected randomly by their National Insurance numbers.
2 How much time do British teenagers doing GCSEs spend doing homework each day?
   Population: all British teenagers in Years 10 and 11.
   Sample: a sample of 600 teenagers in Years 10 and 11 from a selection of different schools throughout the country.
3 What proportion of British MPs would vote for entry into the Euro?
   Population: all British MPs.
   Sample: 100 MPs skilfully selected to reflect MPs in different parties and regions of Britain.

SAMPLING

Some key points on sampling are as follows.

First, the population must be very clearly defined. For example, regarding 'full-time' workers:

- How many hours constitutes full-time?
- Is overtime included?

Secondly, the property of interest must be very clearly defined. For example, take 'average income':

- What do we mean by 'average': the mean; the median?
- What do we mean by 'income': does it include overtime or a company car, for example?

Thirdly, the sample must be representative of the population. Asking 1000 people in Aberdeen, for example, what their average income is would not be representative of Great Britain as a whole.

We need to choose our sample very carefully in order to minimise:

- sampling error
- sampling variability.

This jargon is explained below.

Types of error in samples

There are several reasons why the characteristics of a sample will not be identical to the characteristics of the population.

Three types of error are described as follows.

SAMPLING VARIABILITY

If we take repeated samples from the same population, the means and standard deviations of the different samples will not be the same.

For example, suppose we are interested in estimating the mean height of a lecture class. We might believe that we could choose one row randomly and take the mean height of people sitting in that row as an estimate. We would expect each mean would be different due to chance and hence our estimate would vary dependent on the row chosen. There might even be one mean which was particularly different, for example if the rugby team were all sitting together in the back row.

SAMPLING ERROR

An estimate from a sample (such as a mean) will not be exactly the same as the population value being estimated: in other words the estimate will be 'in error'.

'Error' here does not imply carelessness, but is an artefact of the method used to select the sample. There may be some bias involved in the sampling method. For example, choosing a sample from a telephone directory will systematically exclude those without phones and people who are ex-directory. Sampling error can be reduced by using an optimum method of choosing a sample.

NON-SAMPLING ERROR

These are other errors, not connected with the sampling method. For example:

- Poor survey questions may be interpreted incorrectly by respondents.
- Interviewers can unconsciously bias the results or record question responses incorrectly.
- Errors can be made when coding or typing responses.

There is a huge amount of statistical theory devoted to estimating sampling error and recommending optimal sampling strategies which minimise error. If in doubt contact an expert!! The next section describes some of the most commonly used sampling strategies.

Representative samples

There are two basic sampling strategies, as follows.

SIMPLE RANDOM SAMPLE

In a random sample, every member of a population has an equal chance of being selected. This is the sampling equivalent of the National Lottery, where we put all the members of the population into a hat and draw out their names.

STRATIFIED SAMPLE

This is used if we know there are specific groups in a population who may be different to each other.

For example, if we are interested in the proportion of MPs voting for entry into the Euro, we know that certain groups of MPs may vote in particular ways, so we want to make sure we include them all. In other words we want the sample to reflect the various strata in the population.

The most commonly used stratification in many samples is by sex and age. This is because as you get older you often change your views (Julie would say you get more conventional but Ian denies this!) and men often have different views to women.

How many members of each stratum should be in a sample?

- The number is usually (but not always) proportionate to the number in the population.
- It is often a good idea to include larger numbers from the more variable and therefore less predictable strata.

How large should a sample be?

This is a tricky question!

The sample size will reflect the size of a population, but will *not* usually be proportional to the population size. As a population gets larger, the sample size needed for an accurate estimate will not get proportionately bigger after a certain point.

The choice of sample size will depend on the following.

VARIABILITY AMONG MEMBERS OF THE POPULATION

Populations with greater variability (a high standard deviation) will need a larger sample size. If the population is very uniform, a small sample will be adequate for obtaining an accurate estimate. To take this to an absurd extreme, if everyone in the population were exactly the same then one would only need to sample *one* person to get a 'perfect' estimate of whatever one was trying to estimate!

LEVEL OF PRECISION NEEDED FOR ESTIMATE

The greater precision that is needed, the larger the sample that should be used. A larger sample will give a more precise estimate. It is worth noting here (as we shall see later) that the increase in precision does not increase uniformly with sample size. After a while the increase in precision for a constant increase in sample size becomes increasingly small.

COST OF SAMPLING

Sampling can be very time-consuming and expensive. At the end of the day you only collect data if you really need to. Therefore the sample size should not be unnecessarily large.

THE SAMPLING DISTRIBUTION FOR THE MEAN

Don't be put off by the title of this section: it's not as bad as it sounds!

We have already said that if we take lots of samples from a population, the means of each sample will be slightly different.

Suppose we take five samples A to E, each of five women, and ask them how many children they have. The hypothetical data are shown in Table 8.1.

TABLE 8.1 Hypothetical data for five samples of five women who were asked how many children they had

Sample	Number of children				
A	0	2	2	1	1
B	3	0	1	0	2
C	2	1	2	2	0
D	2	0	4	1	0
E	1	3	0	2	2

We could then calculate the mean number of children for each sample, as in Table 8.2. For example, the mean number of children in sample A will be:

$$\text{Mean} = \frac{0+2+2+1+1}{5} = \frac{6}{5} = 1.2$$

TABLE 8.2 Mean number of children for the five samples of women

Sample	Mean number of children
A	1.2
B	1.2
C	1.4
D	1.4
E	1.6

The means of the different samples are called the **sample means**.

If the samples are representative, most sample means will be very close to the true population mean. However a small number of samples will have a mean which is some distance away from the population mean. This leads us to:

> *Amazing fact number 1*
> The distribution of sample means will approximately follow the normal distribution.

Figure 8.1 shows the distribution of sample means.

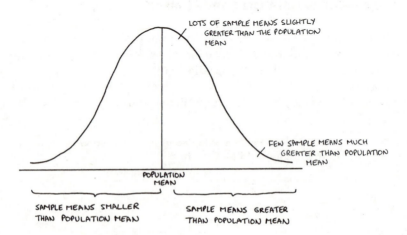

FIGURE 8.1 THE DISTRIBUTION OF SAMPLE MEANS

If we have taken a reasonable number of samples, then:

Amazing fact number 2
The mean of the sample means will approximately equal the true population mean.

If you are getting confused with all these different means, look back at the example of the women and their number of children. The five means in Table 8.2 are the sample means. To find the *mean* of these sample means, we add the five means together and divide by five:

$$\text{Mean of the sample means} = \frac{1.2 + 1.2 + 1.4 + 1.4 + 1.6}{5} = 1.36$$

So the mean of the sample means is 1.36 children, and from amazing fact number 2 we can therefore say that the population mean will probably be around 1.36 as well. In other words, the best estimate of the mean number of children for all British women is 1.36.

Now consider the sample means: will they vary as much as the actual values in the population? In Figure 8.2, which line shows the distribution of all the values in the population and which shows the distribution of the sample means?

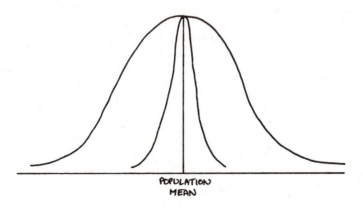

POPULATION MEAN

FIGURE 8.2

The distribution with the much wider spread is the distribution of the whole population. The distribution with the much narrower range is the distribution of sample means.

Why is this?

The values for the whole population will include a few extreme values which make the range wider. But the sample means are *means*! Therefore in calculating them you will have effectively got rid of the extreme values.

To illustrate this, if the sample of five women had 2, 0, 1, 1 and 9 children respectively:

- The population distribution would include the extreme value of 9.
- The sample mean would still only be 2.6, which is not very extreme at all. Taking a mean moderates the effect of extreme values.

So the sample means are less variable than the actual values in the population. This will mean that the standard deviation of the sample means is smaller than the standard deviation of the whole population.

There is, in fact, a formula for calculating the standard deviation of the sample means. The standard deviation of the sample means is known as the **standard error** (SE):

> *Amazing fact number 3*
>
> $$SE = \frac{SD}{\sqrt{n}}$$

In words, the standard error is equal to the standard deviation of the population divided by the square root of the sample size.

We call the standard deviation of the sample means the standard error (SE) to distinguish it from the ordinary standard deviations of samples or populations.

The standard error is very handy. For example, since we know that the sample means follow a normal distribution, we can say that 68% of all sample means will lie between the mean and one standard error on either side, as in Figure 8.3. This idea enables us to estimate the chances of a particular sample mean being much larger or smaller than the population mean. We can

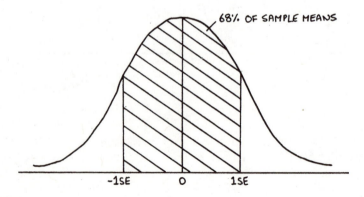

FIGURE 8.3

calculate a Z-score for a sample mean to see how much higher or lower it is than the population mean.

Before looking at some examples, let's now combine the three amazing facts: together they are known as the central limit theorem (for no apparent reason!).

Fantastic theorem number 1: the central limit theorem
If samples of size *n* are selected from a population, the means of the samples are approximately normally distributed with

Mean = population mean

and

$$\text{Standard error} = \frac{SD_{pop}}{\sqrt{n}}$$

How big a sample do we need for this to work?

- If the distribution of the population is normal, a sample size of about 10 or more is needed.
- If the distribution is not normal (if it is skewed, for example), the sample size must be at least 25.

What use is all this? It is mainly useful for seeing whether a sample mean that you have found is different to the population due to chance (sampling variability) or whether the sample is genuinely quite different to the population. It also allows you to estimate the precision of any sample you take. The examples to follow show some applications of the theorem. These methods are the basis for hypothesis testing which is introduced more formally in Chapter 11.

EXAMPLE: THE IQ OF STUDENTS

IQs in the general population are normally distributed with a mean of 100 and a standard deviation of 15. You take a random sample of 40 students and find that their mean IQ is 107. Given that one is prepared to accept that IQ measures intelligence, are the students really brighter than the average population?

What we are really trying to find out here is the chance of a sample of 40 students having a mean IQ of 107 or more due to chance (rather than genuine higher intelligence). This can be shown on a diagram, as in Figure 8.4.

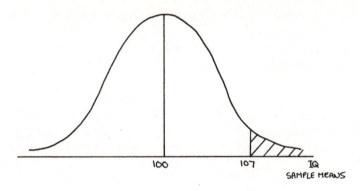

FIGURE 8.4

First we must find out the sampling distribution for the means of samples of size 40. According to the central limit theorem, the sample means will be normally distributed with:

$$\text{Mean} = \text{population mean} = 100$$

$$\text{Standard error} = \frac{\text{SD}}{\sqrt{n}} = \frac{15}{\sqrt{40}} = 2.37$$

Next we can calculate the Z-score using the formula:

$$Z = \frac{\text{sample mean} - \text{population mean}}{\text{standard error}}$$

$$Z = \frac{107 - 100}{2.37} = 2.95$$

A Z-score of 2.95 is quite high. Looking up Z = 2.95 on the normal table (Table A1.1) gives an area of 0.4984 between the mean and Z = 2.95. So the area above Z = 2.95 will be 0.5 – 0.4984 = 0.0016.

This tells us that the probability of getting a sample of 40 people with an IQ of 107 or more just by chance is very low (less than 1%). Therefore we can conclude that we have evidence that the students genuinely are of higher intelligence than the general population.

Note that although the chance of getting a *sample* of 40 students with an IQ of 115 or more is extremely low, the chance of getting an *individual* with an IQ of 115 or more is much higher, because individuals vary much more than sample means. The Z-score for an individual with a score of 107 would be:

$$Z = \frac{\text{observation} - \text{mean}}{\text{SD}} = \frac{107 - 100}{15} = 0.47$$

Looking up a Z-score of 0.47 on the normal table gives an area of 0.1808. Therefore the area above Z = 0.47 will be 0.5 – 0.1808 = 0.3192. So the chance of an individual having an IQ of 107 or more is 0.3192 (around 32%) which is quite reasonable.

EXAMPLE: THE WEIGHT OF STUDENTS

You have been told that the weights of male students are normally distributed with a mean of 70.31 kg and a standard deviation of 2.74 kg. You decide that your lecture class is representative of male students and that, by weight, male students will sit randomly around the lecture theatre. You sample the back row and when you weigh the nine men sitting there, their mean weight is 72.22 kg. Could this result have occurred due to chance, or are the rugby team sitting together in the back row?!

According to the central limit theorem, the mean weights of samples of nine men will be normally distributed with:

$$\text{Mean = population mean = 70.31 kg}$$

$$\text{Standard error} = \frac{2.74}{\sqrt{9}} = 0.91 \text{ kg}$$

What is the probability of having a sample mean of 72.22 kg or more? This is the shaded area in Figure 8.5.

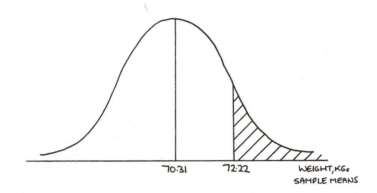

FIGURE 8.5

$$Z = \frac{72.2 - 70.3}{0.91} = 2.09$$

The area between the mean and $Z = 2.09$ is 0.4817 (from the normal table, Table A1.1), and so the area above $Z = 2.09$ will be $0.5 - 0.4817 = 0.0183$.

The probability of a sample of men from the ordinary population of male students having a mean weight of 72.22 kg or more by chance is 0.0183 or 1.83%; in other words the probability is very small. We must conclude that there probably is an abnormal group of people sitting in the back row, presumably the rugby team (are they scared or what?).

EXAMPLE: BOTTLE FILLING

A new EU rule states that wine producers must give you 750 ml in every bottle otherwise they get grief from Brussels. Unfortunately bottle filling machines are subject to variability. To be on the safe side, Monsieur de Vin sets his bottling machine up to put 755 ml of wine in each bottle. The machine has a natural variation which gives a standard deviation of 18 ml.

The next day, Madame Bruxelles, the inspector, comes along and does a random check of 36 of Monsieur de Vin's bottles. What is the chance of Monsieur de Vin getting grief from Brussels?

What we want to know is the proportion of samples which will contain less than 750 ml of wine on average, because Monsieur de Vin would be in trouble if the mean of his sample was less than 750 ml. The proportion is the shaded part in Figure 8.6. (Always draw a diagram to help with these questions.)

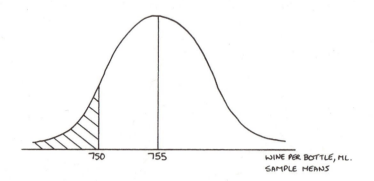

FIGURE 8.6

We can use the central limit theorem, even though we do not know whether the quantities in each bottle are normally distributed, because $n = 36$. Remember that the population in this case (by which we mean this example rather than 12 bottles!) is all of Monsieur de Vin's bottles, and a sample is any 36 randomly selected bottles.

According to the central limit theorem, samples of 36 bottles will be normally distributed with:

$$\text{Mean} = \text{population mean} = 755 \text{ ml}$$

$$\text{Standard error} = \frac{\text{SD}}{\sqrt{n}} = \frac{18}{\sqrt{36}} = 3$$

Now that we know the standard error, we can calculate Z:

$$Z = \frac{750 - 755}{3} = -1.67$$

From the normal table, the area between the mean and $Z = -1.67$ is 0.4525. So the area below $Z = -1.67$ will be $0.5 - 0.4525 = 0.0475$. Therefore the chance of Monsieur de Vin's bottles failing the test is 0.0475 or 4.75%.

What would you do? Risk it? Buy a more reliable machine? Increase the amount the machine should give? Any of these strategies might be successful. In statistics, we often use a 5% risk as a cut-off point. In this example, the chance of the sample failing is less than 5%, so Monsieur de Vin can be over 95% certain that his sample will pass. If he wants to be more confident, he must reset his machine to put more wine in each bottle (but this will increase costs). As in life, it is a question of weighing up the risks, costs and benefits of different strategies.

Guidelines for using the sampling distribution for the mean

From the three examples, it should be clear that the strategy for answering questions involving the sampling distribution for the mean is:

1 Find the mean and standard error of the sample means.
2 Draw a diagram.
3 Calculate the Z-score.
4 Look up the probability on the normal table and draw a conclusion.

PRACTICE QUESTIONS

8.1 Casual workers in a particular occupation are paid a mean wage of £4.60 per hour with a standard deviation of £0.40. The wages are normally distributed.

(a) What is the probability of an individual worker earning £4.50 or less per hour?

(b) What is the probability of obtaining a sample of 20 workers with a mean wage of £4.50 or less?

(c) What is the probability of obtaining a sample of 50 workers with a mean wage of £4.50 or less?

(d) Why are your answers to parts (a), (b) and (c) different?

8.2 Casual workers in another industry are paid on average £5.10 per hour with a standard deviation of £0.50. Workers in a particular firm believe that they are being underpaid. A sample of 30 casual workers from the firm has a mean hourly wage of £4.50. Is this low mean wage likely to be due to chance or are the workers in this firm really hard done by?

Hints: find the mean and standard error of the sample means. Draw a diagram and find the Z-score for the sample. What is the probability of getting a sample with a mean of £4.50 or less by chance?

8.3 The mean age at birth in England and Wales is 28.5 years (Office for National Statistics, 1997e). The standard deviation is approximately 4.6 years. You believe that women in a deprived area are having their births at a younger age than average. You take a sample of 100 births from the local hospital and find the mothers' ages at the time of the birth. The mean age in the sample is 28.0 years. Are these women really having births at a younger age or could the difference be due to sampling variability?

9

GETTING CONFIDENT

A very common statistical question is to estimate the mean of a population from a sample. For example:

- You want to take a sample of students in a Quantitative Methods lecture so as to estimate the mean height of all the students on the course.
- A sociologist wants to know how much income women lose on divorce, so she interviews a sample of divorced women.

In these cases, the strategy is to take a representative sample and then estimate the population mean from the sample.

Do you think that a sample mean would be a good estimate of the population mean?

Suppose the mean height of 16 people in the Quantitative Methods lecture is found to be 1.71 metres. This sample mean will not be exactly the same as the mean height of the whole class (the population mean), but it is a good estimate.

An estimate of the mean like this is called a **point estimate**: we are trying to pin the mean down to an exact figure.

A sample mean is the best point estimate for the population mean.

But, you may be thinking, how can a mean of any sample be a good estimate of a population mean when we know that if we take repeated samples from the same population we will get a different answer for the mean every time? The answer is to remember the results from the last chapter which showed that properly collected samples vary in a systematic way. Therefore the point estimate is the best 'one number' estimate, but what we would really like is, in addition, an estimate of the likely range in which we could be reasonably sure that the true population would lie. This is called an **interval estimate** and is intuitively better than a point estimate.

For example, most people would be happier, if asked to estimate the number of students in a lecture, to say something like 'between 50 and 60' or 'around 50' than to estimate a precise number such as 55. The way to do this is to calculate a **confidence interval** for the population mean.

CONFIDENCE INTERVALS

You can make estimates for any level of confidence you like. However, most often people find the two limits which we are 95% certain the mean will lie between: this is called a **95% confidence interval**. In other words we will calculate a range in which we would expect the true value to lie 19 times out of 20.

Suppose that the mean height of the 16 students is 1.71 metres with a standard deviation of 0.12 metres. We want to calculate an interval estimate for the mean of all the students in the room.

Think about a normal distribution. If we look at the 95% in the middle of the distribution, it can be broken down into two halves, with 47.5% of the area on either side of the mean, as in Figure 9.1.

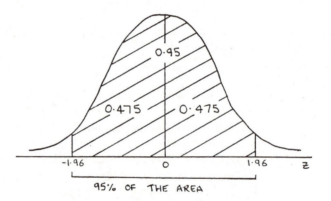

FIGURE 9.1 A GRAPH DEPICTING 95% OF THE AREA UNDER A NORMAL CURVE

If you now look in the *middle* of the normal table (Table A1.1) for the area 0.475, you will find that it corresponds with a Z-score of 1.96. In fact, 1.96 is the magic number that you need to remember for calculating 95% confidence intervals. To work out the possible variation around the sample mean we multiply the standard error by 1.96:

$$1.96 \times \frac{\text{SD}}{\sqrt{n}} = 1.96 \times \frac{0.12}{\sqrt{16}} = 0.0588$$

Thus we have a range spanning 0.0588 on either side of the sample mean where we are 95% confident that the population mean will lie.

To work out the two limits between which the population mean could lie, we need lastly to add and subtract this figure from our sample mean:

$$1.71 + 0.0588 = 1.7688$$

$$1.71 - 0.0588 = 1.6512$$

Therefore we can be 95% confident that the population mean will lie between 1.6512 and 1.7688. This is usually written as follows, with the lower limit first:

$$95\% \text{ CI} = (1.6512, 1.7688)$$

The formula for a 95% confidence interval is therefore:

$$95\% \text{ CI} = \text{sample mean} \pm \left(1.96 \times \frac{\text{SD}}{\sqrt{n}} \right)$$

A confidence interval therefore takes into account both the variability of the sample and the size of the sample. A sample which is larger or less variable will produce a better estimate of the population mean and so the confidence interval will be narrower than it would be for a smaller or more variable sample.

Note that to use this formula we need to remember that fantastic central limit theorem. Either the population must be normally distributed or the sample size must be at least 30. Strictly speaking, the standard error should use the population standard deviation rather than the sample standard deviation, but for confidence intervals we can use the sample standard deviation, providing the population is not too small.

EXAMPLE: FREQUENCY OF INTERCOURSE

Let's return to the data on frequency of sex among married women aged 19–20 in the USA (from Table 5.2). Table 9.1 gives the mean frequency of intercourse in the past four weeks, along with the standard deviation and sample size for each of the three years. The question was whether there was an increase in the frequency of sex over time.

Now that we know how to calculate confidence intervals for the three means, we can answer this question properly. For example, the 95% confidence interval for 1965 would be:

TABLE 9.1 Frequency of intercourse in four weeks before interview for married women aged 19–20 in the US, 1965, 1970 and 1975

	Year of interview		
	1965	**1970**	**1975**
Mean	9.6	9.8	12.1
Standard deviation	1.1	1.3	1.2
n	190	249	219

Source: means from Trussell and Westoff, 1980; other data hypothetical

$$95\% \ \text{CI} = 9.6 \pm \left(1.96 \times \frac{1.1}{\sqrt{190}} \right) = 9.6 \pm 0.14$$
$$= (9.46, \ 9.74)$$

In other words we can be 95% confident that the true value for frequency of intercourse in the population of married women aged 19–20 lies between 9.46 and 9.74 times in a four-week period.

See if you can calculate the 95% confidence intervals for 1970 and 1975 yourself and check that you come up with the following answers:

> 1970:   95% CI = (9.64, 9.96).
> 1975:   95% CI = (11.94, 12.26)

What do you notice about the confidence intervals around the three means?

The confidence intervals for 1965 and 1970 overlap. However the confidence intervals for 1970 and 1975 do not overlap. We should only conclude that there is a real difference if the confidence intervals do not overlap. Therefore the data show no real difference in the frequency of sex among American married women aged 19–20 between the years 1965 and 1970. There is evidence of an increase in frequency, however, between 1970 and 1975.

As we have already noted, we can use confidence intervals other than 95% if we want to, although 95% is the most common. For more precision, we might want to use a 99% CI. Can you work out what the formula for a 99% CI would be? (Hint: only the 1.96 would change.)

It would be:

$$99\% \ \text{CI} = \text{sample mean} \pm \left(2.575 \times \frac{\text{SD}}{\sqrt{n}} \right)$$

Half of 99% is 49.5%, as in Figure 9.2. The figure of 2.575 was found by looking up 0.495 on the normal table and finding it to be halfway between 2.57 and 2.58.

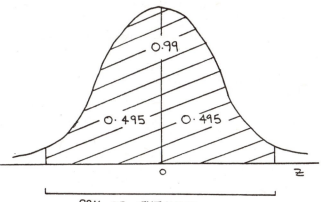

FIGURE 9.2 A GRAPH DEPICTING 99% OF THE AREA UNDER A NORMAL CURVE

Note that the confidence interval gets wider as the precision increases. Why is this? Put simply, if you want to be ever more certain that the true value will lie within your interval estimate then you will need a wider interval. On the other hand if you are happy to be wrong most of the time (which would be rather odd!) then you can have a smaller interval. There is nothing sacrosanct about 95%: it is just a range which has widespread intuitive acceptability among analysts.

HI-LO PLOTS

Confidence intervals can be presented graphically by using a **hi-lo plot**.

A hi-lo plot shows the estimated mean and the confidence interval for one or more populations. They are particularly useful for comparing the means and confidence intervals for several populations side by side. For each population, the length of the vertical line represents the range of the 95% (or whatever value you choose) confidence interval and the middle horizontal line is the mean.

EXAMPLE: CONDOM RETRIEVAL

A researcher wanted to know if there were daily variations in sexual activity in his area, so he thought up a very novel method of measuring the amount of sex occurring each day. Over a 10-week period he counted the number of condoms retrieved daily from Dunmurray sewage plant! Do you think that counting used condoms is a good method of measuring sexual activity?

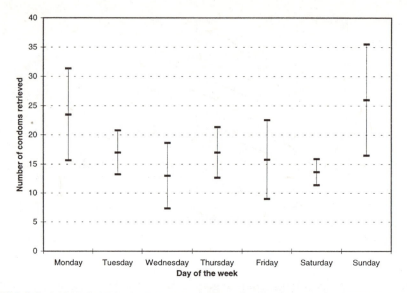

FIGURE 9.3 A HI-LO PLOT SHOWING THE DAILY VARIATION IN CONDOM RETRIEVAL AT DUNMURRAY SEWAGE PLANT OVER A 10-WEEK PERIOD (ADAPTED FROM TITTMAR, 1976)

The results are shown in Figure 9.3. There does appear to be some daily variation in the number of condoms retrieved, with a higher mean on Sundays and Mondays (the days following Saturday and Sunday nights). The 95% confidence intervals for the days Monday to Saturday all overlap, so we cannot make any concrete conclusions about daily differences in condom retrieval for these days. However, the confidence intervals for Saturdays and Sundays do not quite overlap, so we can say that there is a significant difference in condom retrieval between Saturdays and Sundays.

PRACTICE QUESTIONS

9.1 In the National Survey of Sexual Attitudes and Lifestyles (Wellings et al., 1994), female respondents were asked at what age they experienced menarche (began menstruation). To see whether the age at menarche has changed over time, the mean age at menarche was found for women of different ages at interview. The results are shown in Table 9.2.

   (a) Does it appear that the mean age at menarche varies by age at interview?
   (b) Calculate 95% confidence intervals for the mean age at

menarche in each of the four age groups. What can you conclude now about any real variations in the age at menarche?

TABLE 9.2 Age at menarche among British women of different ages at interview (years)

	Age at interview			
	16–24	25–34	35–44	45–59
Mean	13.40	13.42	13.41	13.54
Standard deviation	1.66	1.35	1.52	1.56
n	2172	2810	2481	2606

Source: Wellings et al., 1994

9.2 A sample of 40 students at a college is asked how they rate Tony Blair as a Prime Minister, on a scale of 1 to 20, where 1 is terrible and 20 is excellent. The students' mean score is 12.1 with a standard deviation of 3.5.
(a) Estimate the 'Tony Blair rating' for all students in the college and calculate a 95% confidence interval for your answer.
(b) Calculate a 99% confidence interval for your answer. Is this wider or narrower than the 95% confidence interval? Why?
(c) Suppose that you had obtained the same mean and standard deviation from a sample of 100 students. Calculate a new 95% confidence interval for the 'Tony Blair rating' for all the college's students. Is this wider or narrower than your answer to part (a)? Why?

TABLE 9.3 Prices of three-bedroom houses at an estate agent (£)

75900	88500	79950	81000	90900	72250
72500	69950	83600	91450	77500	

Source: hypothetical data

9.3 You are investigating housing availability for low income families with children in your local area. To get an idea of the price of houses for sale, you look in an estate agent's window and note down the prices of their three-bedroom houses on offer. Table 9.3 gives these prices.

Estimate the mean price of a three-bedroom house in the area and give a 95% confidence interval for your answer. Do you think that this sample of prices is representative?

10

FUN WITH PROPORTIONS

In the last three chapters we have been looking at continuous variables, where different samples and populations can be compared by examining their means. Sometimes, the statistic of interest will be in the form of a proportion rather than a mean. For example, you might be interested in the proportion of senior staff in a company who are female or the proportion of teenagers who regularly take hard drugs.

PROPORTIONS

Take the following example. You want to know what proportion of male students smoke. So you take a representative sample of male students and ask them if they smoke. There are two possible answers: yes or no. Let's assign a value 1 to yes and 0 to no.

The proportion of smokers will be:

$$\text{Proportion} = \frac{1+1+1+\ldots+0+0+0}{\text{total number in sample}} = \frac{\text{number of smokers}}{\text{total number in sample}}$$

The question is: can we use this as an estimate of the proportion of smokers in the whole population (all male students)?

The good news is – yes!

SOME JARGON

- We call the sample proportion p.
- The true population proportion that we are trying to estimate is known as Π. (Π is the Greek capital letter 'pi', pronounced 'pie'.)

Now it's time for another magnificently useful and fantastic theorem! This is like the central limit theorem but refers to a *proportion* rather than a mean.

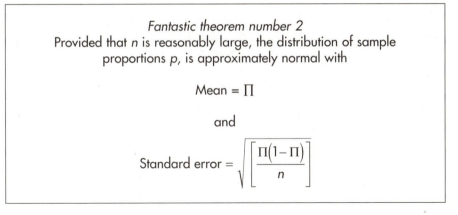

Fantastic theorem number 2
Provided that *n* is reasonably large, the distribution of sample proportions *p*, is approximately normal with

$$\text{Mean} = \Pi$$

and

$$\text{Standard error} = \sqrt{\left[\frac{\Pi(1-\Pi)}{n}\right]}$$

This is similar to the distribution of sample means. What it implies is that if we take repeated samples and find the proportion *p* of each sample, then the mean of all the *p*s will be approximately the population proportion Π, and the standard deviation of the distribution of *p*s will be the standard error given in the equation.

As long as the sample size is reasonably large, we can use the sample proportion *p* as a reasonable approximation to the population proportion in the standard error. Here are some examples putting fantastic theorem number 2 into practice.

EXAMPLE: MOT TESTS

Your car has just failed its MOT, but you reckon that it is perfectly OK and the garage is making things up. On checking the garage's records it appears that, out of the last 100 MOT tests, 55 resulted in a fail. Therefore the sample proportion is 0.55 from a sample where *n* = 100.

National figures state that, in 1997, 36% of MOT tests resulted in a fail (Department of the Environment, Transport and the Regions, 1997). Thus the population proportion is 0.36.

You want to find out whether the garage's result of 0.55 is likely given that the population proportion is 0.36, or whether they are failing lots of cars unnecessarily to make more money.

According to fantastic theorem number 2, the proportions failing in different samples of 100 will be normally distributed with:

$$\text{Mean} = \text{population proportion} = 0.36$$

$$\text{Standard error} = \sqrt{\left[\frac{0.36(1-0.36)}{100}\right]} = \sqrt{\left[\frac{0.23}{100}\right]} = 0.048$$

Now we need to find the chance of having 55 fail results in a sample of 100, so in jargon, we want to find the probability that $p \geq 0.55$.

As we know p, Π and the standard error, we can put these figures into the equation to find a Z-score:

$$Z = \frac{\text{sample proportion} - \text{population proportion}}{\text{standard error}} = \frac{p - \Pi}{SE}$$

$$Z = \frac{0.55 - 0.36}{0.048} = \frac{0.19}{0.048} = 3.96$$

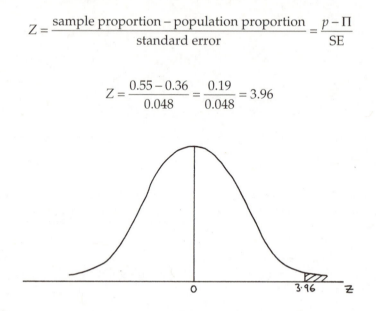

FIGURE 10.1

Figure 10.1 shows this on a diagram. A Z-score of 3.96 is very high and is not on the normal tables (Table A1.1), so the area greater than Z = 3.96 is extremely small. It is very unlikely that the garage would have failed 55 out of 100 MOTs just by chance. Either the customers have particularly dodgy cars or the garage is fiddling things to make more money on fake repairs. Get a new car or try a different garage next time!

But what if the garage had only failed 40 out of 100 cars in the sample? Would this still be a cause for concern?

The sample proportion p is now 0.40, and the population proportion and sample size remain unchanged. The mean and standard error of the sample proportions will therefore be the same. All we need to do is calculate a new Z-score:

$$Z = \frac{0.40 - 0.36}{0.048} = \frac{0.04}{0.048} = 0.83$$

The shaded area in Figure 10.2 shows the probability of getting a sample with a proportion of 0.40 or more. The area between the mean and Z = 0.83 is 0.2967

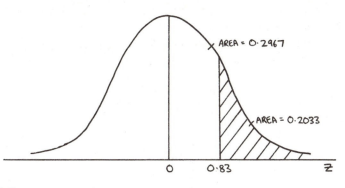

FIGURE 10.2

(from the normal table). Therefore the area above $Z = 0.83$ will be $0.5 - 0.2967 = 0.2033$.

Therefore there is a 20% chance of a garage having a proportion of 0.40 or more of its MOT tests resulting in a fail. This is a reasonable chance and could be due to natural sampling variability. There would probably be no need to be suspicious of the garage if only 40 MOT tests in the sample had been failed.

EXAMPLE: AEROPLANE SEATS

You know that on average only 90% of booked passengers show up for a flight. You want to go to New York at the last moment and are 35th standby passenger for a plane of 330 seats. What is your chance of making it to New York on that plane?

The strategy is to first write down what we know. We know that the sample size n is 330 and that the population proportion Π is 0.90 (90 ÷ 100).

We can then calculate the mean and standard error of the sample proportions:

$$\text{Mean} = \Pi = 0.90$$

$$\text{Standard error} = \sqrt{\left[\frac{\Pi(1-\Pi)}{n}\right]} = \sqrt{\left[\frac{0.9 \times 0.1}{330}\right]} = 0.017$$

So we can say that p is normally distributed with mean = 0.90 and SE = 0.017.

Next we must work out what must happen in order for you to get on the plane. There are 330 seats and you are the 35th standby. Therefore for you to get on, how many booked passengers would turn up? Clearly, if $330 - 35 = 295$ passengers (or fewer) turned up you would make it to New York. But what is the chance of so few people turning up?

The sample proportion p will be 295 ÷ 330 = 0.8939. This is the maximum proportion of passengers you want to show up to ensure success. So you want to find the probability of the proportion turning up being 0.8939 or less.

Now we can calculate the Z-score and draw a diagram (see Figure 10.3):

$$Z = \frac{0.8939 - 0.9}{0.017} = -0.36$$

AREA = 0.1406

AREA = 0.3594

−0.36   0   Z

FIGURE 10.3

From the normal tables (Table A1.1), the area between the mean and Z = –0.36 is 0.1406, and so the area to the left of Z = –0.36 will be 0.5 – 0.1406 = 0.3594.

From this result you can conclude that you have a 36% chance of getting to New York on that plane.

CONFIDENCE INTERVALS FOR PROPORTIONS

You will remember that when we estimated a population mean from a sample we argued that, intuitively, an interval estimate was often preferable to a point estimate, and therefore we calculated a confidence interval as a measure of the range we could be sure that the population mean would lie in.

In the same way we can calculate confidence intervals for proportions, so that when we estimate a population proportion from a sample we can have some idea of how accurate our estimate is.

The formula for a 95% confidence interval is analogous to that for a mean:

95% CI = p ± (1.96 × standard error)

So the actual equation will be as below (putting in the formula for the standard error of a proportion) using the sample proportion p – which in practice will be all we have, because if we knew what the population proportion was we wouldn't need to estimate it:

$$95\% \ \text{CI} = p \pm \left\{ 1.96 \sqrt{\left[\frac{p(1-p)}{n} \right]} \right\}$$

As with means, for a 99% confidence interval, multiply the standard error by 2.575 instead of 1.96. This will make the confidence interval wider, because the wider the range, the more confident you can be that the population proportion will lie in it.

EXAMPLE: NEW AGE TRAVELLERS

Some researchers were interested in the reasons for 'New Age' travellers living on the road. In 1996 they carried out a survey of travellers in the Wessex region. Respondents were asked the question, 'Do you live on the road as a means of preventing homelessness?' Out of the 61 travellers who answered the question, 24 replied 'yes' (Zoe Matthews, unpublished data, 1998).

This gives us a sample proportion of 0.3934 (24 ÷ 61). We can use this sample proportion p as an estimate of the population proportion Π, but we must have some measure of the variation in the sample proportions. In this case, a 95% CI would be:

$$95\% \ \text{CI} = 0.3934 \pm \left\{ 1.96 \sqrt{\left[\frac{0.3934(1-0.3934)}{61} \right]} \right\}$$

$$= 0.3934 \pm 0.1226 = (0.2708, 0.5160)$$

Therefore we can say with 95% confidence that the population proportion will lie between 0.2708 and 0.5160. In other words, between 27.08% and 51.60% of New Age travellers live on the road as a means of preventing homelessness. This is rather a wide confidence interval, so the estimate is not very precise. In this case the confidence interval is wide due to the sample size being quite small.

EXAMPLE: OPINION POLLS

Confidence intervals for proportions are particularly useful when interpreting **opinion polls**.

Table 10.1 compares the results of two British opinion polls published on 8 April 1992, the day before the 1992 general election. The results from the poll in *The Independent* suggested that Labour was in the lead by 3%, while the results published in *The Daily Telegraph* suggested that the Conservatives had a 0.5% lead over Labour. Does this mean that Labour were in the lead or the Conservatives? Which results should we believe?

TABLE 10.1 Percentage of people intending to vote Conservative or Labour in two opinion polls held on 7 April 1992

Opinion poll	Number in sample	% intending to vote:	
		Conservative	Labour
NOP/*Independent*	1746	39.0	42.0
Gallup/*Telegraph*	2478	38.5	38.0

Source: Butler and Kavanagh, 1992.

As a good statistician, you are a little wary of the papers' claims, so you decide to calculate 95% confidence intervals for all the results.

The percentages must first be converted into proportions, so for example the 39% intending to vote Conservative according to *The Independent* poll is a proportion of 0.39. The 95% confidence interval for the proportion voting Conservative would be:

$$95\% \ \text{CI} = 0.39 \pm \left\{ 1.96 \sqrt{\left[\frac{0.39(1 - 0.39)}{1746} \right]} \right\}$$

$$= 0.39 \pm 0.0229 = (0.3671, 0.4129)$$

Converted back into percentages, this could be written as:

$$95\% \ \text{CI} = (36.71\%, 41.29\%)$$

Try the other three yourself and see if you come up with the results in Table 10.2.

If you look at the ranges of the confidence intervals, it is obvious that we cannot draw any concrete conclusions about who would win the elections from these data. Because the ranges for the percentages voting Conservative

TABLE 10.2 95% confidence intervals for the percentage of people intending to vote Conservative or Labour in two opinion polls held on 7 April 1992

Opinion poll	% intending to vote (95% confidence interval):	
	Conservative	Labour
NOP/*Independent*	39.0	42.0
	(36.71, 41.29)	(39.68, 44.32)
Gallup/*Telegraph*	38.5	38.0
	(36.58, 40.42)	(36.09, 39.91)

Source: Original data from Butler and Kavanagh, 1992.

and Labour overlap each other, we cannot say from *The Independent* or *The Daily Telegraph* polls that either party was in the lead.

Moral of the story: don't believe everything you read about opinion polls, even in the 'quality' newspapers! In fact, in the end the Conservatives won with a 7.6% lead, which the polls had failed to predict (Butler and Kavanagh, 1992)! This was blamed on various factors such as late switching and differential turnout among Conservative and Labour supporters.

PRACTICE QUESTIONS

10.1 You decide to take a representative sample of students – 50 males and 50 females – and ask them if they believe it is usually not a good idea to have a one-night stand. You will find that 21 of the males and 35 of the females respond by saying that one-night stands are usually not a good idea.

(a) You want to apply your results to the whole student population, so calculate the 95% confidence intervals for the proportions of male and female students who believe that one-night stands are usually not a good idea. Can you say that there is a definite difference in the beliefs of males and females from your sample?

(b) Because the ranges of possible values for Π are quite large, you decide to rerun the survey with larger samples of 150 males and 150 females. This time you find that 65 males and 110 females believe that one-night stands are usually not a good idea. Now what figures can you be 95% confident that the population proportions will lie between?

10.2 The National Survey of Sexual Attitudes and Lifestyles (Wellings et al., 1994) found that 13.1% of British men aged 16–59 had had an HIV test (half of these were due to blood donation). If you take a random sample of 100 people, what is the chance that:

(a) 20 or more will have had an HIV test?
(b) 10 or fewer will have had an HIV test?
(c) Between 15 and 18 will have had an HIV test?

10.3 A local market research company takes a random sample of 200 adults in a town and asks them whether they support the council's plans for building a multiplex cinema complex on a greenfield site outside the town. Only 80 of the adults say that they support the proposal.

(a) Estimate the proportion of the adult population who support the proposal and calculate a 95% confidence interval for your answer.
(b) Calculate a 99% confidence interval. Explain why it is different to the 95% confidence interval.
(c) A member of the council claims that the market research company has got it wrong and that 60% of the population support the cinema proposal. Do you think the council member could be right?

Hint: what is the chance of getting a sample of 200 people with the observed proportion supporting the proposal if the true population proportion is 0.6?

11

HOW TO DECIDE HOW TO DECIDE

We have already been using the normal distribution to find out the probability of something happening (see Chapter 8). In a similar way, it can be used for formal decision-making. Chapters 11 and 12 provide a brief introduction to hypothesis testing.

We often want to know whether a sample is likely to come from a particular population or whether a sample is genuinely different to the population.

For example, your company wants to carry out a survey and you have been asked to find a market research company to do the work. One of the companies that tenders for the job claims that their staff are very clever, with professional staff having a mean intelligence quotient (IQ) of 120 with a standard deviation of 10.

You decide to check out the company properly and set an IQ test for a random sample of 36 professional staff. You find that the mean IQ of the 36 staff is 114. It appears that the staff you have tested have a lower IQ on average than the company claims. There are two possible reasons for this:

- The company's claim is *true*: the staff do have a mean IQ of 120. By chance you selected a sample of the staff with the lowest IQs.
- The company's claim is *false*: their staff do not have a mean IQ of 120.

Which explanation is likely to be the correct one? How do we decide what to decide?

HYPOTHESES

First of all we must write down a **hypothesis** about what we expect to happen if the company's claim is true. This is known as the **null hypothesis** or H_0. The null hypothesis is something of a 'Life is boring and nothing exciting (or out of the usual) is happening' hypothesis. In this example, our null hypothesis is that the company staff do have a mean IQ of 120, so we could write:

H_0: The company staff have a mean IQ of 120

The question we are then asking is 'Do our sample data support this hypothesis?

From Chapter 8, we know that any sample will not behave exactly as we would expect under our null hypothesis. Nevertheless, providing our hypothesis is sensible, we would expect our sample value to fall in a region of values fairly close to the population value that is specified by the null hypothesis. For example, if you had found that the mean IQ in your sample was 119, you would probably be fairly happy to say that the population mean could be 120. However, faced with a mean IQ in your sample of 114, you are rightly more sceptical of the truth of the null hypothesis. Where do we draw the line between believing and not believing the company's claim?

If, as in this case, the sample value falls a long way from our expectation, then we must ask:

- Is our hypothesis sensible?
- Is the sample result too much of a coincidence just to be a fluke? In other words, is it highly probable that some alternative hypothesis is true?

Secondly, we write down an **alternative hypothesis** known as H_A or H_1. In this case we would be thinking it more likely that the company's claim is false, so we could write:

$$H_A = \text{the company staff do not have a mean IQ of 120}$$

Note that the population mean is usually written as μ. In this example the two hypotheses could be written more concisely as:

H_o: $\mu = 120$ (the sample comes from a population that has a mean of 120)
H_A: $\mu \neq 120$ (the sample does not come from a population that has a mean of 120)

Now we are faced with the really tricky problem. How can we decide whether to believe the null hypothesis or whether to go for the alternative hypothesis? Hypothesis testing is all about finding strategies to make this decision.

What we need is a range of possible sample values within which we will be happy to accept the null hypothesis, but if the population value lies outside that range we would decide not to believe the null hypothesis (we call this 'rejecting' the null hypothesis). So what we are trying to do is decide whether to accept or reject the null hypothesis.

We concentrate on the null hypothesis because it is easier to prove that something is untrue than to prove that it is true. To prove the hypothesis 'all cats have a tail' definitively, you would have to check every cat in the world! But as soon as you find just one cat without a tail you have proved that the statement is definitely false. This is why we either reject the null hypothesis or say there is no evidence to reject it and therefore accept it.

SIGNIFICANCE TESTING: THE CONFIDENCE INTERVAL METHOD

The process of examining the null hypothesis in the light of sample evidence is called a **significance test**. It is possible to do this using confidence intervals. This is not the method generally used by most people, but it may help you to understand what is going on more easily.

STEPS IN SIGNIFICANCE TESTING USING CONFIDENCE INTERVALS

Step 1: *write down the hypotheses*
State the null hypothesis (what you would have expected to happen) and the alternative hypothesis (what actually appears to be happening). This should be done in terms of a population mean.

Step 2: *find the statistic for the sample*
Calculate the mean for your sample.

Step 3: *find a confidence interval*
Find a 95% confidence interval for the sample mean.

Step 4: *draw a conclusion*
Does your population value fall within this range? If *yes*, accept H_o; if *no*, reject H_o.

EXAMPLE: COMPANY STAFF IQ

Let's go through the four steps for the example about the IQs of a company's staff.

1 Write down the hypotheses:

H_o: $\mu = 120$ (the staff have a mean IQ of 120)
H_A: $\mu \neq 120$ (the staff do not have a mean IQ of 120)

Note that the hypotheses can be written either in statistical jargon or in words.

2 Find the statistic for the sample:
The mean IQ in our sample is 114. The sample mean is usually written $\bar{x}$, so we would write:

$$\bar{x} = 114$$

3 Calculate a range from the sampling distribution. Suppose we are prepared to be wrong one time in 20 (wrong 5% of the time and right 95% of the

time). Then, for a normal distribution, we want to find the values that we are 95% certain that the population mean would lie between if the null hypothesis were true (if the company's staff did have a mean IQ of 120). This is shown in Figure 11.1.

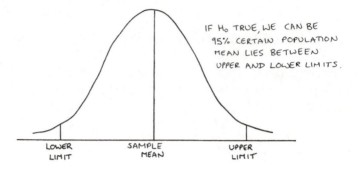

FIGURE 11.1 THE UPPER LIMIT AND LOWER LIMIT

This is just like calculating a confidence interval. The value 1.96 is used because we are testing at the 5% level; in other words we are calculating a 95% confidence interval. Remember that the company claimed the standard deviation for their staff was 10. Therefore the confidence interval will be:

$$95\% \ \mathrm{CI} = \text{sample mean} \ \pm \ 1.96 \times \frac{\text{standard deviation}}{\sqrt{n}}$$

$$= 114 \pm 1.96 \times \frac{10}{\sqrt{36}} = 114 \pm 3.27 = (110.73, \ 117.27)$$

4   Draw a conclusion. The population mean, 120, does not lie in the range (110.73, 117.27). The sample is very unlikely to have come from a population with a mean of 120. Therefore we can reject the null hypothesis H_o and accept the alternative hypothesis H_A. We conclude that the staff in the company do not have a mean IQ of 120. The sample is significantly different to their claim, sufficient to make us believe that they were not telling the truth!

THE TEST STATISTIC METHOD

The way we have just tackled this problem was a good introduction, but there is a much more commonly used method for testing hypotheses: the **test statistic method**.

Remember that we are wanting the range where we accept H_o to cover the middle 95% of the possible sample means. This corresponds to 47.5% either side of the population mean, as in Figure 11.2. Therefore the 5% of sample means outside this range will consist of 2.5% of sample means at either end of the distribution.

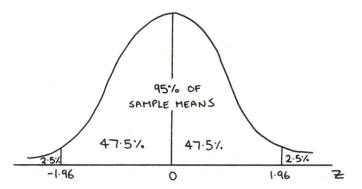

FIGURE 11.2 Z-SCORES FOR THE MIDDLE 95% OF SAMPLE MEANS

In terms of Z-scores, looking up 0.475 (the area 47.5%) in the middle of the normal table (Table A1.1) gives us a Z-score of 1.96 (check this yourself).

We want to reject the null hypothesis if the sample value is particularly extreme. So we can use 1.96 and –1.96 as the cut-off points. The points 1.96 and –1.96 are known as the **critical values**. If the Z-score in the sample lies in the **critical region** above 1.96 or below –1.96, we can reject H_o.

How can we find the Z-score for our sample? The formula is similar to the Z-score formula we learnt in Chapter 6, but the sample mean is compared to the population mean assumed under the null hypothesis, and because we are dealing with a sample, the standard error is used rather than the standard deviation.

$$Z = \frac{\text{sample mean} - \text{population mean}}{\text{standard error}} = \frac{\bar{x} - \mu}{SD / \sqrt{n}}$$

In this case, the Z-score will be:

$$Z = \frac{114 - 120}{10 / \sqrt{36}} = -3.6$$

The Z-score calculated like this is known as the **test statistic**. The test statistic –3.6 is much less than –1.96 (see Figure 11.3), so it definitely lies in the critical region. We reject the null hypothesis and conclude that the company staff are extremely unlikely to have a mean IQ of 120. It is highly improbable that the

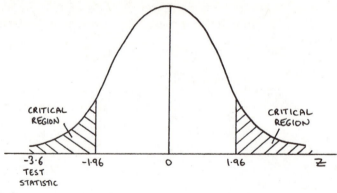

FIGURE 11.3

sample comes from a population with a mean of 120 and a standard deviation of 10.

STEPS FOR A HYPOTHESIS TEST: TEST STATISTIC METHOD
As a summary, here are the four steps needed for carrying out a hypothesis test comparing a sample mean to a population mean. Each step is important. If you forget to write down hypotheses at the beginning, the results will be meaningless.

Step 1: *write down the hypotheses*
Write down the null and alternative hypotheses.

Step 2: *find the sample statistic*
Find the sample mean. You may be told this or may need to calculate the mean yourself from some data.

Step 3: *calculate the test statistic*
Calculate the test statistic Z:

$$Z = \frac{\bar{x} - \mu}{SD / \sqrt{n}}$$

Step 4: *compare the test statistic with the critical values*
Compare the test statistic with the critical values, as in Figure 11.4. Draw a conclusion about the hypotheses and explain in words what this means.

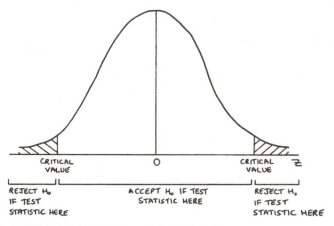

FIGURE 11.4 CRITICAL REGIONS FOR A HYPOTHESIS TEST

EXAMPLE: CLASS SIZES

A group of parents believe that class sizes in their local primary schools are too high. They find that in a sample of 22 classes in the town, the mean number of children per class is 33. According to national education figures, class sizes nationally are normally distributed with a mean of 30 children and a standard deviation of 8 children. Are class sizes in the town significantly different to class sizes nationally?

Let's go through the four steps:
1   Write down the hypotheses:

H_O: $\mu = 30$ (class sizes in the town are no different to the national average)
H_A: $\mu \neq 30$ (class sizes in the town are different to the national average)

2   Find the sample statistic: we have been told that the mean class size in the town is 33.

3   Calculate the test statistic:

$$Z = \frac{33 - 30}{8 / \sqrt{22}} = 1.76$$

4   Compare the test statistic with the critical values: the test statistic 1.76 lies between –1.96 and 1.96, as shown in Figure 11.5. Therefore we do not have sufficient evidence to reject H_o. We must accept the null hypothesis that

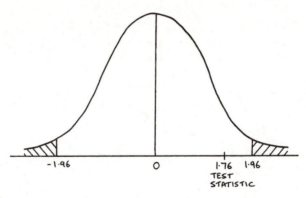

FIGURE 11.5

class sizes in the town are not significantly different to class sizes nationally.

IMPORTANT NOTE

In both these examples, we knew the standard deviation of the population. Often, we will not know the standard deviation of the population, but can instead calculate the standard deviation for the sample. The sample standard deviation can then be used to calculate the test statistic, but this should only be done if the sample size is at least 30. Otherwise a different test must be used (see Chapter 12).

TESTS FOR PROPORTIONS

So far, we have looked at hypothesis tests for a mean, where we are comparing the mean of a sample with that specified by a hypothesis. Sometimes, however, we may have a sample proportion which we want to compare to a population proportion. The method is the same as that for a Z test using means, except for the calculation of the test statistic.

The following formula gives the calculation of a Z-statistic to compare a sample proportion p with the population proportion Π. The standard error for a proportion, rather than the standard error for a mean, is used on the bottom line. Note that we always use the hypothesised population proportion Π to calculate the standard error.

$$Z = \frac{p - \Pi}{\sqrt{\left[\dfrac{\Pi(1-\Pi)}{n}\right]}}$$

EXAMPLE: RACIAL DISCRIMINATION

A London clothing store claims that it does not racially discriminate. Half of its employees come from ethnic minorities and half do not. You observe that 23 out of 28 people who were fired last year came from an ethnic minority. Is the store discriminating against such employees?

1 State the hypotheses:

H_o: Π = 0.5 (the proportion of those fired coming from ethnic minorities is the same as the proportion in the company's workforce, i.e. 0.5)

H_A: Π ≠ 0.5 (the proportion of those fired coming from ethnic minorities is different to 0.5)

2 Find the sample statistic. The proportion fired who come from an ethnic minority will be 23 divided by 28:

$$p = \frac{23}{28} = 0.82$$

3 Calculate the test statistic:

$$Z = \frac{p - \Pi}{\sqrt{\left[\frac{\Pi(1-\Pi)}{n}\right]}} = \frac{0.82 - 0.5}{\sqrt{\left[\frac{0.5(1-0.5)}{28}\right]}} = 3.39$$

4 For a Z test at the 5% level, the critical values are −1.96 and 1.96. The test statistic 3.39 is much greater than 1.96 and lies in the critical region. Therefore we should reject H_o and conclude that there is evidence that the company is guilty of racial discrimination.

THE LEVEL OF SIGNIFICANCE

All the examples so far use tests at the 5% level of significance. But what if we want to be extremely cautious and test at the 1% level (we are only prepared to be wrong 1 time in 100)?

Steps 1 to 3 are the same. Only Step 4 changes: we use different critical values. The critical region now only covers 1% of the area rather than 5%. In a two-tailed (two-sided) test, the 1% region is split between the two tails with 0.5% on each side, as shown in Figure 11.6. Therefore the percentage of the total area between the mean and a critical value will be 49.5%. Looking up the area 0.495 in the middle of the normal table (Table A1.1) gives a Z-score of 2.575. So the critical values for a two-tailed test at the 1% level are –2.575 and 2.575.

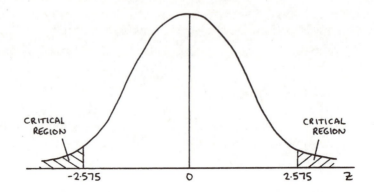

FIGURE 11.6 CRITICAL REGIONS FOR A TWO-SIDED TEST AT THE 1% LEVEL

In this chapter's first example, about the IQ of company staff, the test statistic was –3.6, so we would still reject H_o at the 1% level. In the second example, regarding class sizes, H_o was not rejected at the 5% level so it cannot possibly be rejected at the 1% level. In some cases, you may reject H_o at the 5% level but not reject it at the 1% level (if the test statistic lies between 1.96 and 2.575, or between –2.575 and –1.96 for a two-sided test). You are more likely to reject H_o at the 5% level than the 1% level because the rejection region is larger.

Note that you may want to memorize the critical values for each type of test. However, if you know how to work out the Z-score from the area as shown in the diagrams, you should be able to work out the critical values for a one- or two-tailed test at any level of significance, providing you have the normal tables with you.

ONE-SIDED TESTS

The tests we have carried out so far have been **two-sided tests**, otherwise known as **two-tailed tests**. In a two-sided test, the aim is to discover whether the sample mean or proportion is *different* to the population mean or proportion, not whether it is either larger or smaller.

Sometimes we are fairly sure that the sample mean is, for example, larger than the population mean. In other words, we know in which **direction** the difference is. In the example about class sizes, the parents were fairly sure that the class sizes in their town were *bigger* than the national average. So instead of testing to see whether their class sizes were *different* to the national average, we could test to see whether they are bigger.

To do this we use a **one-sided test**. The procedure is similar apart from the hypotheses and the critical values.

For a one-sided test, the null hypothesis is the same as for a two-sided test, but the alternative hypothesis becomes directional. The new hypotheses might be:

H_o: μ = 30 (class sizes in the town are the same as the national average)
H_A: μ > 30 (class sizes in the town are greater than the national average)

The test statistic will still be 1.76. However the critical values are different. In a two-sided test, the 5% critical region was split into the two tails of the distribution. With a one-sided test, the 5% critical region is all at one end; which end depends on whether you are testing for a sample mean being greater or less than the population mean. In this case, we expect the sample mean to be greater, so the critical region will be on the right-hand side which is higher than the mean, as shown in Figure 11.7. With 5% at the end, the area between the mean and the critical value will be 45%. If you look up the area 0.45 in the middle of the normal tables (Table A1.1), this gives a Z-score of 1.645. (Check this yourself: in fact you will see that 1.645 is the mean of the two nearest Z-scores.)

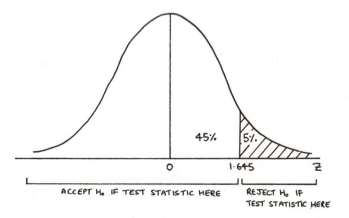

FIGURE 11.7 CRITICAL REGION FOR A ONE-SIDED TEST (WHERE THE SAMPLE STATISTIC IS EXPECTED TO BE BIGGER THAN THE POPULATION STATISTIC)

So for a one-sample test, the critical value at the 5% level is 1.645, or –1.645 if you are testing for the sample mean being less than the population mean.

In this example, the test statistic of 1.76 lies in the critical region, so we can reject the null hypothesis and conclude that the class sizes in the town are significantly bigger than the national average.

This is a different conclusion than the one reached using a two-tailed test.

It is always easier to reject the null hypothesis using a one-sided test, because the Z-score does not need to be as large for it to lie in the critical region. The null hypothesis can be rejected on weaker evidence and so one-tailed tests should be used with caution. It is essential that you use them only when you are absolutely certain of the direction of the effect. You should always remember that if you specify a one-tailed hypothesis then you do not have the option of moving to a two-tailed hypothesis if your sample turns out to have a mean or proportion which has a value in the opposite direction.

EXAMPLE: TRAIN TIMES

An independent rail company claims that 95% of trains run on time (defined as departing within 5 minutes of the scheduled departure time). A group of angry commuters claim that their trains are always late. To back up their case, they take a random sample of 40 trains and find that only 33 of them left on time according to the company's definition. Have the commuters got a good case against the rail company?

The commuters are convinced that a *smaller* proportion of trains run on time than the company claims. We therefore use a one-sided test.

1 Hypotheses:

$$H_o: \Pi = 0.95$$
$$H_A: \Pi < 0.95$$

2 Sample proportion:

$$p = \frac{33}{40} = 0.825$$

3 Test statistic:

$$Z = \frac{0.825 - 0.95}{\sqrt{\left[\frac{0.95(1-0.95)}{40}\right]}} = -3.63$$

4 Because we are testing to see whether the proportion on time is *smaller* than 0.95, the critical region will be below the mean, as in Figure 11.8. The critical value will be −1.645. As −3.63 is smaller than −1.645, it lies in the critical region. We can reject the null hypothesis and conclude that there is evidence that the proportion of trains running on time is significantly lower than 0.95. The commuters do have a good case against the rail company.

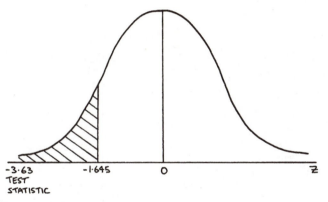

FIGURE 11.8

Note that if we had used a two-sided test for this example, the null hypothesis would still have been rejected because –3.63 is less than the –1.96 critical value used in a two-sided test at the 5% level.

PRACTICE QUESTIONS

11.1 You are interested in the drinking habits of school children and carry out a survey of 34 girls aged 14 from a local school. The mean number of units of alcohol consumed by the girls in the previous week was 2.8 units with a standard deviation of 0.8 units.

National data suggest that mean weekly alcohol consumption among girls aged 14 is 2.5 units per week (Office for National Statistics, 1997b). Carry out a test at the 5% level to determine whether alcohol consumption among girls in the sample is significantly different to the national average.

11.2 A group of 11 professional male social workers has a mean weekly income of £542. However the New Earnings Survey of 1997 states that the mean weekly income of full-time male workers with professional occupations in health and social work is £688.80 (Office for National Statistics, 1997d) with a standard deviation of £321.

The social workers complain to the higher authorities that they are badly off. Carry out a one-sided test at the 5% level to see whether their claim is justified.

11.3 When a politician was elected onto the city council, 63.8% of voters thought that local crime prevention was an important issue. Since then, several measures have been taken to reduce crime and the politician wonders whether attitudes have changed. In a recent survey of 350 voters, 204 still thought that local crime prevention was an important issue. Perform a hypothesis test at the 1% level to determine whether there has been a significant change in this attitude over time.

11.4 The mean hourly rate of pay for white males in full-time employment was £8.34 in 1994–5 (Office for National Statistics, 1996a). A researcher is studying people of Pakistani and Bangladeshi origin in Britain and finds that the comparable rate of pay in her sample of 55 men is £6.92 with a standard deviation of £2.12.

Carry out a two-sided test to see whether the difference is significant:

(a) at the 5% level
(b) at the 1% level.

11.5 A researcher claims that anybody conducting a small-scale postal survey on an issue of local concern will have a response rate of 40%. You recently tried to do a small-scale postal survey about the need for local sports facilities and only had 18 replies from a sample of 60.

Does your experience provide any evidence at the 5% level to suggest that the researcher's claim might be incorrect?

11.6 A local health centre asks all smokers registered with the practice whether they would like to give up smoking. Of 124 smokers, 89 say that they would like to give up.

A national survey carried out in 1995 (Office for National Statistics, 1996a) suggested that 68% of adult smokers would like to give up smoking. Is the proportion of smokers at the health centre who want to give up significantly different to the national proportion?

12

MORE TRICKY DECISIONS

So far we have carried out Z tests comparing a sample to a population. This can only be done if we know the standard deviation of the population, or if not, providing the sample size is 30 or greater. It should be noted that in our experience, most social scientists use data which satisfy these assumptions.

If we do not know the population standard deviation and the size of the sample is below 30, a slightly different approach must be used. We will look at two methods for testing small samples where the population standard deviation is unknown.

1 The one-sample t **test** compares the sample mean with the population mean, just like a Z test. It is very similar, but t tables are used instead of the normal tables. The t test can only be used when the data are normally distributed.
2 The one-sample **sign test** compares the median of the sample with the population median. This test can be used when the data do not follow the normal distribution; in other words it is suitable for skewed data. It can also be used if we want to compare medians rather than means.

Figure 12.1 may help you to decide which is the most appropriate test to use for a particular set of data. When presented with a problem, always write down what you know first, as this will help you decide which test to use. For example, if you realise that you do not know the population standard deviation, but there are 40 people in the sample, you can use a Z test. If you find that you do not know the population standard deviation and there are fewer than 30 people in the sample, drawing a stem and leaf plot can help you to decide whether the data are normally distributed or not.

Because we are dealing with small samples, it is harder to reject the null hypothesis using these tests than with a conventional Z test. Smaller samples are less reliable and so we must be more certain of a difference before rejecting H_o. Where possible, the better strategy is still to obtain a larger sample to work from.

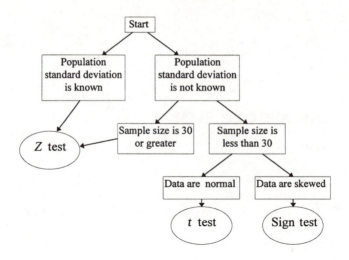

FIGURE 12.1 HOW TO DECIDE WHICH TEST TO USE

THE *T* TEST

A *t* test is only used when the population standard deviation is unknown, the sample size is less than 30 and the sample data are normally distributed. A *t* test is very similar to a Z test, but rather than using the normal distribution, the *t* **distribution** must be used instead, to take account of the small sample size.

The t distribution

The *t* distribution is similar to the normal distribution, but there is a separate curve for each value of *t*, as shown in Figure 12.2. As the value of *t* increases, the *t* curves get taller and thinner. Once the sample size reaches 30 or more,

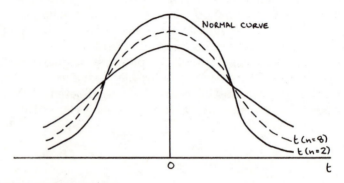

FIGURE 12.2 THE *T* DISTRIBUTION

the t curve is approximately the same as the normal distribution. This is why we can use the normal distribution as an approximation where $n \geq 30$.

Procedure for a t test

A t test is very similar to a Z test. As before, the hypotheses should be written down and the sample statistic found. The test statistic has the same formula as for the Z test:

$$t = \frac{\bar{x} - \mu}{SD / \sqrt{n}}$$

The main difference lies in finding the critical values. These are found using t tables (see Table A1.2 in Appendix 1).

The t curve to use is the curve for $n-1$ degrees of freedom. So if the sample size is 15, t_{n-1} is t_{14}. To find the value of t for 14 degrees of freedom, find 14 in the first column (which gives the degrees of freedom) and look horizontally along.

For a two-tailed test at the 5% level, look down the $t_{df}(0.025)$ column. This is because for such a test there will be 95% in the middle of the distribution and 2.5% (0.025) at each end, as shown in Figure 12.3. So for a 5% level test with 14 degrees of freedom, the t value from the table is 2.1448 and the critical values will be –2.1448 and 2.1448.

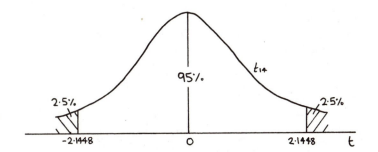

FIGURE 12.3 CRITICAL REGIONS FOR A TWO-SIDED TEST AT THE 5% LEVEL WITH 14 DEGREES OF FREEDOM

Similarly, for a two-tailed test at the 1% level, look down the $t_{df}(0.005)$ column, because there will be 99% in the middle of the distribution and 0.5% (0.005) in each tail. Can you work out which columns you would use for one-tailed tests at the 5% and 1% levels? (Sketch a diagram to help.)

EXAMPLE: DRINKING HABITS

National research has shown that the mean weekly alcohol consumption among women aged 16–24 is 9.5 units (Office for National Statistics, 1998a). You wonder whether your fellow students are different in this respect and undertake a survey of drinking in the previous week. The number of units consumed by a sample of female students in the previous week is shown in Table 12.1.

TABLE 12.1 Units of alcohol consumed by 14 female students in the previous week

11	0	12	23	17	6	1
17	11	14	0	18	14	5

To carry out a hypothesis test at the 5% level, let's follow the key steps as before. A *t* test must be used because we do not know the population standard deviation and the sample size is less than 30.

1 Write down hypotheses:

H_o: $\mu = 9.5$ (alcohol consumption among female students is the same as the national mean for women aged 16–24)

H_A: $\mu \neq 9.5$ (alcohol consumption among female students is different from the national mean for women aged 16–24)

2 Find sample statistics. From the data, we can calculate that the mean number of units consumed in the previous week by the sample was 10.64 with a standard deviation of 7.26 units. (Check these figures yourself for practice.)

3 Calculate the test statistic:

$$t = \frac{\bar{x} - \mu}{\text{SD} / \sqrt{n}} = \frac{10.64 - 9.5}{7.26 / \sqrt{14}} = 0.59$$

4 Compare the test statistic with the critical values. With a sample size of 14, there will be 13 degrees of freedom. From the *t* tables (Table A1.2), $t_{13}(0.025)$ = 2.1604. The critical values will be –2.1604 and 2.1604. The null hypothesis will be rejected if the test statistic is less than –2.1604 or greater than 2.1604 (see Figure 12.4). The test statistic 0.59 lies between –2.1604 and 2.1604 and so the null hypothesis is accepted. From this sample, there is no evidence that alcohol consumption among female students is different from national levels for females aged 16–24.

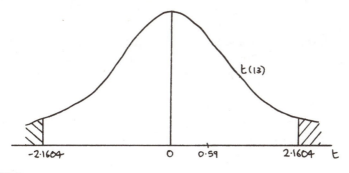

FIGURE 12.4

EXAMPLE: PSYCHOMETRIC TESTING

A group of social science graduates applying for management jobs in a company have to take psychometric tests. Their scores for the test are shown in Table 12.2. They later discover that the mean score for the test among all applicants is 62. They are so modest that they believe that they will definitely get the jobs due to their superior intelligence. Is there any evidence that the social science graduates really are better than the mean at the psychometric tests?

TABLE 12.2 Psychometric test scores for nine social science graduates applying for management jobs in a company

71	63	62	74	69	67	59	65	68	65	66	67

The hypotheses could be written as follows:

H_o: $\mu = 62$ (the performance of the social science graduates is the same as the mean)

H_A: $\mu > 62$ (the performance of the social science graduates is better than the mean)

Note that this is a one-sided test.

The sample statistics must be calculated from the data. The mean score from the sample of students is 66.33 with a standard deviation of 4.03.

Next the test statistic is calculated:

$$t = \frac{\bar{x} - \mu}{SD / \sqrt{n}} = \frac{66.33 - 62}{4.03 / \sqrt{9}} = 3.22$$

Finally, the critical values must be found and a conclusion drawn. With a sample size of 12, there will be 11 degrees of freedom. For a one-sided test at the 5% level, there will be 5% of the area in one tail, so the $t(0.05)$ column should be used. From Table A1.2, $t_{11}(0.05) = 1.7959$, so the critical value will be 1.7959. Figure 12.5 illustrates this process.

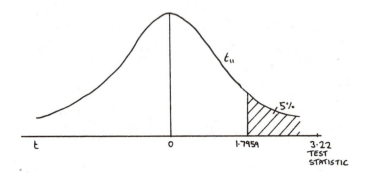

FIGURE 12.5

The test statistic 3.22 lies in the critical region and so the null hypothesis can be rejected. There is evidence that the sample of social science graduates have done significantly better than the mean in the psychometric tests.

THE SIGN TEST

If the distribution of a set of data is skewed, the median is a better measure of the average than the mean because it is not affected by extreme values. The sign test compares the median of a sample with a population median and is used with small samples of skewed data. It can also be used when the population median is known rather than the population mean.

Idea behind a sign test

The mean has a sampling distribution, as described by the central limit theorem, which helps us to compare a sample mean with a population mean. However, the median does not have a similar sampling distribution. (This is why the sign test is known as a **non-parametric test**: 'non-parametric' tells us that there is no sampling distribution.)

All we know is that the median lies in the middle of the distribution. In the population, we know that half of the observations will lie above the median and half below it. If there is no evidence that the sample is no different to the population, we would expect that about half of the observations in the sample will lie above the population median and half below it. If the sample is genuinely different to the population, the proportion of observations above the median will be markedly greater or lower than 0.5.

EXAMPLE: SALARIES

The salaries of a group of hypothetical Politics students who graduated in 1997 are shown in Table 12.3. The median salary of graduates in 1997 from that university was £15 000. Are the salaries of Politics students significantly different to the median?

TABLE 12.3 Starting salaries of hypothetical politics students graduating in 1997 (£)

15 500	16 200	19 500	13 900	14 200
15 400	15 500	17 000	14 900	14 800
14 700	15 900	15 500	16 600	18 000

The hypotheses are always written in terms of the proportion of observations above the median. Here π_m is the proportion of observations above the median in the population and p_m is the proportion in the sample. So we can write:

H_o: π_m = 0.5 (the salaries of Politics graduates come from a population with half the observations above £15 000)

H_A: Π_m ≠ 0.5 (the salaries of Politics graduates do not come from a population with half the observations above £15 000)

To find the test statistic p_m, the proportion of salaries above the median in the sample must first be found. To do this, put a plus or minus sign by each observation to indicate whether it is above (+) or below (−) the median:

15 500	+	16 200	+	19 500	+	13 900	−	14 200	−
15 400	+	15 500	+	17 000	+	14 900	−	14 800	−
14 700	−	15 900	+	15 500	+	16 600	+	18 000	+

The proportion above the median will be the number of plus signs divided by the total number in the sample:

$$p_m = \frac{\text{number of} + \text{signs}}{\text{total number}} = \frac{10}{15} = 0.67$$

(If you have one or more observations equal to the median, take half of them to be above and half below.)

A Z test statistic can then be found in the same way as that for a hypothesis test for a proportion. If the null hypothesis is true, the population proportion above the median will be 0.5 and the standard error of the population if the null hypothesis was true would be

$$\sqrt{\left[\frac{0.5(1-0.5)}{15}\right]}$$

The Z test statistic in this case would be:

$$Z = \frac{p_m - \Pi_m}{\sqrt{\left[\frac{\Pi_m(1-\Pi_m)}{n}\right]}} = \frac{0.67 - 0.5}{\sqrt{\left[\frac{0.5(1-0.5)}{15}\right]}} = 1.32$$

For a two-tailed test at the 5% level, the critical values will be −1.96 and 1.96. The test statistic 1.32 lies between −1.96 and 1.96, so we have no reason to reject the null hypothesis. We must accept the null hypothesis that the salaries of Politics students are not significantly different to the median.

Even though it appeared that the salaries in the sample were higher than the median, we cannot reject the null hypothesis. Non-parametric tests are less likely to find a significant difference between the sample and the population than tests based on the normal distribution (Z tests). Remember that the sign test does not use all the information from the data. It only takes account of whether each observation is above or below the median and not its actual value. Therefore we recommend this test is used only when the assumptions surrounding the use of the Z test are clearly not satisfied. Finally it should be noted that there are a plethora of non-parametric tests for use in different situations and you are advised to consult a more specialised book (there are many) on non-parametric tests if appropriate.

EXAMPLE: BOOK PRICES

The median cost of textbooks in the local bookshop in 1997 was £13.99. In early 1998 you took a sample of 25 textbooks from the shop and found that 18 of them cost more than £13.99. Is there any evidence that the price of textbooks increased in 1998? (Use a two-tailed test at the 5% level.)

This problem is phrased slightly differently in that some of the work is done for us; we know that 18 out of 25 books in the sample cost more than the median price of the 1997 population. Otherwise, the method is the same, as the workings below show:

$$H_o: \Pi_m = 0.5$$
$$H_A: \Pi_m \neq 0.5$$

$$p_m = \frac{18}{25} = 0.72$$

$$Z = \frac{0.72 - 0.5}{\sqrt{\left[\dfrac{0.5(1-0.5)}{25}\right]}} = 2.2$$

For a two-tailed test at the 5% level, the critical values are −1.96 and 1.96. The test statistic 2.2 is greater than 1.96 and so we can reject the null hypothesis. There is evidence to suggest that the price of textbooks did increase in 1998, so you should go and complain! You will probably be told that the global economy is to blame and the poor bookseller can do nothing!

PRACTICE QUESTIONS

12.1 National data suggest that the mean weekly household expenditure among lone mother families with at least one dependent child is £158 (Central Statistical Office, 1995). From interviewing 16 lone mothers in your local area, you find that they spend on average £149 per week with a standard deviation of £33. Is there any evidence at the 5% level that the household expenditure of lone mothers in your area is different to the national average?

12.2 A class of 25 children is asked how much pocket money they receive weekly. The mean amount received was found to be £1.56 with a standard deviation of £0.45.

You find data which suggest that the mean amount of pocket money received by children in the country is £1.80. Use a one-tailed test at the 5% level to determine whether the children are receiving less pocket money than average.

12.3 The median amount charged for an adult weekday swim in a leisure pool in the London metropolitan area in 1997–8 was £2.50 (CIPFA, 1997). Table 12.4 shows the amount charged for a similar swim in 10 other metropolitan districts of England. Use a sign test (5% level) to determine whether the cost of swimming in a leisure pool in other metropolitan districts is different to the cost in London.

TABLE 12.4 Amount charged for an adult weekday swim in a leisure pool in 10 metropolitan districts, England, 1997

District	Cost of a swim (£)
Manchester	2.20
Oldham	1.50
Bolton	3.60
Liverpool	1.25
Rotherham	2.20
South Tyneside	1.70
Birmingham	2.00
Dudley	2.10
Bradford	2.10
Leeds	1.95

Source: CIPFA, 1997

12.4 A charity runs an annual sponsored bike ride. Last year the median amount raised per rider was £63.20. This year the charity hopes that the riders have brought in more sponsorship money. To see whether this is the case, they take a sample of 20 riders and check how much money each raised. The results (to the nearest 10p) are shown in Table 12.5.

TABLE 12.5 Sponsorship money raised by 20 riders in a charity ride (£ to nearest 10p)

23.40	52.00	39.20	48.50
65.10	69.90	68.80	101.30
110.70	44.70	82.20	88.60
77.30	72.60	99.40	61.10
60.30	71.40	59.80	66.70

Carry out a sign test (5% level) to find out whether the amount of sponsorship money raised per rider has changed significantly since last year.

13

CORRELATION AND REGRESSION

Frequently you may have found yourself wanting to compare two variables with each other, for example, to answer questions such as:

- Is the social deprivation level of a district related to the level of unemployment in the district?
- Is the number of units of alcohol a student drinks in an average week related to how often they miss the Quantitative Methods class in a term due to a hangover?

You may also want to predict the value of one variable from the other, for example:

- If a district has an unemployment rate of 13%, how socially deprived would we expect it to be?
- If student X drinks 25 units in an average week, how many classes is he/she likely to miss in the semester?

Fortunately, statistics help us to address these sorts of questions.

Correlation measures the association between two variables, in other words the strength of the relationship between the values of the two variables.

Regression is the prediction of the values of one variable from the values of another variable.

In many ways one can think of correlation and regression as being descriptive statistics on two variables as opposed to one.

CORRELATION

Correlation measures the **association** between two continuous variables.

Here are some examples of variables whose values are associated:

1 The number of years of education that women in developing countries have and the number of children they have. With more years of education, women tend to have fewer children.

2 The sales of Zimmer frames and the number of people over 70 years old in the population. In populations with a high proportion of over 70s, we would expect sales of Zimmer frames to be high.
3 The mean temperature and number of riots in a month. When the temperature is high, one might expect more rioting in cities as people spend more time hanging around outside and get frazzled by the heat.

In some cases, two variables may be closely associated, but that does not mean that there is a **causal** relationship between them. If the value of one variable increases as the other variable increases (or decreases), it does not necessarily mean that one variable explains the other or could be used to predict the other. This can be seen in the two examples following.

EXAMPLE: IQ AND MENARCHE

Early research found that a high IQ and early menarche (starting menstrual periods) were associated among females. However it was clear that having a high IQ did not cause the menarche to be early; neither did an early menarche cause a high IQ! In fact a third factor, social class, was influencing both variables (see Figure 13.1). Girls of higher social class were better nourished and therefore experienced menarche earlier than girls of lower social class. Girls of higher social class also had higher IQs due, probably, to better education and opportunity in the home compared with those of a lower social class. Therefore IQ and age at menarche were only associated because of the confounding effect of social class.

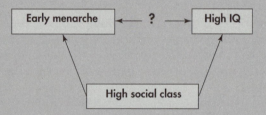

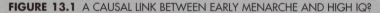

FIGURE 13.1 A CAUSAL LINK BETWEEN EARLY MENARCHE AND HIGH IQ?

EXAMPLE: AIDS AND AMPHETAMINES

Early research into the causes of AIDS found an association between the risk of contracting HIV and taking amphetamines anally. The researchers could have therefore concluded that taking amphetamines anally caused HIV infection. However they soon realised that there was a third variable involved in these cases: homosexuality (see Figure 13.2). Male homosexuals were particularly likely to be taking amphetamines anally and were also more likely to contract the HIV virus for other reasons, so this is why an association was found.

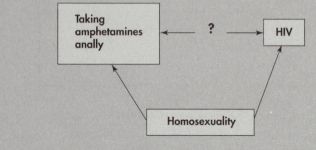

FIGURE 13.2 A CAUSAL LINK BETWEEN AND HIV AND TAKING AMPHETAMINES ANALLY?

Scatter graphs

When you are trying to examine the association between two variables X and Y, always draw a **scatter graph** (also known as a scatterplot or scattergram) before doing anything else.

Table 13.1 provides data for the total fertility rate (TFR) and percentage of women using contraception in 10 countries. The total fertility rate is the total number of children a woman would expect to have during her lifetime if current levels of childbearing prevailed. These data can be plotted on a scatter graph as in Figure 13.3.

TABLE 13.1 Total fertility rate and contraceptive prevalence in 10 countries

Country	Total fertility rate, 1994	% of women using contraception (any method), 1987–94
UK	1.8	82
USA	2.1	71
Gambia	5.4	12
Indonesia	2.8	55
Mexico	3.0	53
Brazil	2.3	66
Uganda	7.1	15
Slovakia	1.8	74
Niger	7.3	4
Botswana	4.7	33

Source: UNDP, 1997

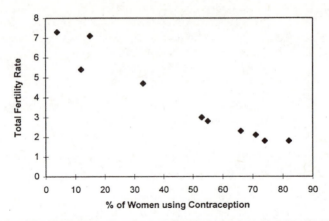

FIGURE 13.3 TOTAL FERTILITY RATE AND THE PERCENTAGE OF WOMEN USING CONTRACEPTION IN TEN COUNTRIES (UNDP, 1997)

TIPS FOR DRAWING SCATTER GRAPHS

Remember all the rules for drawing graphs discussed in Chapter 3. In particular, take care in choosing the scale.

If you are interested in causation, as opposed simply to association, it is important to decide which of the two variables is the **dependent variable** and which is the **independent variable**. If you are trying to predict one variable from the other, the variable being predicted is the dependent variable. In this example, we know that the level of childbearing is likely to depend on the level of contraceptive use and so the total fertility rate is the dependent variable and contraceptive prevalence is the independent variable. Often it will be obvious which variable is dependent, but sometimes it is not clear and in such cases it does not matter which is which.

Deciding which variable is dependent is important, because on a scatter graph the dependent variable should always go on the Y axis. The independent variable is therefore plotted on the X axis.

Figure 13.3 shows that, in general, countries where a high percentage of women are using contraception have low total fertility rates, while countries where contraceptive prevalence is low tend to have high total fertility rates. This makes substantive sense.

Occasionally, you may want to plot scores of variables that have been standardised (Z-scores). Because Z-scores are negative as well as positive, you will need a cross-shaped axis, as in Figure 13.4, which shows some standardised weights and heights (hypothetical data). The graph shows in general that the taller a person is, the heavier they are likely to be. We call this type of relationship a positive correlation.

INTERPRETING SCATTER GRAPHS

Figure 13.5 shows five examples of patterns which a scatter graph might exhibit.

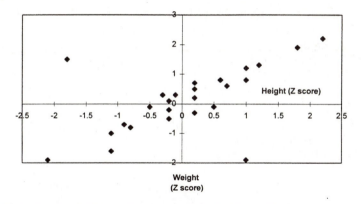

**Weight
(Z score)**

FIGURE 13.4 STANDARDISED WEIGHTS AND HEIGHTS OF 25 PEOPLE

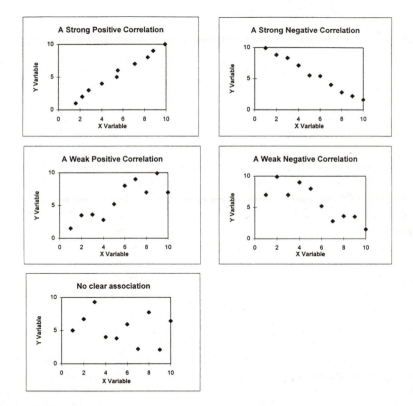

FIGURE 13.5 DIFFERENT TYPES OF PATTERN FOUND ON SCATTER GRAPHS

If when the values of the X variable are high the values of the Y variable are also high, and when the values of the X variable are low the values of the Y variable are also low, a **positive correlation** exists between the two variables. The points on a scatter graph showing a positive correlation will follow an upwards slope from left to right. Gross national product (GNP) and the number of televisions per 1000 population in different countries would have a positive correlation, for example, because richer countries will have more consumer goods per head.

On the other hand, if when the X values are high the Y values are low and vice versa, a **negative correlation** exists. The points on a scatter graph showing a negative correlation will slope downwards from left to right. An example of a negative correlation would be the value of cars and their ages: as cars become older, their value drops.

If all the points lie in a fairly straight line, we have a **strong correlation** between the two variables. If they are more spread out, we have **weak correlation**. Therefore a correlation can be strong and positive, weak and positive, strong and negative or weak and negative! Note that the distinction between strong and weak is fairly arbitrary. You might want to describe a correlation as fairly strong, for example.

Finally, if the points appear to be randomly scattered all over the graph and show no clear pattern, we say that there is *no association* (no correlation) between the two variables.

You may be thinking that this is all a bit vague: ideally we want to quantify *how* weak or strong a correlation between two variables is. This can be done!

The correlation coefficient

To quantify an association – in other words, to measure its strength numerically – we can calculate the **Pearson product moment correlation coefficient**, named after a statistician called Karl Pearson. You will be pleased to know that this is called the correlation coefficient or *r* for short.

Take a deep breath: here is the formula!

$$r = \frac{\sum\left[(X_i - \overline{X})(Y_i - \overline{Y})\right]}{\sqrt{\left[\sum(X_i - \overline{X})^2 \sum\left(Y_i - \overline{Y}\right)^2\right]}}$$

The formula is honestly not as bad as it looks, although it can be time-consuming to work out by hand. After all, you should now be very familiar with expressions like $\sum(Y_i - \overline{Y})$ for calculating a standard deviation.

The way to handle a scary-looking equation like this is to draw up a worksheet to do each bit separately before finally putting them together in the equation.

STEPS IN CALCULATING THE CORRELATION COEFFICIENT

The following tabulation calculates the correlation coefficient for the data on total fertility rate and contraceptive prevalence in 10 countries (from Table 13.1). The procedure is as follows.

Step 1

Write down a list of all the observations for the two variables X and Y in the first two columns (A and B). Remember that X is contraceptive prevalence and Y is the total fertility rate.

Step 2

For each variable, add up all the values of the observations and divide by the total number of them to obtain the means $\bar{X}$ and $\bar{Y}$ at the bottom of each column.

Step 3

In columns C and D, calculate the residuals $(X - \bar{X})$ and $(Y - \bar{Y})$ by subtracting the mean from each value.

Step 4

In columns E and F, square the answers that you got in columns C and D to obtain $(X - \bar{X})^2$ and $(Y - \bar{Y})^2$.

Step 5

In column G, multiply the values in column C by the values in column D to obtain $(X - \bar{X})(Y - \bar{Y})$.

Step 6

For columns E, F and G add up all the values in each column to obtain a total at the bottom of each column. These are the numbers that will go into the equation.

Note that a common mistake is to miss out column G and get an answer of zero for the top line of the equation, through thinking that the sum of the X residuals is zero and the sum of the Y residuals is zero, and so zero times zero equals zero. In fact you need to multiply *each* X residual by the corresponding Y residual and *then* sum these answers (as in column G). Your answer is unlikely to be zero.

A	B	C	D	E	F	G
X	Y	$(X - \bar{X})$	$(Y - \bar{Y})$	$(X - \bar{X})^2$	$(Y - \bar{Y})^2$	$(X - \bar{X})(Y - \bar{Y})$
82	1.8	35.5	−2.03	1260.25	4.12	−72.07
71	2.1	24.5	−1.73	600.25	2.99	−42.39
12	5.4	−34.5	1.57	1190.25	2.46	−54.17
55	2.8	8.5	−1.03	72.25	1.06	−8.76
53	3.0	6.5	−0.83	42.25	0.69	−5.40
66	2.3	19.5	−1.53	380.25	2.34	−29.84
15	7.1	−31.5	3.27	992.25	10.69	−103.01
74	1.8	27.5	−2.03	756.25	4.12	−55.83
4	7.3	−42.5	3.47	1806.25	12.04	−147.48
33	4.7	−13.5	0.87	182.25	0.76	−11.75
$\bar{X} = 46.5$ $\bar{Y} = 3.83$			Totals	7282.50	41.27	−530.70
				$\Sigma(X - \bar{X})^2$	$\Sigma(Y - \bar{Y})^2$	$\Sigma(X - \bar{X})(Y - \bar{Y})$

Now you are ready to put all these figures into the equation, which has magically been reduced to three numbers:

$$r = \frac{-530.70}{\sqrt{(7282.50 \times 41.27)}} = -0.97 \text{ (to two decimal places)}$$

Eureka! There is just one problem here: what does an r value of -0.97 actually mean?

A BRIEF GUIDE TO r, THE UNIVERSE AND EVERYTHING

The correlation coefficient r takes values between $+1$ and -1. This is what the different values of r indicate:

- $r = +1$: perfect positive correlation (all the points lie in a straight line).
- r between 0 and 1: positive but not perfect correlation.
- $r = 0$: no association between the two variables.
- r between -1 and 0: negative but not perfect correlation.
- $r = -1$: perfect negative correlation (all the points lie in a straight line).

The nearer r is to $+1$ or -1, the stronger the relationship between the two variables. Values near zero indicate a very weak relationship.

In the example, the result $r = -0.97$ indicates a very strong negative correlation between contraceptive prevalence and the total fertility rate (as we would expect from the scatter graph).

In other words, countries with a low percentage of women using contraception tend to have high total fertility rates and vice versa. Because the relationship is so strong, a country's total fertility rate could safely be predicted from its contraceptive prevalence.

Note that in the social sciences, we would almost never get a perfect correlation between two variables because people never behave in exactly the way we would expect! A value as close to -1 as the example is quite rare.

WARNING

The correlation coefficient measures **linear** association: how close the data points are to a straight line. However, with some relationships, the data follow a curved pattern. This is called a **curvilinear** relationship, as in Figure 13.6. In such cases r is *not* a good measure of the strength of association between the two variables. This is one reason why it is important to draw a scatter graph before doing any calculations: if it shows a curvilinear association, you should not calculate the correlation coefficient because it will be misleading.

REGRESSION: PREDICTING Y FROM X

When describing just one variable, we can summarise the data using means,

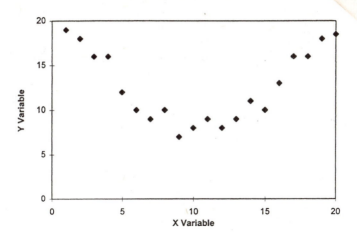

FIGURE 13.6 A SCATTER GRAPH SHOWING A CURVILINEAR ASSOCIATION

medians and so on. But with two variables, we summarise their relationship using the equation of a straight line.

If X and Y are the two variables, the equation of a straight line is:

$$Y = a + bX$$

where a is the Y intercept and b is the gradient (explained in a moment).

(Note that you may or may not remember from your schooldays that the equation of a straight line was '$Y = mX + c$'. This means exactly the same thing – we just use slightly different letters in statistics, so 'a' is equivalent to 'c', and 'b' is equivalent to 'm'. If this means nothing to you, then just ignore it!)

If we calculate the values of a and b, this equation can be used to predict the value of the Y variable from any given value of the X variable. The problem is, how can we fit the best straight line to a set of data? With just two points, as in Figure 13.7, it's easy! But with three or more points, there are lots of possibilities. Figure 13.8 shows some possible lines for a dataset with only three points. In a larger dataset with a strong correlation, it is usually possible to judge by eye roughly where the best fit line might go, but even so we would probably all draw it slightly differently. And if the correlation is weak and there is a lot of scatter, it is very difficult to judge where the line should be. So we have to calculate the line of best fit, known as the **regression line**.

The line of best fit will be the line that minimises the vertical distance between the line and all the points. In jargon, the best fit line will minimise $\sum d_i^2$, where d_i are the vertical distances between the line and each point as shown in Figure 13.9.

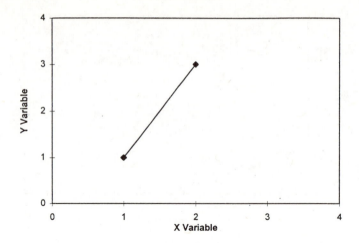

FIGURE 13.7 FINDING THE BEST STRAIGHT LINE THROUGH TWO POINTS

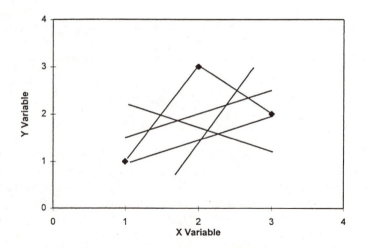

FIGURE 13.8 FINDING THE BEST STRAIGHT LINE THROUGH THREE POINTS

This line is described by the equation $Y = a + bX$. To find the values of a and b to put into the equation, the following formulae are needed:

$$b = \frac{\sum \left(X_i - \bar{X} \right)\left(Y_i - \bar{Y} \right)}{\sum \left(X_i - \bar{X} \right)^2}$$

$$a = \bar{Y} - b\bar{X}$$

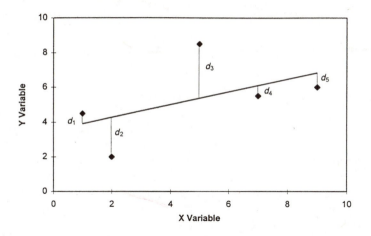

FIGURE 13.9 DISTANCES BETWEEN THE LINE AND THE POINTS

If you look back at the calculation of the correlation coefficient, you will see that we have already calculated all the numbers we need to put into these equations! So very little extra work is needed.

The value of b for the contraception and fertility example is calculated as follows:

$$b = \frac{-530.70}{7282.50} = -0.07 \text{ (to two decimal points)}$$

This value for b, along with the two means $\bar{X}$ and $\bar{Y}$, is used in the equation to find the value of a:

$$a = \bar{Y} - b\bar{X} = 3.83 - (-0.07 \times 46.5) = 7.09$$

We now know the values of a and b. These are known as the **regression coefficients**. The equation of a straight line is $Y = a + bX$, so the equation of the regression line for these data will be:

$$Y = 7.09 + (-0.07\ X)$$

Note that in this equation, the + and – signs will cancel each other out to give a – sign, so the equation can be written as:

$$Y = 7.09 - 0.07\ X$$

The X variable represents the percentage using contraception and the Y variable represents the total fertility rate (TFR), so the variable names can also be put into the equation:

TFR = 7.09 – 0.07 × percentage using contraception

And there we have it! But what on earth does it mean?!

Interpreting the regression coefficients, a and b

The regression coefficients *a* and *b* must always be interpreted in the *context* of the analysis that you are doing.

How should *a* be interpreted? In this case, *a* = 7.09. Looking at the equation TFR = 7.09 – 0.07 × percentage using contraception, we can see that if the percentage using contraception were zero, then –0.07 × 0 would equal 0 and so the TFR would take the value 7.09. Therefore we can **predict** that if no women in a country are using contraception, the total fertility rate will be 7.09. Thus:

> *a* is the value of *Y* when *X* = 0.

In other words, *a* is the value of *Y* when the regression line crosses the *Y* axis (this is where *X* = 0). It is sometimes called the *Y* intercept. In this case the *Y* intercept is 7.09, so a quick sketch of the regression line would look something like Figure 13.10.

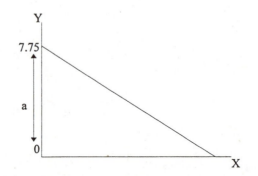

FIGURE 13.10 A SKETCH GRAPH SHOWING THE REGRESSION LINE AND Y INTERCEPT

Be warned however, that *X* = 0 will not always be a sensible possibility, for example if the variable were the cost of textbooks in a bookshop: none are free! Or again, if the *X* variable was the age of the woman and the *Y* variable was the number of children she had: very few (alright then, none) babies aged 0 have children themselves! Always check the context of the data and ask yourself if what you are saying makes sense!

In general, we don't interpret *a* too much; *b* is far more interesting.

> b is a measure of the 'gradient' or steepness of the line.

Suppose you need to estimate the TFR for countries with different percentages of women using contraception. This can be done by putting different percentages into the equation and calculating the resulting TFR. For example, if 10% of women were using contraception, the equation would be:

$$TFR = 7.09 - (0.07 \times 10) = 6.39$$

We would therefore expect the TFR to be 6.39 in a country with 10% contraceptive prevalence.

Table 13.2 shows some more values of the TFR predicted using the equation. Check that you can do these calculations yourself and get the same answers.

TABLE 13.2 Some values of the total fertility rate estimated from contraceptive prevalence using the regression equation

% women using contraception	Total fertility rate (estimated)
0	7.09
1	7.02
2	6.95
25	5.34
40	4.29
80	1.49
100	0.09

Can you spot what happens every time contraceptive prevalence increases by 1%? The TFR actually falls by 0.07 each time. This is true for all values of contraceptive prevalence, whether it increases from 0% to 1% or 78% to 79%.

Therefore we can say that the TFR increases by b when we increase contraceptive prevalence by 1% (one unit of X). Since b is negative in this case, the TFR actually falls. Similarly, if contraceptive prevalence increased by 10%, the TFR would fall by $10 \times 0.07 = 0.7$.

WARNING

Can you see what is wrong with the TFR that we estimated for a country where 100% of women are using contraception? A value of 0.09 for the TFR is unrealistically low (indeed any childbearing would be the result of contraceptive failure) and would imply that nearly all women are childless! It is also unlikely that 100% of women would be using contraception in any country, because at any one time, some women would be pregnant and others would not be in a relationship and would have no need for contraception.

This problem has arisen because we have estimated from outside the range of our original data. If you look right back to the values we were first given (Table 13.1), you will find that the highest contraceptive prevalence for any of the countries was 82%. We can confidently make predictions about points on the part of the line which comes within the range of the data (4% to 82% of women using contraception). But making predictions outside this range (known as extrapolation) is dangerous! Figure 13.11 shows this.

Do not make inferences outside the range of your data unless you are really sure that they are sensible. If in doubt, don't!

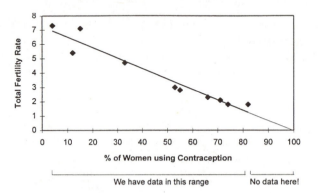

FIGURE 13.11 TOTAL FERTILITY RATE AND THE PERCENTAGE OF WOMEN USING CONTRACEPTION IN 10 COUNTRIES: THE RANGE OF THE DATA

The regression line: summary

From the findings above, we can make some general rules which apply to any regression line.

- The equation of a regression line is $Y = a + bX$.
- b is the change in Y for a change of one unit in X.
- If b is positive, Y increases as X increases.
- If b is negative, Y decreases as X increases.
- If $b = 0$, the line will be horizontal and there is no relationship between the two variables.

EXAMPLE: TEENAGE PREGNANCY RATES IN SOUTHAMPTON

Research by Steve Clements (unpublished) compares rates of conceptions among girls aged 15–19 in the different electoral wards of Southampton. One aim of the research was to find out whether high rates of teenage conceptions were linked to social deprivation. Table 13.3 shows teenage conception rates in 1996 and values of the Carstairs index in 1991 for each ward. The Carstairs index measures deprivation in terms of unemployment, car ownership and social class composition. Higher values indicate greater deprivation.

TABLE 13.3 Teenage conception rates and the Carstairs index of deprivation in 15 Southampton wards

Ward	Conception rate per 1000 female population aged 15–19, 1996	Carstairs index,[1] 1991
Bargate	110.90	2.03
Bassett	53.25	0.15
Bitterne	113.40	1.09
Bitterne Park	91.45	0.02
Coxford	43.82	0.86
Freemantle	93.38	0.65
Harefield	94.11	0.25
Millbrook	80.85	1.09
Peartree	65.30	0.40
Portswood	54.24	0.37
Redbridge	82.17	1.10
St Lukes	55.35	1.10
Shirley	49.21	0.02
Sholing	83.19	0.19
Woolston	115.17	0.68

[1] The Carstairs index is a deprivation index calculated from 1991 Census data (see text).

Source: Steve Clements, unpublished

How strongly related are teenage conception rates and deprivation? Can we successfully predict the teenage conception rate of a ward from its Carstairs index value?

Y is the dependent variable, the variable being predicted. In this case the teenage conception rate may be affected by the level of deprivation, so the teenage conception rate is the Y variable.

The first step as always is to draw a scatter graph, as in Figure 13.12. There appears to be quite a lot of scatter on the graph, with no obvious pattern, although you may be able to detect a slight positive correlation.

If we were to calculate the regression line for these data, the working would be as follows:

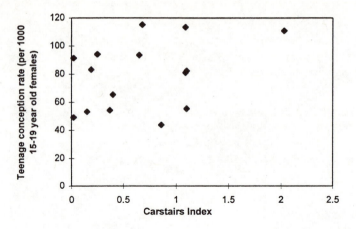

FIGURE 13.12 TEENAGE CONCEPTION RATES AND THE CARSTAIRS INDEX IN 15 SOUTHAMPTON WARDS (STEVE CLEMENTS, UNPUBLISHED)

X	Y	$(X - \bar{X})$	$(Y - \bar{Y})$	$(X - \bar{X})^2$	$(X - \bar{X})(Y - \bar{Y})$
2.03	110.90	1.36	31.85	1.85	43.32
0.15	53.25	−0.52	−25.80	0.27	13.42
1.09	113.40	0.42	34.35	0.18	14.43
0.02	91.45	−0.65	12.40	0.42	−8.06
0.86	43.82	0.19	−35.23	0.04	−6.69
0.65	93.38	−0.02	14.33	0.00	−0.29
0.25	94.11	−0.42	15.06	0.18	−6.33
1.09	80.85	0.42	1.80	0.18	0.76
0.40	65.30	−0.27	−13.75	0.07	3.71
0.37	54.24	−0.30	−24.81	0.09	7.44
1.10	82.17	0.43	3.12	0.18	1.34
1.10	55.35	0.43	−23.70	0.18	−10.19
0.02	49.21	−0.65	−29.84	0.42	19.40
0.19	83.19	−0.48	4.14	0.23	−1.99
0.68	115.17	0.01	36.12	0.00	0.36
$\bar{X} = 0.67$	$\bar{Y} = 79.05$		Total:	4.29	70.63

$$b = \frac{\sum(X - \bar{X})(Y - \bar{Y})}{\sum(X - \bar{X})^2} = \frac{70.63}{4.29} = 16.46$$

$$a = \bar{Y} - b\bar{X} = 79.05 - (16.46 \times 0.67) = 68.02$$

So, as $Y = a + bX$, the regression line will be:

Teenage conception rate = 68.02 + 16.46 Carstairs index

What does the value 16.46 tell us? It indicates that for every increase of one in the Carstairs index, the predicted teenage conception rate will increase by 16.46 per 1000.

Using this equation, we could try to predict some teenage conception rates for wards with different values of the Carstairs index. What would the estimated rate be in a ward with a Carstairs index value of 1.1?

$$\text{Teenage conception rate} = 68.02 + (16.46 \times 1.1) = 86.13$$

QUESTIONS: TEENAGE CONCEPTION RATES

Try predicting the teenage conception rates for wards with the following index values (answers at the end of the chapter):

(a) Carstairs index value of 0.5
(b) Carstairs index value of 0.8
(c) Carstairs index value of 1.6.

Note that your answers will not be the same as the observed rates for wards with the same index values in the actual data, because we are making a prediction and the observed results are unlikely to be exactly the same as our prediction.

Measuring how well a regression line fits the data

Figure 13.13 shows this regression line plotted on the graph. We can see that most of the points are not that close to the line. In other words the regression line does not 'fit' the data particularly well. This means that any predictions we make will not be very reliable.

In order to measure how well a line fits the data, we must return to r, the correlation coefficient. You should remember that when all the points lie exactly on the regression line, the line is a perfect fit and $r = 1$ or $r = -1$. If $r = 0$, then there is no association and the line is useless.

For this purpose, it does not matter whether the correlation is positive or negative; we only want to see whether the line is a good fit. To get rid of the + and − signs we can take the square of r (multiply r by r) and use that as the measure of fit. A value of $r^2 = 1$ indicates a perfect fit, while a value of $r^2 = 0.8$ would be an excellent fit in the social sciences. Even values around $r^2 = 0.5$ are considered, with many social science data, to indicate a good fit. However, lower values would indicate that the line does not fit the data very well.

Let's calculate r^2 for the teenage conception data, using the formula for r. Most of the values needed have already been calculated in the working for the regression line, with the exception of $\Sigma(Y - \bar{Y})^2$ which equals 8278.53 (you could calculate this column yourself for practice).

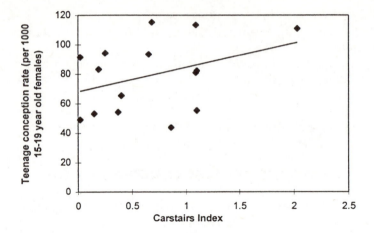

FIGURE 13.13 TEENAGE CONCEPTION RATES AND THE CARSTAIRS INDEX IN 15 SOUTHAMPTON WARDS, WITH REGRESSION LINE (STEVE CLEMENTS, UNPUBLISHED)

$$r = \frac{\sum\left[\left(X_i - \overline{X}\right)\left(Y_i - \overline{Y}\right)\right]}{\sqrt{\left[\sum\left(X_i - \overline{X}\right)^2 \times \sum\left(Y_i - \overline{Y}\right)^2\right]}}$$

$$r = \frac{70.63}{\sqrt{4.29 \times 8278.53}} = 0.37$$

Therefore $r^2 = 0.37^2 = 0.14$.

This suggests that the line is a relatively poor fit to the data, so we should not really use it to predict teenage conception rates. Therefore if the scatter graph does not show a clear association, it is always a good idea to check r^2 first, in order to avoid unnecessary calculation of the regression line.

We have already said that r^2 is a measure of how well the regression line fits the data. Another way of putting this is to say that r^2 *is the proportion of variation in Y which is explained by X*; $1 - r^2$ is therefore the proportion of the variation in Y *not* explained by X.

In this case, only 0.14 or 14% of the variation in teenage conception rates is explained by differences in the level of deprivation between wards. The Carstairs index does not explain 86% of the variation. There must be other factors involved in determining rates of teenage conceptions which the researcher needs to investigate, such as proximity to family planning clinics.

What about our first example, the total fertility rates and contraceptive prevalence in 10 countries? In Figure 13.11 the data all seem to lie fairly close to the regression line. For these data, we found that $r = -0.97$ and so $r^2 = 0.94$. This indicates that the regression line fits these data extremely well and so we can predict a country's total fertility rate from its contraceptive prevalence with very reliable results. Contraceptive prevalence explains 94% of the difference in total fertility rates between the 10 countries.

ANSWERS: TEENAGE CONCEPTION RATES

(a) Rate = 68.02 + (16.46 × 0.5) = 76.25.
(b) Rate = 68.02 + (16.46 × 0.8) = 81.19.
(c) Rate = 68.02 + (16.46 × 1.6) = 94.36.

PRACTICE QUESTIONS

13.1 Students entering higher education are usually vetted by their grades in A level exams. However, are such grades really good predictors of performance in higher education?

Table 13.4 shows the number of points achieved at A level by an anonymous group of students and also their mean mark in their first-semester exams of their first year in higher education.   Note that the points score for A level is calculated, where an A grade is 10 points, a B grade 8 points, a C grade 6 points, a D grade 4 points and an E grade 2 points. The number of points for each subject can then be added up to give a points score for each student.

TABLE 13.4 A level point scores and mean first semester marks for a group of 18 higher education students

A Level points score[1]	Mean first semester marks (%)
18	54
18	48
16	52
18	65
14	46
12	65
20	52
18	57
20	63
18	53
26	64
16	54
20	43
16	58
28	60
22	64
22	60
22	54

[1] See text for explanation of A level points scores.

Source: anonymised student records

(a) Which variable will be the dependent variable Y?

   (b) Draw a scatter graph of the data. What does it show?

   (c) Calculate the correlation coefficient. What does the result mean?

   (d) Calculate r^2. How good a predictor of first-semester performance are A level grades for these students?

13.2 In developing countries, unsafe water is often linked to illness. Table 13.5 shows data on life expectancy in 1994 in 10 developing countries, along with the percentage of their populations with access to safe water in 1990–6.

TABLE 13.5 Life expectancy at birth and percentage of population with access to safe water in 10 developing countries

Life expectancy at birth, 1994 (years)	% of population with access to safe water, 1990–6
79.0	100
72.4	71
70.1	85
69.3	68
68.2	80
55.9	57
57.2	29
54.4	28
45.6	48
33.6	34

Source: UNDP, 1997

   (a) Draw a scatter graph. What does it tell you about the relationship between access to safe water and life expectancy?

   (b) Calculate the correlation coefficient. What does your answer mean?

   (c) Calculate the regression coefficients a and b.

   (d) Write down, in words, the equation for the regression line.

   (e) If nobody in a population had access to safe water, what would we predict life expectancy to be? Is this realistic?

   (f) Predict the life expectancy of a country with a percentage of the population with access to safe water of: (i) 40%, (ii) 52%, (iii) 90%.

14

ANALYSING TABLES

Much of this book has concentrated on methods for analysing continuous data. This final chapter describes a method for analysing **categorical data**. The **chi-squared test** can be used to find out whether there is a significant relationship between two categorical variables. The Greek letter chi is written χ, so in short this is known as the χ^2 **test**.

CATEGORICAL DATA AND CONTINGENCY TABLES

We often want to classify people into different categories. These might be demographic or socio-economic categories such as age, sex or educational qualifications. Other types of survey question also categorise people by their response to a particular question, for example 'yes' or 'no', or perhaps 'strongly agree', 'agree', 'disagree', 'strongly disagree' or 'not sure' about a particular statement.

Categorical data consist of **counts**: in other words the number of people in each category. Tables 14.1 and 14.2 shows some data from a hypothetical local survey of 100 people. The people were first asked whether they were aged 'below 40' or '40 or above' and then whether they supported or opposed proposals for a new out-of-town superstore in their area. The data simply show the number of people in each age group and the number of people who supported, opposed or were not sure about the superstore. Tables 14.1 and 14.2 are **one-way contingency tables** because they contain counts for only one variable.

TABLE 14.1 Age group of respondents to a local survey

Under 40	40 or above	Total
50	50	100

TABLE 14.2 Opinions of respondents to a local survey

Mainly support superstore	Mainly oppose superstore	Not sure	Total
27	52	21	100

Often we may want to see whether there is a relationship between two variables, for example whether opinions vary by age. To do this, the first step is to produce a **two-way contingency table** where people are classified by both age and opinion. In Table 14.3, each cell contains the number of people of a particular age and opinion. Thus for example there were 20 people aged under 40 who mainly support the superstore proposal. Note that the table contains the *row totals* (the totals for each age group: 50 and 50), the *column totals* (the totals for each opinion: 27, 52 and 21) and a *grand total* of 100 people.

TABLE 14.3 Opinions of respondents to a local survey by age group

Age group	Opinion			Total
	Mainly support superstore	Mainly oppose superstore	Not sure	
Under 40	20	17	13	50
40 or above	7	35	8	50
Total	27	52	21	100

You may be able to spot some interesting patterns from Table 14.3. It would appear that those supporting the superstore proposal are mainly under 40, while those opposing the proposal are more likely to be 40 or above. If age had no influence on opinion we might expect the proportion of people supporting and opposing to be similar in both age groups. To investigate this further we could calculate row percentages or column percentages (see Chapter 2 to revise this topic). For example, of the supporters, 74% ((20 ÷ 27) × 100) are under 40 and 26% are 40 or above (this is a column percentage). If age did not affect opinion behaviour we might expect about 50% of the supporters to be under 40 and 50% to be 40 or above, given that we have the same number of respondents in each age group. Therefore it seems that there is some kind of relationship between age and opinion.

However, even if the percentages show an apparent association, we need to test whether this association is significant or not. Does age really influence opinion, or have we obtained these results by chance?

THE CHI-SQUARED TEST

The chi-squared test for independence tests whether two variables are independent from each other. If not, we have evidence that the two variables are associated in some way.

Note that the chi-squared test only uses tables of counts. It cannot be used for tables of percentages because the test needs to take into account the total number of people in the sample when determining whether an association is significant. You should not use a chi-squared test for tables containing means, proportions or anything else other than counts.

We will start with a worked example using some real data.

EXAMPLE: EDUCATION AND VOTING IN THE 1987 ELECTION

The data in Table 14.4 come from the British Election Study 1987 cross-sectional survey. The sample consists of 852 salaried workers who were eligible to vote in 1987. Respondents are classified by whether they have been university educated or not and which of the three main parties they voted for in the 1987 election (15 people who voted for a minority party have been excluded from this analysis). Note that the row and column totals are included here, whereas if you had collected the data you would need to work them out yourself first.

TABLE 14.4 Observed values for university education and vote among salaried workers in the 1987 British election

| Education | Political party voted for | | | |
	Conservative	Alliance	Labour	Total
University educated	80	80	45	205
Not university educated	387	161	84	632
Total	467	241	129	837

Source: British Election Study 1987 cross-sectional survey, from Heath et al., 1991

It would be useful to carry out a test to establish whether there is any relationship between university education and voting behaviour.

Step 1
The first stage in any kind of test is always to write down the null and alternative hypotheses. In this case we might write:

H_o: there is *no* association between university education and party voted for

H_A: there *is* an association between university education and party voted for

In order to decide whether to accept or reject the null hypothesis, we must calculate a test statistic and then compare it to a critical value from the χ^2 tables.

Step 2
The counts in the original table are known as the **observed values**: they tell us what the survey actually found. For the χ^2 test we need to calculate a table of **expected values**. These are the values which we would expect to get in each cell if there were no association between the two variables. The test then

compares the observed and expected values to see whether they are significantly different.

To calculate the expected value for each cell, we use the formula:

$$\text{Expected value} = \frac{\text{column total} \times \text{row total}}{\text{grand total}}$$

For example, for Conservative voters with university education:

$$\text{Expected value} = \frac{467 \times 205}{837} = 114.38 \text{ (to two decimal places)}$$

TABLE 14.5 Expected values for university education and vote in the salariat in the 1987 British election

Education	Political party voted for			Total
	Conservative	**Alliance**	**Labour**	
University educated	114.38	59.03	31.59	205
Not university educated	352.62	181.97	97.41	632
Total	467	241	129	837

Table 14.5 shows the expected values for all six cells. If you have calculated them correctly, the row and column totals should be the same for the expected values as for the observed values: this is a useful check.

Step 3
Now we are ready to calculate the test statistic. The formula for the χ^2 test statistic is as follows:

$$\chi^2 = \sum \frac{(O - E)^2}{E}$$

where O represents the observed values and E the expected values.

It is best to do this calculation on a worksheet as shown in the following tabulation, where the calculation using O and E is done for each cell and then the results are summed at the end. Once you understand how this works you will be able to miss out some of the columns and just do them on a calculator, but this first example shows the workings in detail.

O	E	$(O-E)$	$(O-E)^2$	$\dfrac{(O-E)^2}{E}$
80	114.38	−34.38	1181.98	10.33
80	59.03	20.97	439.74	7.45
45	31.59	13.41	179.83	5.69
387	352.62	34.38	1181.98	3.35
161	181.97	−20.97	439.74	2.42
84	97.41	−13.41	179.83	1.85

Total 31.09

Therefore the χ^2 test statistic in this case is 31.09.

Step 4

Next we must find a critical value from the χ^2 tables (Table A1.3). To do this we must know the significance level we want to use (usually 5%) and the degrees of freedom.

Have a look at the χ^2 table. Along the top is the significance level. To carry out a test at the 5% level we need to look down the column headed $\chi^2_{df}(0.05)$. Along the side (in the first column) are the number of degrees of freedom (df).

To find the number of degrees of freedom for a two-way contingency table, we use the following formula:

$$df = (\text{number of rows} - 1) \times (\text{number of columns} - 1)$$

In this case the table has two rows and three columns, so the number of degrees of freedom will be $(2 - 1) \times (3 - 1) = 1 \times 2 = 2$.

Now refer back to the χ^2 table. Look across the row where df = 2 and down the column where the significance level is 5% and you should come to a value of 5.99. This is the critical value of χ^2 for this test.

Step 5

The null hypothesis can be rejected if the test statistic is greater than the critical value, 5.99. The test statistic we calculated in step 3 was 31.09 which is clearly much greater than 5.99. Therefore we can reject the null hypothesis and accept the alternative hypothesis that there is an association between university education and party voted for in the 1987 election.

STEPS FOR CARRYING OUT A χ^2 TEST

The steps taken in the example are the same for any chi-squared test of independence. The following procedure describes how to carry out a chi-squared test on any two-way table.

Step 1: *write down the hypotheses*

Write down a null hypothesis and alternative hypothesis appropriate to the variables in the table.

H_0: there is no association between the two variables

This means that the two variables are independent; neither variable influences the other.

H_A: there is an association between the two variables

This suggests that there is some kind of relationship between the two variables.

Step 2: *calculate a table of expected values*
Remember the formula:

$$\text{Expected value} = \frac{\text{column total} \times \text{row total}}{\text{grand total}}$$

Always check that your expected values still add up to the same row and column totals as in the original table.

Step 3: *calculate the χ^2 test statistic*

The formula is

$$\chi^2 = \sum \frac{(O - E)^2}{E}$$

where O represents the observed values and E the expected values.
    To calculate this, draw up a worksheet as in the examples, where you calculate $(O - E)^2 \div E$ for each cell of the table and then sum the results at the end.

Step 4: *find the critical value*
Find the critical value from the χ^2 table (Table A1.3). For a test at the 5% level, look down the column headed $\chi^2_{df}(0.05)$. For a test at the 1% level, look down the column headed $\chi^2_{df}(0.01)$. To decide which row to look across, the number of degrees of freedom (df) must be calculated using the formula:

$$df = (\text{number of rows} - 1) \times (\text{number of columns} - 1)$$

Finally look down the column with the correct significance level and across the row with the correct number of degrees of freedom and read off the critical value.

With practice, you may become very familiar with some values from the table, for example 3.84 for a two-by-two table at the 5% level of significance.

Step 5: *draw conclusions*
Now is the time to make a decision about the hypotheses.

The critical region (see Figure 14.1) is the area to the right of the critical value. If the test statistic lies in the critical region, there is evidence to reject the null hypothesis; if not, we must accept it. Therefore the rule is:

> Test statistic greater than critical value → reject null hypothesis.
> Test statistic less than (or equal to) critical value → accept null hypothesis.

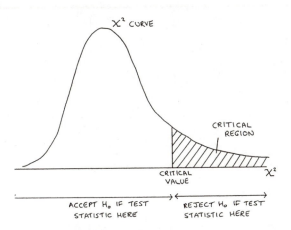

FIGURE 14.1 CRITICAL REGION FOR χ^2 TESTS

Some people find it easier to remember the rule; others can more easily memorise the diagram.

Once you have decided whether to accept or reject the null hypothesis, always write a sentence explaining what this means in terms of the two variables. For example you might write, 'We accept the null hypothesis and conclude that, at the 5% level, there is no significant relationship between age and opinion'; or 'We reject the null hypothesis and conclude that, at the 5% level, there is a significant association between age and opinion.'

EXAMPLE: ARE WOMEN BETTER AT STATISTICS?

Table 14.6 shows the results from a quantitative methods course taken by students at Southampton in 1997–8. The students are categorised by gender and by whether they achieved a high mark (55% or better) or a low mark (below 55%). Only students who completed both the course-work and the exam are included here.

TABLE 14.6 Observed values for quantitative methods marks for male and female students in 1997–8

| Marks | Sex | | |
	Male	Female	Total
Low[1]	53	53	106
High	36	56	92
Total	89	109	198

[1] 'Low' indicates marks of below 55%; 'High' indicates 55% or higher.

Source: authors' data

The data seem to suggest that while men and women are equally likely to achieve a high or low mark, there is a greater proportion of men achieving low marks than high marks. Are women significantly better at quantitative methods than men?

Step 1

H_o: there is no association between gender and achievement in quantitative methods

H_A: there is an association between gender and achievement in quantitative methods

Step 2

Table 14.7 shows the expected values. To calculate the expected value for women with high marks, for example, multiply the row total 92 by the column total 109 and divide your answer by the grand total 198. This gives an expected value of 50.65. Note that we are using two decimal places for accuracy, although whole people are more realistic!

TABLE 14.7 Expected values for quantitative methods marks

| Marks | Sex | | |
	Male	Female	Total
Low	47.65	58.35	106
High	41.35	50.65	92
Total	89	109	198

Step 3

Next we draw up a worksheet to calculate the test statistic. It does not matter in which order you put the observed values, as long as you put the expected values in the same order!

O	E	$(O-E)$	$(O-E)^2$	$\dfrac{(O-E)^2}{E}$
53	47.65	5.35	28.62	0.60
36	41.35	−5.35	28.62	0.69
53	58.35	−5.35	28.62	0.49
56	50.65	5.35	28.62	0.57
				Total 2.35

The χ^2 test statistic is 2.35.

Step 4

This table has two rows and two columns so there will be $(2-1) \times (2-1) = 1$ degrees of freedom. From the χ^2 table (Table A1.3), the critical value for a 5% level test with one degree of freedom is 3.84.

Step 5

The test statistic 2.35 is less than the critical value 3.84, so it does not lie in the rejection region. The null hypothesis cannot be rejected, so we must conclude that there is no significant association between gender and achievement in quantitative methods.

EXAMPLE: CONCERN OVER HIV

A study by Roger Ingham et al. (1996) carried out in-depth interviews with 86 young British adults who had reported having two or more sexual partners in the last 12 months. Table 14.8 shows data from a question asking the respondents how concerned they were about avoiding HIV and other sexually transmitted infections (STIs). The respondents have also been classified into male or female. We shall carry out a test to determine whether there is a significant difference in concern between males and females.

TABLE 14.8 Observed values for level of concern to avoid HIV/STIs among a sample of sexually active young adults in Britain

Level of concern about HIV/STIs	Sex		
	Female	Male	Total
Low	6	13	19
Mixed, medium, ambivalent	11	14	25
High	26	16	42
Total	43	43	86

Source: Ingham et al., 1996

H_o: there is *no* association between gender and concern over HIV/STIs
H_A: there is an association between gender and concern over HIV/STIs

The expected values are shown in Table 14.9.

TABLE 14.9 Expected values for levels of concern to avoid HIV/STIs

Level of concern about HIV/STIs	Sex		Total
	Female	Male	
Low	9.5	9.5	19
Mixed, medium, ambivalent	12.5	12.5	25
High	21.0	21.0	42
Total	43	43	86

The test statistic is calculated as shown in the following tabulation:

O	E	(O–E)	(O–E)²	$\frac{(O-E)^2}{E}$
6	9.5	–3.5	12.25	1.29
11	12.5	–1.5	2.25	0.18
26	21.0	5.0	25.00	1.19
13	9.5	3.5	12.25	1.29
14	12.5	1.5	2.25	0.18
16	21.0	–5.0	25.00	1.19

Total 5.32

The χ^2 test statistic is 5.32. The table has three rows and two columns so there are $(3-1) \times (2-1) = 2$ degrees of freedom. For a test at the 5% level, the critical value from Table A1. 3 will be 5.99. The test statistic is slightly less than the critical value.

Therefore there is not sufficient evidence to reject the null hypothesis at the 5% level, and we must accept the alternative hypothesis that there is no significant association between gender and concern about avoiding HIV and other STIs.

You may be surprised that there is no significant association, given the apparent differences in the table. This may be due to the small size of the sample. In a small sample, any difference has to be large in order to be significant, while in a much bigger sample a smaller difference between observed and expected values may be significant.

RESTRICTIONS ON THE χ^2 TEST

It has already been noted that the χ^2 test can only be used for tables containing counts. In addition, for the results of a χ^2 test to be valid *each expected value should be five or above.*

If you have cells with expected values below five, either you can go and collect more data or you can collapse the categories of your table as shown in the following example. In Table 14.10, the expected values for 15–19-year-olds are both below five. This is because the sample of 15–19-year-olds is very small, so one solution would be to collect more data from this age group. Alternatively you could collapse the categories of the table by combining the data for 15–19-year-olds with those from 20–24-year-olds, as in Table 14.11. This gives fewer cells in the table but it means that all the expected values are now well above five.

TABLE 14.10 Example of a table with expected values below five

Agreement with statement		Age group 15–19	20–24	25–29	Total
Agree:	observed	1	15	23	39
	expected	1.56	15.08	22.36	
Disagree/not sure:	observed	2	14	20	36
	expected	1.44	13.92	20.64	
Total		3	29	43	75

TABLE 14.11 Example of a table after collapsing categories

Agreement with statement		Age group 15–24	25–29	Total
Agree:	observed	16	23	39
	expected	16.64	22.36	
Disagree/not sure:	observed	16	20	36
	expected	15.36	20.64	
Total		32	43	75

RESIDUALS

In the first example, we concluded that there *was* an association between university education and voting behaviour among salaried workers in the 1987 British election. However, simply concluding that there is an association does not tell us very much. We want to know what kind of association there is: for example, which parties the university educated are more or less likely to vote for than would be expected if university education did not affect voting behaviour.

By calculating **standardised residuals** we can discover more about the association between education and voting behaviour. A residual r can be calculated for each cell in the table using the following formula:

$$r = \frac{O - E}{\sqrt{E}}$$

For those with a university education who voted Conservative, the residual will be:

$$r = \frac{80 - 114.38}{\sqrt{114.38}} = -3.21$$

Table 14.12 shows the residuals for all six cells of the table.

TABLE 14.12 Standardised residuals for education and voting example

| Education | Political party voted for | | |
	Conservative	Alliance	Labour
University educated	−3.21	2.73	2.39
Not university educated	1.83	−1.55	−1.36

Interpreting residuals

What do the residuals in Table 14.12 tell us?

First, we can look at whether the residual in each cell is positive or negative. A positive residual indicates that there are more people in the cell than we would expect if there were no association: in other words the observed value is greater than the expected value. Similarly, a negative residual tells us that there are fewer people than we would expect in that cell.

Table 14.12 shows, for example, that those without university education are more likely to vote Conservative than we would expect if there were no association, and less likely to vote either Alliance or Labour.

Secondly, we can look at the size of the residual to see whether the difference between observed and expected values is significant. To determine significance at the 5% level, the value of each residual can be compared to 1.96 or −1.96. In practice, 2 and −2 are used for ease. Therefore a residual of greater than 2 or less than −2 is significant, while any values between −2 and 2 are not significant.

In the example, all the residuals for those with university education are significant, while the residuals for those without university education are not significant.

We can conclude that salaried workers with university education were significantly less likely to have voted Conservative and significantly more likely to have voted Alliance or Labour in the 1987 election than we would expect if university education did not influence voting behaviour. Those without university education are more likely to vote Conservative and less likely to vote Alliance or Labour than we might expect, but these results are not significant at the 5% level.

ENDPIECE

It should be noted that it is possible to extend the ideas of χ^2 tests to tables with more than two variables. We typically use statistical techniques known as loglinear models to analyse such tables. These techniques are beyond the scope of this book but they are great fun and we really hope you now feel inspired to move on to even greater heights with your quantitative methods.

PRACTICE QUESTIONS

14.1 The study of sexually active young British adults by Roger Ingham et al. (1996) asked respondents whether they had planned their first experience of intercourse or not. Table 14.13 shows the results from this question.

TABLE 14.13 Whether first sexual intercourse was planned by respondent (interviews of 86 sexually active young adults in Britain)

Was first intercourse planned by respondent?	Sex	
	Female	Male
Yes	14	7
Somewhat/sort of	11	7
No	18	29

Source: Ingham et al., 1996

(a) Calculate row and column totals and a grand total for the table. What tentative conclusions, if any, might you draw from the table?

(b) Carry out a χ^2 test at the 5% level to find out whether there is any association between gender and whether first intercourse was planned or not.

14.2 Does educational level affect childbearing? Table 14.14 shows the number of children ever born to a large sample of women aged over 40 at interview, who are presumed to have completed childbearing. The women are also classified by whether their highest qualification is A level or equivalent or higher, or below A level standard. (Women with foreign qualifications have been excluded from this analysis.) The data come from the 1995–6 British General Household Survey.

**TABLE 14.14 Number of children ever born to a sample of
women aged 40 or above by highest educational
qualification**

Highest educational qualification	Number of children born			
	0	1 or 2	3 or more	Total
A level equivalent or higher	116	364	190	670
Below A level or none	225	1143	721	2089
Total	341	1507	911	2759

Source: 1995–6 General Household Survey: Office for National Statistics Social Survey
Division (computer file), The Data Archive (distributor), Colchester, Essex, 6 June 1997, SN
3690

(a) Carry out a χ^2 test at the 5% level to determine whether there
    is an association between highest educational qualification and
    the number of children ever born.
(b) Would your conclusion change if you carried out the test at the
    1% level?
(c) Calculate standardised residuals. What do they tell you about
    the association between education and childbearing?

14.3 Research in Warwickshire in the early 1990s studied residential
placements of children (Cliffe and Berridge, 1991). The placements
of children with siblings also in care were compared with the
placements of those without siblings. The results of the study are
shown in Table 14.15.

**TABLE 14.15 Residential placements for children with and
without siblings, Warwickshire, early 1990s**

Placement type	Sibling status		Total
	With siblings	Without siblings	
Foster care	53	128	181
Home on trial	8	9	17
Residential	0	11	11
Other	4	14	18
Total	65	162	227

Source: Cliffe and Berridge, 1991 (National Children's Bureau)

(a) Calculate the expected values. What do you notice?
(b) If you have calculated the expected values correctly, two of
    them will be below five. To overcome this problem, draw up a
    new contingency table which combines the 'home on trial' and
    'residential' categories. Recalculate the expected values to
    check that they are all above five.

(c) Carry out a χ^2 test at the 5% level on the new table to see whether having a sibling or not has any effect on residential placements.

Appendix 1

STATISTICAL TABLES

THE NORMAL DISTRIBUTION

An area in Table A1.1 is the proportion of the area under the entire curve in Figure A1.1 which lies between the mean ($Z = 0$) and a positive Z-score. The area between the mean and a negative Z-score will be identical to the area between the mean and a positive Z-score due to symmetry.

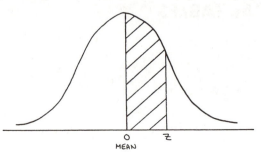

FIGURE A1.1

TABLE A1.1 The normal distribution

z	0.00	0.01	0.02	0.03	0.04	0.05	0.06	0.07	0.08	0.09
0.0	0.0000	0.0040	0.0080	0.0120	0.0160	0.0199	0.0239	0.0279	0.0319	0.0359
0.1	0.0398	0.0438	0.0478	0.0517	0.0557	0.0596	0.0636	0.0675	0.0714	0.0753
0.2	0.0793	0.0832	0.0871	0.0910	0.0948	0.0987	0.1026	0.1064	0.1103	0.1141
0.3	0.1179	0.1217	0.1255	0.1293	0.1331	0.1368	0.1406	0.1443	0.1480	0.1517
0.4	0.1554	0.1591	0.1628	0.1664	0.1700	0.1736	0.1772	0.1808	0.1844	0.1879
0.5	0.1915	0.1950	0.1985	0.2019	0.2054	0.2088	0.2123	0.2157	0.2190	0.2224
0.6	0.2257	0.2291	0.2324	0.2357	0.2389	0.2422	0.2454	0.2486	0.2517	0.2549
0.7	0.2580	0.2611	0.2642	0.2673	0.2703	0.2734	0.2764	0.2794	0.2823	0.2852
0.8	0.2881	0.2910	0.2939	0.2967	0.2995	0.3023	0.3051	0.3078	0.3106	0.3133
0.9	0.3159	0.3186	0.3212	0.3238	0.3264	0.3289	0.3315	0.3340	0.3365	0.3389
1.0	0.3413	0.3438	0.3461	0.3485	0.3508	0.3531	0.3554	0.3577	0.3599	0.3621
1.1	0.3643	0.3665	0.3686	0.3708	0.3729	0.3749	0.3770	0.3790	0.3810	0.3830
1.2	0.3849	0.3869	0.3888	0.3907	0.3925	0.3944	0.3962	0.3980	0.3997	0.4015
1.3	0.4032	0.4049	0.4066	0.4082	0.4099	0.4115	0.4131	0.4147	0.4162	0.4177
1.4	0.4192	0.4207	0.4222	0.4236	0.4251	0.4265	0.4279	0.4292	0.4306	0.4319
1.5	0.4332	0.4345	0.4357	0.4370	0.4382	0.4394	0.4406	0.4418	0.4429	0.4441
1.6	0.4452	0.4463	0.4474	0.4484	0.4495	0.4505	0.4515	0.4525	0.4535	0.4545
1.7	0.4554	0.4564	0.4573	0.4582	0.4591	0.4599	0.4608	0.4616	0.4625	0.4633
1.8	0.4641	0.4649	0.4656	0.4664	0.4671	0.4678	0.4686	0.4693	0.4699	0.4706
1.9	0.4713	0.4719	0.4726	0.4732	0.4738	0.4744	0.4750	0.4756	0.4761	0.4767
2.0	0.4772	0.4778	0.4783	0.4788	0.4793	0.4798	0.4803	0.4808	0.4812	0.4817
2.1	0.4821	0.4826	0.4830	0.4834	0.4838	0.4842	0.4846	0.4850	0.4854	0.4857
2.2	0.4861	0.4864	0.4868	0.4871	0.4875	0.4878	0.4881	0.4884	0.4887	0.4890
2.3	0.4893	0.4896	0.4898	0.4901	0.4904	0.4906	0.4909	0.4911	0.4913	0.4916
2.4	0.4918	0.4920	0.4922	0.4925	0.4927	0.4929	0.4931	0.4932	0.4934	0.4936
2.5	0.4938	0.4940	0.4941	0.4943	0.4945	0.4946	0.4948	0.4949	0.4951	0.4952
2.6	0.4953	0.4955	0.4956	0.4957	0.4959	0.4960	0.4961	0.4962	0.4963	0.4964
2.7	0.4965	0.4966	0.4967	0.4968	0.4969	0.4970	0.4971	0.4972	0.4973	0.4974
2.8	0.4974	0.4975	0.4976	0.4977	0.4977	0.4978	0.4979	0.4979	0.4980	0.4981
2.9	0.4981	0.4982	0.4982	0.4983	0.4984	0.4984	0.4985	0.4985	0.4986	0.4986
3.0	0.4987	0.4987	0.4987	0.4988	0.4988	0.4989	0.4989	0.4989	0.4990	0.4990

z = 3.5: proportion = 0.4998
z = 4.0: proportion = 0.49997

Source: adapted from Fisher and Yates, 1974; reprinted with the permission of Addison Wesley Longman Ltd

THE *T* DISTRIBUTION

Table A1.2 gives critical values for the *t* distribution. The left-hand column gives the number of degrees of freedom, and the remaining columns give the values for various significance levels, i.e. the proportion of the area in one tail of the distribution in Figure A1.2.

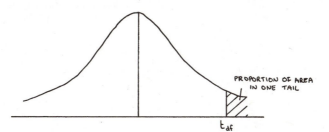

FIGURE A1.2

TABLE A1.2 The *t* distribution

df	$t_{df}(0.1)$	$t_{df}(0.05)$	$t_{df}(0.025)$	$t_{df}(0.01)$	$t_{df}(0.005)$
1	3.0777	6.3138	12.7062	31.8205	63.6567
2	1.8856	2.9200	4.3027	6.9646	9.9248
3	1.6377	2.3534	3.1824	4.5407	5.8409
4	1.5332	2.1318	2.7764	3.7469	4.6041
5	1.4759	2.0150	2.5706	3.3649	4.0321
6	1.4398	1.9432	2.4469	3.1427	3.7074
7	1.4149	1.8946	2.3646	2.9980	3.4995
8	1.3968	1.8595	2.3060	2.8965	3.3554
9	1.3830	1.8331	2.2622	2.8214	3.2498
10	1.3722	1.8125	2.2281	2.7638	3.1693
11	1.3634	1.7959	2.2010	2.7181	3.1058
12	1.3562	1.7823	2.1788	2.6810	3.0545
13	1.3502	1.7709	2.1604	2.6503	3.0123
14	1.3450	1.7613	2.1448	2.6245	2.9768
15	1.3406	1.7531	2.1314	2.6025	2.9467
16	1.3368	1.7459	2.1199	2.5835	2.9208
17	1.3334	1.7396	2.1098	2.5669	2.8982
18	1.3304	1.7341	2.1009	2.5524	2.8784
19	1.3277	1.7291	2.0930	2.5395	2.8609
20	1.3253	1.7247	2.0860	2.5280	2.8453
21	1.3232	1.7207	2.0796	2.5176	2.8314
22	1.3212	1.7171	2.0739	2.5083	2.8188
23	1.3195	1.7139	2.0687	2.4999	2.8073
24	1.3178	1.7109	2.0639	2.4922	2.7969
25	1.3163	1.7081	2.0595	2.4851	2.7874
26	1.3150	1.7056	2.0555	2.4786	2.7787
27	1.3137	1.7033	2.0518	2.4727	2.7707
28	1.3125	1.7011	2.0484	2.4671	2.7633
29	1.3114	1.6991	2.0452	2.4620	2.7564
30	1.3104	1.6973	2.0423	2.4573	2.7500
∞[1] 1.2816	1.6449	1.9600	2.3263	2.5758	

Where have you seen this before?

[1] df = ∞ (last row of table) gives critical values of the normal (z) distribution.

Source: adapted from Fisher and Yates, 1974; reprinted with the permission of Addison Wesley Longman Ltd

THE CHI-SQUARED DISTRIBUTION

Table A1.3 gives critical values for the chi-squared distribution. The left-hand column gives the number of degrees of freedom, and the remaining columns give the values for various significance levels, i.e. the proportion of the area in the critical region in Figure A1.3.

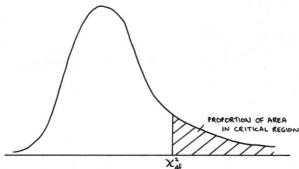

FIGURE A1.3

TABLE A1.3 The chi-squared distribution

df	$\chi^2_{df}(0.1)$	$\chi^2_{df}(0.05)$	$\chi^2_{df}(0.025)$	$\chi^2_{df}(0.01)$	$\chi^2_{df}(0.005)$
1	2.7055	3.8415	5.0239	6.6349	7.8794
2	4.6052	5.9915	7.3778	9.2103	10.5966
3	6.2514	7.8147	9.3484	11.3449	12.8382
4	7.7794	9.4877	11.1433	13.2767	14.8603
5	9.2364	11.0705	12.8325	15.0863	16.7496
6	10.6446	12.5916	14.4494	16.8119	18.5476
7	12.0170	14.0671	16.0128	18.4753	20.2777
8	13.3616	15.5073	17.5345	20.0902	21.9550
9	14.6837	16.9190	19.0228	21.6660	23.5894
10	15.9872	18.3070	20.4832	23.2093	25.1882
11	17.2750	19.6751	21.9200	24.7250	26.7568
12	18.5493	21.0261	23.3367	26.2170	28.2995
13	19.8119	22.3620	24.7356	27.6882	29.8195
14	21.0641	23.6848	26.1189	29.1412	31.3193
15	22.3071	24.9958	27.4884	30.5779	32.8013
16	23.5418	26.2962	28.8454	31.9999	34.2672
17	24.7690	27.5871	30.1910	33.4087	35.7185
18	25.9894	28.8693	31.5264	34.8053	37.1565
19	27.2036	30.1435	32.8523	36.1909	38.5823
20	28.4120	31.4104	34.1696	37.5662	39.9968
21	29.6151	32.6706	35.4789	38.9322	41.4011
22	30.8133	33.9244	36.7807	40.2894	42.7957
23	32.0069	35.1725	38.0756	41.6384	44.1813
24	33.1962	36.4150	39.3641	42.9798	45.5585
25	34.3816	37.6525	40.6465	44.3141	46.9279
26	35.5632	38.8851	41.9232	45.6417	48.2899
27	36.7412	40.1133	43.1945	46.9629	49.6449
28	37.9159	41.3371	44.4608	48.2782	50.9934
29	39.0875	42.5570	45.7223	49.5879	52.3356
30	40.2560	43.7730	46.9792	50.8922	53.6720

Source: adapted from Fisher and Yates, 1974; reprinted with the permission of Addison Wesley Longman Ltd

Appendix 2

ANSWERS TO PRACTICE QUESTIONS

CHAPTER 2

2.1 Your table should look something like Table A2.1. The biggest gender differences shown in the table are that a greater proportion of males than females are single and a much larger proportion of females than males are widowed. The latter probably reflects the fact that women tend to live longer than men. A slightly greater proportion of females than males are divorced, which may be due to the higher remarriage chances for men than women.

TABLE A2.1 Legal marital status of males and females (all ages) in Britain, 1991 (column %)

	Sex	
Marital status	Males	Females
Single	44.78	37.72
Married	47.93	45.43
Widowed	3.01	11.40
Divorced	4.28	5.45
Total %	100.00	100.00
Total number	26 574 954	28 313 890

Source: Office of Population Censuses and Surveys and General Register Office Scotland, 1993

2.2 (a) Your table should look something like Table A2.2.

TABLE A2.2 Voting patterns of salaried workers in the 1987 British election, by whether university educated or not

	Party voted for				Total
Education	Conservative	Alliance	Labour	Other	% (n)
University educated	39	39	22	1	101% (207)
Not university educated	60	25	13	2	100% (645)

Source: British Election Study 1987 cross-sectional survey, from Heath et al., 1991

    (b) (i) 22%

       (ii) 60%

      (iii) The university educated are more likely to have voted Alliance or Labour than those without university education, while those without university education are much more likely to have voted Conservative in the 1987 election.

CHAPTER 3

3.1 (a) An example of an abridged frequency table is shown in Table A2.3. Intervals of width 10 are probably the most appropriate here.

TABLE A2.3 Percentage of 1-year-olds fully immunised against measles in 30 of the poorest African countries, 1995

% fully immunised against measles	Frequency (number of countries)
10–19	1
20–29	1
30–39	2
40–49	8
50–59	5
60–69	4
70–79	5
80–89	4
Total	30

Source: UNICEF 1997, in UNDP, 1997

(b) An appropriate graph to present these data would be a histogram or a stem and leaf plot. There is a high proportion of countries with 40–49% of 1-year-olds fully immunised against measles, but few countries with a lower percentage than this. The remaining countries are evenly spread within the 50–89% group.

3.2 See Figure A2.1 for the stem and leaf plot. The plot clearly shows that the percentage of males smoking in different countries is higher than the percentage of females smoking. For females, the greatest number of countries fall in the 25–29% interval, while for males, the greatest number fall into the 35–39% interval.

```
        MEN                          WOMEN

                         1  | 0 3 3 4

                         1* | 7 8

                         2  | 1 2 4

                 6       2* | 5 6 7 8 9 9 9

             3 1 0       3  | 0 0 2 2 2 3

     9 7 7 6 5 5 5       3* | 8

             2 1         4  |

       9 9 8 6 6         4* |

             4 0         5  |

               8         5* |

             6 3         6  |
```

FIGURE A2.1 A STEM AND LEAF PLOT SHOWING THE PERCENTAGE OF MEN AND WOMEN WHO SMOKE IN 23 INDUSTRIALISED COUNTRIES, 1986–94 (UN 1994, IN UNDP, 1997)

3.3 (a) A bar chart would be best for presenting these data. A pie chart would not be suitable because the different percentages do not make up parts of a whole.

   (b) A line graph would be suitable for presenting changes in asylum seekers over time. Two lines, one for the UK and one for France, could be plotted on the same graph.

   (c) These data could be plotted on two stacked bars, one for males and one for females. Alternatively they could be presented using a multiple bar chart, with one colour for males and one for females. Either way, it would be a good idea to convert the data into percentages first so that males and females can be more easily compared.

CHAPTER 4

4.1 (a) Mean = 145.8 book titles.·
   Median = 8th observation = 100 book titles.

   (b) Iceland is a clear outlier with a far higher rate than the other countries.

   (c) If Iceland is removed from the data:
   Mean = 117.86
   Median = 7.5th observation = 93.5.
   The mean changes more than the median when Iceland is removed because the mean is affected more by extreme values.

4.2 Here the methods for grouped data must be used.

   Mean: mid-points are 25, 35, 45, 55, 65.
   Sum of (mid-point × frequency) = 12 060.
   Mean = 12 060 ÷ 298 = 40.47 years (40 years).

   Median = 149.5th observation.
   This lies in the 30–39 group.
   From interpolation (draw a diagram!), median = 39.52 years (39 years).
   The mean and median age of elected candidates was 49 years, so it appears that the defeated candidates were younger on average.

4.3 Mean: mid-points are 2.5, 7.5, 15, 25, 40, 60.
   Sum of (mid-point × frequency) = 8350.
   Mean = 8350 ÷ 560 = 14.9107; mean = £14 911 to nearest pound.

   Median = 280.5th observation.
   This lies in the 10–19.99 group.
   From interpolation the median income is £12 410. (not 12.41!).

   The mean is greater than the median, which implies that the data are positively skewed.

4.4　(a)　£386.60.
　　　(b)　£287.90.
　　　(c)　£950.10.
　　　(d)　The middle 50% lies between the upper and lower quartiles. Therefore the highest and lowest incomes of this group are £456.00 and £250.00.
　　　(e)　Managers and administrators in financial intermediation appear to be paid the most and those in the hotel and restaurant industry to be paid the least.

4.5　The cumulative frequencies must first be calculated.
　　　Median = 90th observation = 2 feeds.
　　　Lower quartile = 45th observation = 0 feeds.
　　　Upper quartile = 135th observation = 4 feeds.

CHAPTER 5

5.1　(a)　Assessment 1:　mean $= \dfrac{556}{10} = 55.6$.

　　　　　Assessment 2:　mean $= \dfrac{543}{10} = 54.3$.

　　　The students did not improve between the two assessments: the mean mark fell slightly.

　　　(b)　*Assessment 1*
　　　　Standard deviation = 4.81.

　　　　Workings:

X	$\bar{X}$	$X - \bar{X}$	$(X - \bar{X})^2$
53	55.6	−2.6	6.76
61	55.6	5.4	29.16
54	55.6	−1.6	2.56
59	55.6	3.4	11.56
59	55.6	3.4	11.56
48	55.6	−7.6	57.76
53	55.6	−2.6	6.76
49	55.6	−6.6	43.56
60	55.6	4.4	19.36
60	55.6	4.4	19.36
Total			208.40

$$SD = \sqrt{\left[\frac{208.40}{10-1}\right]} = 4.81.$$

Assessment 2
Standard deviation = 16.45.

Workings:

X	$\bar{X}$	$X - \bar{X}$	$(X - \bar{X})^2$
55	54.3	0.7	0.49
77	54.3	22.7	515.29
57	54.3	2.7	7.29
70	54.3	15.7	246.49
61	54.3	6.7	44.89
50	54.3	−4.3	18.49
41	54.3	−13.3	176.89
60	54.3	5.7	32.49
17	54.3	−37.3	1391.29
55	54.3	0.7	0.49
Total			2434.10

$$SD = \sqrt{\left[\frac{2434.10}{10-1}\right]} = 16.45.$$

The students' performance was much more variable in the second assessment, because the standard deviation is much larger.

5.2 (a) The data must first be ordered:
     0 0 0 0 1 1 1 1 1 1 1 2 2 2 2 3 3 3 12 16

$$\text{Median} = \frac{n+1}{2} = \frac{21}{1} = 10.5\text{th observation.}$$

10th observation = 1; 11th observation = 1.
Therefore the median number of sexual partners is one.

$$\text{Upper quartile} = \frac{3 \times 21}{4} = 15.75\text{th observation.}$$

15th observation = 2; 16th observation = 3.
Three-quarters (0.75) of the way between 2 and 3 will be 2.75; therefore the upper quartile will be 2.75 sexual partners.

$$\text{Lower quartile} = \frac{21}{4} = 5.25\text{th observation.}$$

5th observation = 1; 6th observation = 1.
Therefore the lower quartile is one sexual partner.

Interquartile range = upper quartile – lower quartile
= 2.75 – 1 = 1.75.

(b) These data are very skewed. They are positively skewed because most women in the sample have had a small number of partners, while two women have had a much larger number of partners. When data are skewed it is better to use the median and interquartile range as measures of the average and spread than to use the mean and standard deviation.

5.3 A box plot is shown in Figure A2.2.
Partial workings for calculating the boxplot are as follows:

Ordered data:

0	0	0	0	0	5	8	10	11	12	13	14	15	18	22
23	26	29	31	32	33	35	37	4	44	55	60	61	65	122

Median = 15.5th observation = 22.5 seconds.
Upper quartile = 23.25th observation = 38 seconds.
Lower quartile = 7.75th observation = 9.5 seconds.
Interquartile range = 38 – 9.5 = 28.5 seconds.

Lower fence = lower quartile – (1.5 × IQR) = 9.5 – (1.5 × 28.5) = –33.25.
First observation above lower fence = 0 seconds.
Upper fence = upper quartile + (1.5 × IQR) = 38 + (1.5 × 28.5) = 80.75
First observation below upper fence = 65 seconds.

Outlier = 122 seconds.

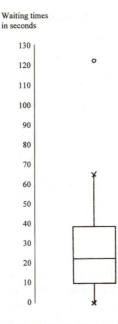

Waiting times
in seconds

FIGURE A2.2 A BOX PLOT OF WAITING TIMES TO PAY AT A PETROL STATION

Comment: the distribution is slightly positively skewed. Half of customers wait for less than 22.5 seconds and three-quarters for less than 38 seconds. The manager might be concerned about the 25% of customers who wait for more than 38 seconds. There is one outlier, a customer who had to wait for over 2 minutes, but this could have been caused by exceptional circumstances.

CHAPTER 6

6.1 (a) Mean price = 157p.
Standard deviation = 40p.
(b) Mean price = 177p (157 + 20).
Standard deviation = 40p (no change).
(c) Mean price = 208p (177 × 1.175).
Standard deviation = 47p (40 × 1.175).

6.2 Answers are given to two decimal places. The means and standard deviations for each variable are as follows:

% total income earned by women: mean = 29.88; SD = 6.20.
% seats in parliament held by women: mean = 9.85; SD = 5.25.
Maternal mortality rate: mean = 383.13; SD = 279.04.

The following working shows the Z-scores for each variable. The signs for the maternal mortality variable have been reversed so that positive values become negative and negative values become positive. The final column shows the mean Z-score for each country.

		Z-SCORES		
Country	% total income earned by women	% seats in parliament held by women	Maternal mortality rate	Z-score index
Philippines	0.18	−0.26	0.37	0.10
India	−0.63	−0.49	−0.67	−0.60
Thailand	1.15	−0.62	0.66	0.40
Malaysia	0.02	0.09	1.09	0.40
Indonesia	0.50	0.52	−0.96	0.02
China	1.31	2.12	1.03	1.49
Bangladesh	−1.11	−0.14	−1.67	−0.97
Pakistan	−1.43	−1.23	0.15	−0.84

A high index value indicates high female empowerment, while a low index value indicates low female empowerment. From the three variables used, it appears that Chinese women are by far the most empowered, followed by women in Thailand and Malaysia. Women are least empowered in Bangladesh and Pakistan.

CHAPTER 7

7.1 (a) 68.2% of the observations lie within one standard deviation either side of the mean; in other words between 85 and 115.

(b) See Figure A2.3.

$$Z = \frac{80 - 100}{15} = -1.33.$$

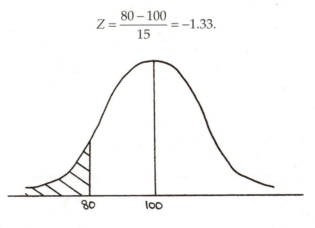

FIGURE A2.3

Area between $Z = -1.33$ and mean is 0.4082.
Area to left of $Z = -1.33$ is: $0.5 - 0.4082 = 0.0918$.
The proportion of the population with an IQ below 80 is 0.0918.

(c) See Figure A2.4.

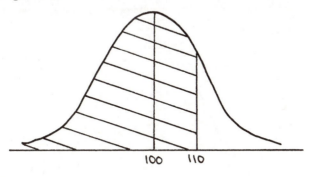

FIGURE A2.4

$$Z = \frac{110 - 100}{15} = 0.67 \text{ (to two decimal places).}$$

Area between mean and $Z = 0.67$ is 0.2486.
Add the 0.5 to the left of the mean: $0.5 + 0.2486 = 0.7486$.
The proportion of the population with an IQ below 110 is 0.7486.

(d) See Figure A2.5.

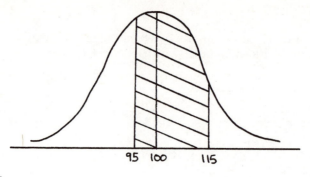

FIGURE A2.5

For the 95: $Z = \dfrac{95-100}{15} = 0.33$.

Area between mean and $Z = 0.33$ is 0.1293.

For the 115: $Z = \dfrac{115-100}{15} = 1$.

Area between mean and $Z = 1$ is 0.3413.
The areas are on opposite sides of the mean, so they can be added together: $0.1293 + 0.3413 = 0.4706$.
The proportion of the population with an IQ between 95 and 115 is 0.4706.

(e) See Figure A2.6.

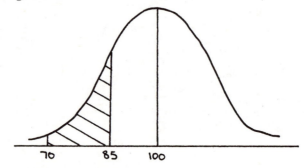

FIGURE A2.6

For the 70: $Z = \dfrac{70-100}{15} = -2$.

Area between mean and $Z = -2$ is 0.4772.

For the 85: $Z = \dfrac{85 - 100}{15} = -1$.

Area between mean and $Z = -1$ is 0.3413.

The areas are on the same side of the mean (both below the mean) and so the smaller area should be subtracted from the larger area: $0.4772 - 0.3413 = 0.1359$.

The proportion of the population with an IQ between 70 and 85 is 0.1359.

(f) See Figure A2.7.

We cannot look up the Z-score for the top 10% directly, but we know that 50% of the observations lie above the mean and we are able to look up the Z-score for the 40% just above the mean. The area 0.4 is looked up in the middle of the tables; the nearest is 0.3997 which gives a Z-score of 1.28. This can then be substituted into the equation for Z, where we know the Z-score, the mean and the standard deviation, and the equation is then rearranged to find the answer:

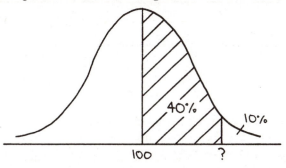

FIGURE A2.7

$$1.28 = \dfrac{? - 100}{15}$$

$? = (1.28 \times 15) + 100 = 119.2$.

The top 10% of the population will have an IQ greater than 119.2.

7.2 (a) See Figure A2.8.

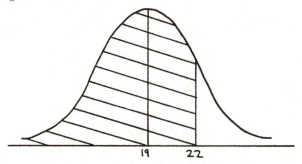

FIGURE A2.8

$$Z = \frac{22 - 19}{3} = 1.$$

Area between mean and $Z = 1$ is 0.3413.
Add 0.5 for the area below the mean: $0.5 + 0.3413 = 0.8413$.
The proportion of students taking less than 22 minutes is 0.8413.
(b) See Figure A2.9.

$$Z = \frac{15 - 19}{3} = -1.33.$$

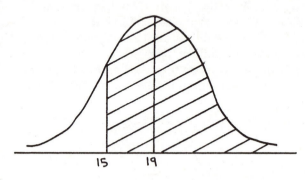

FIGURE A2.9

Area between mean and $Z = -1.33$ is 0.4082.
Add 0.5 for the area above the mean: $0.5 + 0.4082 = 0.9082$.
The proportion of students who take more than 15 minutes is 0.9082.
(c) See Figure A2.10.

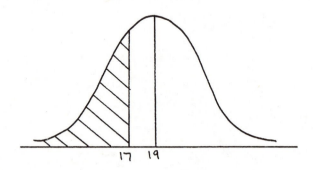

FIGURE A2.10

$$Z = \frac{17 - 19}{3} = -0.67.$$

Area between mean and $Z = -0.67$ is 0.2486.
Area to the left of $Z = -0.67$ is: $0.5 - 0.2486 = 0.2514$.
The proportion of students who take less than 17 minutes is 0.2514.

(d) Here we need to find out the proportion of students who take more than 20 minutes as these students are the ones who will be late for the lecture. See Figure A2.11.

$$Z = \frac{20 - 19}{3} = 0.33.$$

Area between mean and $Z = 0.33$ is 0.1293.
Area to the right of $Z = 0.33$ is: $0.5 - 0.1293 = 0.3707$.

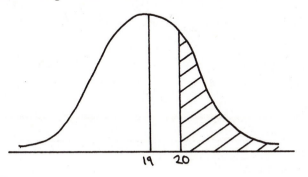

FIGURE A2.11

The proportion of students who would be late is 0.3707.
(e) See Figure A2.12.

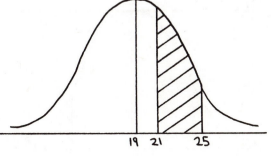

FIGURE A2.12

For the 21: $Z = \frac{21 - 19}{3} = 0.67.$

Area between mean and $Z = 0.67$ is 0.2486.

For the 25: $Z = \frac{25 - 29}{3} = 2.$

Area between mean and $Z = 2$ is 0.4772.

The two areas are on the same side of the mean (both above the mean), so the smaller area should be subtracted from the larger area: 0.4772 − 0.2486 = 0.2286.

The proportion of students who take between 21 and 25 minutes to reach the campus is 0.2286.

7.3 (a) See Figure A2.13.

$$Z = \frac{35 - 58}{10} = -2.3.$$

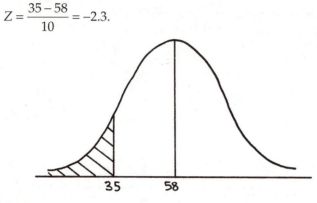

FIGURE A2.13

Area between mean and $Z = -2.3$ is 0.4893.
Area to the left of $Z = -2.3$ is: 0.5 − 0.4893 = 0.0107.
The proportion of students who fail the exam is 0.0107.

(b) See Figure A2.14.

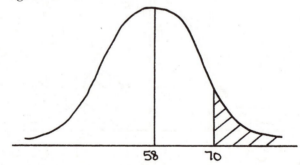

FIGURE A2.14

$$Z = \frac{70 - 58}{10} = 1.2.$$

Area between mean and $Z = 1.2$ is 0.3849.
Area to the right of $Z = 1.2$ is: 0.5 − 0.3849 = 0.1151.
The proportion of students who get an A grade is 0.1151.

(c) We cannot directly find the Z-score corresponding to the top 40%, but we know that 50% of students will get a mark above the mean and we can find the Z-score for the 10% just above the mean (see Figure A2.15). For an area of 0.1, the nearest Z-score is 0.25 (for the area 0.987). This can now be put into the Z-score equation and rearranged:

$$0.25 = \frac{?-58}{10}$$

$$? = (0.25 \times 10) + 58 = 60.5$$

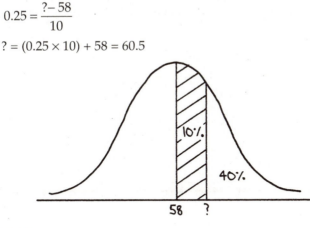

FIGURE A2.15

Therefore 40% of the students obtained a mark higher than 60.5%.

CHAPTER 8

8.1 (a) See Figure A2.16.

$$Z = \frac{4.50 - 4.60}{0.40} = -0.25.$$

Area between mean and $Z = -0.25$ is 0.0987.
Area to left of $Z = -0.25$ is: $0.5 - 0.0987 = 0.4013$.
The probability of an individual worker earning £4.50 or less per hour is 0.4013.

(b) The diagram will be the same as for part (a), i.e. Figure A2.16. Samples of 20 workers will be normally distributed with a mean of £4.60 and a standard error of:

$$SE = \frac{SD}{\sqrt{n}} = \frac{0.40}{\sqrt{20}} = 0.09.$$

Now Z can be calculated using the standard error:

$$Z = \frac{4.50 - 4.60}{0.09} = -1.11.$$

Area between the mean and $Z = -1.11$ is 0.3665.
Area to the left of $Z = -1.11$ is: $0.5 - 0.3665 = 0.1335$.
The probability of obtaining a sample of 20 workers with a mean of £4.50 or less is 0.1335.

(c) The diagram will again be the same as for part (a), i.e. Figure A2.16. Samples of 50 workers will be normally distributed with a mean of £4.60 and a standard error of:

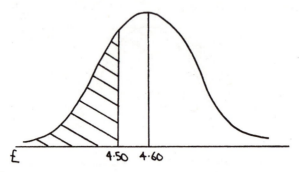

FIGURE A2.16

$$SE = \frac{SD}{\sqrt{n}} = \frac{0.40}{\sqrt{50}} = 0.06.$$

$$Z = \frac{4.50 - 4.60}{0.06} = -1.67.$$

Area between the mean and $Z = -1.67$ is 0.4525.
Area to the left of $Z = -1.67$ is: $0.5 - 0.4525 = 0.0475$.
The probability of obtaining a sample of 50 workers with a mean of £4.50 or less is 0.0475.

(d) The chance of individuals in a population having a particularly high or low score is usually fairly high. However, the chance of a sample of people having such an extreme mean score is always lower because a mean will never be as extreme as the observations. Sample means vary much less than individual scores. This is why the probability in part (b) is lower than in part (a).

The larger the sample size, the more representative the sample should be of the population and the less likely you are to get an extreme mean by chance. This is why the probability in part (c) is lower than the probability in part (b): the sample size is larger.

8.2 See Figure A2.17.
Samples of size 30 will be normally distributed with a mean of £5.10 and a standard error of:

$$SE = \frac{SD}{\sqrt{n}} = \frac{0.50}{\sqrt{30}} = 0.09.$$

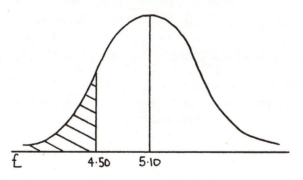

FIGURE A2.17

The Z-score for the workers will be:

$$Z = \frac{4.50 - 5.10}{0.09} = -6.67.$$

This is an extremely low Z-score and cannot be looked up on the tables. Thus we can only conclude that the probability of getting a sample of 30 workers with a mean of £4.50 or less is extremely small. It is likely that the workers are genuinely being underpaid.

8.3 Samples of size 100 will be normally distributed with a mean of 28.5 years and a standard error of:

$$SE = \frac{SD}{\sqrt{n}} = \frac{4.6}{\sqrt{100}} = 0.46.$$

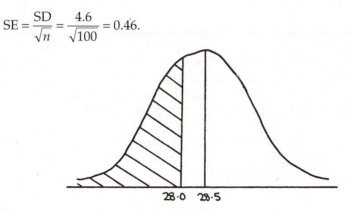

FIGURE A2.18

We are interested in the probability of getting a sample of 100 women with a mean age at birth of 28.0 or lower, as in Figure A2.18.

$$Z = \frac{28.0 - 28.5}{0.46} = -1.09.$$

The area between the mean and $Z = -1.09$ is 0.3621.

The area to the left of $Z = -1.09$ is: $0.5 - 03621 = 0.1379$.

The chance of getting a sample of 100 women with a mean age at birth of 28.0 or less is reasonably high (nearly 14%). So we can conclude that the lower sample mean could have occurred due to chance (sampling variation): there is no evidence that the mean age at birth for women in the deprived area is different to average.

CHAPTER 9

9.1 (a) The mean age at menarche is similar among women aged 16–24, 25–34 and 35–44 at interview. It is, however, slightly higher among women aged 45–59 at interview.

(b) Age $16 - 24$: 95% CI $= 13.40 \pm 1.96 \times \dfrac{1.66}{\sqrt{2172}} = (13.33, \; 13.47)$.

Age $25 - 34$: 95% CI $= 13.42 \pm 1.96 \times \dfrac{1.35}{\sqrt{2810}} = (13.37, \; 13.47)$.

Age $35 - 44$: 95% CI $= 13.41 \pm 1.96 \times \dfrac{1.52}{\sqrt{2481}} = (13.35, \; 13.47)$.

Age $45 - 59$: 95% CI $= 13.54 \pm 1.96 \times \dfrac{1.56}{\sqrt{2606}} = (13.48, \; 13.60)$.

The confidence intervals for the age groups 16–24, 25–34 and 35–44 overlap and so there was no real change in the age at menarche between these age groups. The confidence interval for the 45–59 age group does not overlap with the other confidence intervals, so we can conclude that there is a real difference in the age at menarche between the 45–59 age group and the younger age groups.

9.2 (a) The best estimate for the 'Tony Blair rating' for all students is the sample mean, 12.1.

(b) 95% CI $= 12.1 \pm 1.96 \times \dfrac{3.5}{\sqrt{40}} = (11.02, \; 13.18)$.

99% CI $= 12.1 \pm 2.575 \times \dfrac{3.5}{\sqrt{40}} = (10.67, \; 13.53)$.

This is wider than the 95% confidence interval. If we want to be more confident that the population mean lies within the interval, the interval must be widened.

(c) 95% CI $= 12.1 \pm 1.96 \times \dfrac{3.5}{\sqrt{100}} = (11.41, \; 12.79)$.

With a larger sample size, the confidence interval is narrower. This is because a larger sample is more representative of the population and will provide a more precise estimate of the population mean.

9.3 Sample mean = £80 318.18.
Sample standard deviation = £7585.42.
Best estimate of population mean is £80 318.18.

$$95\% \text{ CI} = 80\,318.18 \pm 1.96 \times \frac{7585.42}{\sqrt{11}} = (£75\,835.48, \ £84\,800.88).$$

The sample of prices may not be particularly representative because the sample size is rather small and, if the sample is drawn from one estate agent only, we cannot be sure that the prices will be similar in all estate agents.

CHAPTER 10

10.1 (a) *Males*

$$\text{Sample proportion} = \frac{21}{50} = 0.42.$$

Best estimate of population proportion = 0.42.

$$95\% \text{ CI} = 0.42 \pm \left\{ 1.96 \sqrt{\left[\frac{0.42 \times (1 - 0.42)}{50} \right]} \right\} = (0.2832, \ 0.5568).$$

Females

$$\text{Sample proportion} = \frac{35}{50} = 0.7.$$

Best estimate of population proportion = 0.7.

$$95\% \text{ CI} = 0.7 \pm \left\{ 1.96 \sqrt{\left[\frac{0.7 \times (1 - 0.7)}{50} \right]} \right\} = (0.5730, \ 0.8270).$$

Although the confidence intervals are quite wide, they do not overlap, so we can say that male students are definitely less likely than female students to believe that one-night stands are usually not a good idea.

(b) *Males*

Sample proportion $= \dfrac{65}{150} = 0.4333.$

Best estimate of population proportion = 0.4333.

$$95\% \text{ CI} = 0.4333 \pm \left\{ 1.96 \sqrt{\left[\frac{0.4333 \times (1 - 0.4333)}{150} \right]} \right\} = (0.3540, \ 0.5126).$$

Females

Sample proportion $= \dfrac{110}{150} = 0.7333.$

Best estimate of population proportion = 0.7333.

$$95\% \text{ CI} = 0.7333 \pm \left\{ 1.96 \sqrt{\left[\frac{0.7333 \times (1 - 0.7333)}{150} \right]} \right\} = (0.6625, \ 0.8041).$$

The confidence intervals for males and females do not overlap, so there is a significant gender difference in attitudes.

10.2 Proportions in samples of size 100 will be normally distributed with:
Mean proportion = 0.131.

$$\text{Standard error} = \sqrt{\left[\frac{\Pi(1 - \Pi)}{n} \right]} = \sqrt{\left[\frac{0.131 \times (1 - 0.131)}{100} \right]} = 0.03.$$

Note that for these questions the percentages must be converted into proportions.

(a) See Figure A2.19.

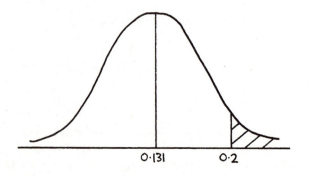

FIGURE A2.19

$$Z = \frac{0.2 - 0.131}{0.03} = 2.3.$$

Area between mean and $Z = 2.3$ is 0.4893.
Area to right of $Z = 2.3$ is: $0.5 - 0.4893 = 0.0107$.
The chance that 20 or more people in the sample have had an HIV test is 0.0107 (a very low chance).

(b)   See Figure A2.20.

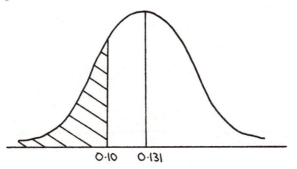

FIGURE A2.20

$$Z = \frac{0.10 - 0.131}{0.03} = -1.03.$$

Area between mean and $Z = -1.03$ is 0.3485.
Area to the left of $Z = -1.03$ is: $0.5 - 0.3485 = 0.1515$.
The chance of getting a sample where 10 or fewer people have had an HIV test is 0.1515.

(c)   See Figure A2.21.

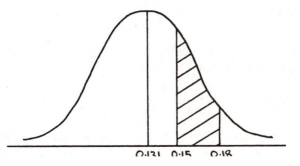

FIGURE A2.21

For 15: $Z = \frac{0.15 - 0.131}{0.03} = 0.63.$

Area between mean and $Z = 0.63$ is 0.2357.

For 18: $\quad Z = \dfrac{0.18 - 0.131}{0.03} = 1.63.$

Area between mean and $Z = 1.63$ is 0.4484.

The two areas are both above the mean, so the smaller area is subtracted from the larger area: $0.4484 - 0.2357 = 0.2127$.
The chance of getting a sample where between 15 and 18 people have had an HIV test is 0.2127.

10.3 (a) Sample proportion supporting proposal $= \dfrac{80}{200} = 0.4.$

The best estimate of the population proportion is 0.4.

$$95\% \text{ CI} = 0.4 \pm \left\{ 1.96 \sqrt{\left[\frac{0.4 \times (1 - 0.4)}{200} \right]} \right\} = (0.3321, \ 0.4679).$$

(b) $\quad 99\% \text{ CI} = 0.4 \pm \left\{ 2.575 \sqrt{\left[\frac{0.4 \times (1 - 0.4)}{200} \right]} \right\} = (0.3108, \ 0.4892).$

The 99% confidence interval is wider than the 95% confidence interval because if we want to be more certain that the population proportion lies within the range, the range must be wider.

(c) If the true population proportion is 0.6, sample proportions of samples of 200 people will be normally distributed with a mean of 0.6 and a standard error of:

$$\text{Standard error} = \sqrt{\left[\frac{0.6 \times (1 - 0.6)}{200} \right]} = 0.03.$$

What is the chance of getting a sample with a proportion of 0.4 or less from this distribution? See Figure A2.22.

$$Z = \frac{0.4 - 0.6}{0.03} = -6.67.$$

This Z-score is extremely low and tells us that the chance of getting a sample of 200 with a proportion of 0.4 is extremely small. It is very unlikely that the sample did come from a population with a proportion of 0.6 supporting, and so the council member is almost certainly wrong in saying that 60% of the population support the proposal.

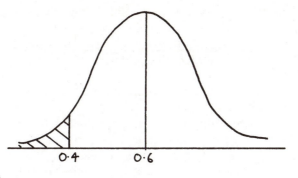

FIGURE A2.22

CHAPTER 11

11.1 This is a two-sided test for a mean.

H_o: $\mu = 2.5$ (alcohol consumption among 14-year-old girls from the local school is the same as the national average).
H_A: $\mu \neq 2.5$ (alcohol consumption among 14-year-old girls from the local school is different to the national average).

Sample mean = 2.8.

Test statistic: $Z = \dfrac{2.8 - 2.5}{0.8 / \sqrt{34}} = 2.19.$

The critical values are −1.96 and 1.96. The test statistic 2.19 is greater than 1.96 and so lies in the critical region. We can reject the null hypothesis and conclude that there is evidence that alcohol consumption among girls in the sample is significantly different to the national average.

11.2 The question asks for a one-sided test.
H_o: $\mu = £688.80$ (social workers in the sample earn the same as the national average).
H_A: $\mu < £688.80$ (social workers in the sample earn less than the national average).

Sample mean = £542.

Test statistic: $Z = \dfrac{542 - 688.80}{321 / \sqrt{11}} = -1.52.$

For a one-sided test at the 5% level, the critical value is −1.645. The test statistic does not fall in the critical region to the left of −1.645 (it is greater than −1.645) and so we must accept the null hypothesis and conclude that the social workers' claim cannot be justified.

You may be surprised at this result, given that the income in the sample is so much lower than the average. However, the standard deviation is very large and the sample size quite small, both of which make it less likely that the null hypothesis will be rejected.

11.3 This is a two-sided test for a proportion.

$H_0: \Pi = 0.638$ (the proportion of people believing that crime prevention is an important issue has not changed).
$H_A: \Pi \neq 0.638$ (the proportion of people believing that crime prevention is an important issue has changed over time).

Sample proportion $= \dfrac{204}{350} = 0.5829$.

Test statistic: $Z = \dfrac{p - \Pi}{\sqrt{\left[\dfrac{\Pi(1 - \Pi)}{n}\right]}} = \dfrac{0.5829 - 0.638}{\sqrt{\left[\dfrac{0.638 \times (1 - 0.638)}{350}\right]}} = -2.14$.

The critical values for a two-sided test at the 5% level are –1.96 and 1.96. The test statistic –2.14, is less than –1.96 and so the null hypothesis can be rejected. We conclude that there is evidence to suggest that the proportion of people believing that crime prevention is an important issue has changed significantly over time.

11.4 The question asks for a two-sided test.

$H_0: \mu = £8.34$ (the hourly pay rate of Pakistani and Bangladeshi men in Britain is the same as the hourly pay rate for white men).
$H_A: \mu \neq £8.34$ (the hourly pay rate of Pakistani and Bangladeshi men in Britain is different to the hourly pay rate for white men).

Sample mean = £6.92.

Test statistic: $Z = \dfrac{6.92 - 8.34}{2.12 / \sqrt{55}} = -4.97$.

(a) The critical values for a two-sided test at the 5% level are –1.96 and 1.96. The test statistic –4.97 lies well below –1.96, so the null hypothesis can be rejected. It appears that there is evidence that the hourly pay rate for men of Pakistani and Bangladeshi origin is different to the rate for white men.

(b) For a test at the 1% level, the critical values would be –2.575 and 2.575. The test statistic is still lower than –2.575, so the conclusion remains the same.

11.5 As we do not know what the outcome might be, a two-sided test will be used.

$H_o: \Pi = 0.4$ (the response rate on a postal survey about an issue of local concern is 40%).

$H_A: \Pi \neq 0.4$ (the response rate on a postal survey about an issue of local concern is different to 40%).

Sample proportion $= \dfrac{18}{60} = 0.3$.

Test statistic: $Z = \dfrac{0.3 - 0.4}{\sqrt{\left[\dfrac{0.4 \times (1 - 0.4)}{60}\right]}} = -1.58$.

The critical values are –1.96 and 1.96, so the test statistic –1.58 does not lie in the critical region. The null hypothesis must be accepted. There is no evidence at the 5% level to suggest that the researcher's claim is incorrect, so we must assume that it is correct from the evidence we have.

11.6 This will be a two-sided test for a proportion.

$H_o: \Pi = 0.68$ (the proportion of adult smokers at the health centre who want to give up smoking is the same as the national proportion).

$H_A: \Pi \neq 0.68$ (the proportion of adult smokers at the health centre who want to give up smoking is different to the national proportion).

Sample proportion $= \dfrac{89}{124} = 0.7177$.

Test statistic: $Z = \dfrac{0.7177 - 0.68}{\sqrt{\left[\dfrac{0.68 \times (1 - 0.68)}{124}\right]}} = 0.90$.

For a two-sided test, the critical values will be –1.96 and 1.96. The test statistic 0.90 does not lie in the critical region outside these values and so the null hypothesis must be accepted. Smokers at the health centre are not significantly different to those in the country as a whole in their desire to give up.

CHAPTER 12

12.1 This is a two-sided test. The population standard deviation is unknown and the sample size is less than 30, so a t test should be used.

H_0: $\mu = £158$ (the weekly household expenditure of lone mothers in your area is the same as the national average).

H_A: $\mu \neq £158$ (the weekly household expenditure of lone mothers in your area is different to the national average).

Test statistic: $t = \dfrac{149 - 158}{33 / \sqrt{16}} = -1.09.$

From a sample of 16, there are 15 degrees of freedom. For a two-sided test at the 5% level, $t_{15} = 2.1314$ (look down the $t_{df}(0.025)$ column in Table A1.2 because there is 2.5% in each tail). The critical values are -2.1314 and 2.1314. The test statistic lies inside this range, so the null hypothesis must be accepted. The household expenditure of lone mothers in your area is no different to the national average.

12.2 The question asks for a one-tailed test and a t test is used because the standard deviation of the population is not known and the sample size is less than 30.

H_0: $\mu = £1.80$ (the children are receiving the average amount of pocket money).

H_A: $\mu < £1.80$ (the children are receiving less pocket money than average).

Test statistic: $t = \dfrac{1.56 - 1.80}{0.45 / \sqrt{25}} = -2.67.$

With a sample of 25, there will be 24 degrees of freedom. For a one-sided test at the 5% level there is 5% in one tail of the distribution, so we look down the $t_{df}(0.05)$ column in Table A1.2 to obtain $t_{24} = 1.7109$. The critical value will be -1.7109 because we are trying to find out whether the children are getting significantly *less* pocket money than the mean.

The test statistic -2.67 is less than -1.7109, so the null hypothesis can be rejected. The children are receiving significantly less pocket money than the mean.

12.3 $\Pi_m = 0.5$ (the charges for swimming in leisure pools in metropolitan districts come from a population where half the observations are above £2.50; charges in metropolitan districts are the same as charges in London).

$\Pi_m \neq 0.5$ (the charges for swimming in leisure pools in metropolitan districts do not come from a population where half the observations are above £2.50; charges in metropolitan districts are different to charges in London).

There are nine negative signs (observations below £2.50) and one positive sign (observation above £2.50). Thus the sample proportion is:

$$p_m = \frac{\text{number of plus signs}}{\text{total}} = \frac{1}{10} = 0.1$$

Test statistic: $\quad Z = \dfrac{p_m - \Pi_m}{\sqrt{\left[\dfrac{\Pi_m(1-\Pi_m)}{n}\right]}} = \dfrac{0.1 - 0.5}{\sqrt{\left[\dfrac{0.5 \times (1-0.5)}{10}\right]}} = -2.53.$

The critical values at the 5% level are –1.96 and 1.96. The test statistic is greater than 1.96, so the null hypothesis can be rejected. The charges for leisure pool swimming in metropolitan districts are significantly different to the charges for swimming in London.

12.4 $\Pi_m = 0.5$ (sponsorship amounts come from a population with half the observations above £63.20; the amount raised per rider has not changed since last year).

$\Pi_m \neq 0.5$ (sponsorship amounts do not come from a population with half the observations above £63.20; the amount raised per rider has changed since last year).

There are 12 positive signs (amounts over £63.20) in the sample. The sample proportion is:

$$p_m = \frac{12}{20} = 0.6.$$

Test statistic: $\quad Z = \dfrac{0.6 - 0.5}{\sqrt{\left[\dfrac{0.5 \times (1-0.5)}{20}\right]}} = 0.89.$

The critical values are –1.96 and 1.96. The test statistic lies within this range, so the null hypothesis must be accepted. There has been no significant change in sponsorship money per rider since last year.

CHAPTER THIRTEEN

13.1 (a) The mean first-semester exam marks will be the Y variable because they may depend on the A level scores.

   (b) The scatter graph (Figure A2.23) does not show a very strong association between A level scores and first-semester exam results.

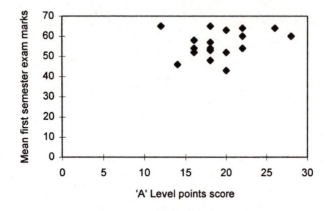

FIGURE A2.23 'A' LEVEL POINTS SCORE AND MEAN FIRST SEMESTER EXAM MARK FOR 18 STUDENTS (ANONYMOUS STUDENT RECORDS)

   (c) Calculation of the correlation coefficient:

X	Y	$(X-\bar{X})$	$(Y-\bar{Y})$	$(X-\bar{X})^2$	$(Y-\bar{Y})^2$	$(X-\bar{X}) \times (Y-\bar{Y})$
18	54	−1.11	−2.22	1.23	4.93	2.46
18	48	−1.11	−8.22	1.23	67.57	9.12
16	52	−3.11	−4.22	9.67	17.81	13.12
18	65	−1.11	8.78	1.23	77.09	−9.75
14	46	−5.11	−10.22	26.11	104.45	52.22
12	65	−7.11	8.78	50.55	77.09	−62.43
20	52	0.89	−4.22	0.79	17.81	−3.76
18	57	−1.11	0.78	1.23	0.61	−0.87
20	63	0.89	6.78	0.79	45.97	6.03
18	53	−1.11	−3.22	1.23	10.37	3.57
26	64	6.89	7.78	47.47	60.53	53.60
16	54	−3.11	−2.22	9.67	4.93	6.90
20	43	0.89	−13.22	0.79	174.77	−11.77
16	58	−3.11	1.78	9.67	3.17	−5.54
28	60	8.89	3.78	79.03	14.29	33.60
22	64	2.89	7.78	8.35	60.53	22.48
22	60	2.89	3.78	8.35	14.29	10.92
22	54	2.89	−2.22	8.35	4.93	−6.42
$\bar{X}= 19.11$	$\bar{Y} = 56.22$		Totals	265.74	761.14	113.48

Correlation coefficient: $r = \dfrac{113.48}{\sqrt{(265.74 \times 761.14)}} = 0.25.$

This indicates a very weak positive correlation between A level scores and first semester exam marks among the 18 students.

(d) $r^2 = 0.25^2 = 0.06$.

A level scores are not a good predictor of first semester exam marks among this group of students; A level scores only explain 6% of the difference in mean exam marks. Perhaps motivation, ability to work independently or other factors are more important than past achievements.

13.2 (a) Figure A2.24 shows a positive relationship between life expectancy at birth and the percentage of the population with access to clean water in the 10 countries. Note that life expectancy is the dependent variable here because life expectancy may depend in part on water quality.

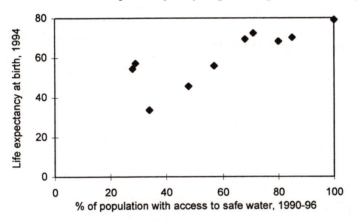

FIGURE A2.24 LIFE EXPECTANCY AT BIRTH AND PERCENTAGE OF POPULATION WITH ACCESS TO CLEAN WATER IN 10 DEVELOPING COUNTRIES (UNDP, 1997)

(b) Calculation of correlation coefficient and regression coefficients:

X	Y	$(X-\bar{X})$	$(Y-\bar{Y})$	$(X-\bar{X})^2$	$(Y-\bar{Y})^2$	$(X-\bar{X})$ $(Y-\bar{Y})$
100	79.0	40	18.43	1600	339.66	737.20
71	72.4	11	11.83	121	139.95	130.13
85	70.1	25	9.53	625	90.82	238.25
68	69.3	8	8.73	64	76.21	69.84
80	68.2	20	7.63	400	58.22	152.60
57	55.9	-3	-4.67	9	21.81	14.01
29	57.2	-31	-3.37	961	11.36	104.47
28	54.4	-32	-6.17	1024	38.07	197.44
48	45.6	-12	-14.97	144	224.10	179.64
34	33.6	-26	-26.97	676	727.38	701.22
$\bar{X} = 60$	$\bar{Y} = 60.57$		Totals	5624	1727.58	2524.80

Correlation coefficient: $r = \dfrac{2524.80}{\sqrt{(5624 \times 1727.58)}} = 0.81$.

A correlation of 0.81 indicates a strong positive correlation: countries where a high percentage of the population has access to safe water are likely to have high life expectancy at birth.

(c) Here you should have already calculated the values to put into the equations during the calculation in (b) to find the correlation coefficient.

$$b = \frac{\sum \left(X_i - \overline{X} \right)\left(Y_i - \overline{Y} \right)}{\sum \left(X_i - \overline{X} \right)^2} = \frac{2524.80}{5624} = 0.45.$$

$$a = \overline{Y} - b\overline{X} = 60.57 - \left(0.45 \times 60 \right) = 33.57.$$

(d) The regression line is $Y = a + bX$:

Life expectancy at birth = 33.57 + (0.45 × % with access to safe water).

(e) Life expectancy = 33.57 + (0.45 × 0) = 33.57 years.

This is a realistic figure for life expectancy at birth, but it may be unrealistic to expect that nobody in a country has access to safe water. In any case, the value of 0% with access to safe water is outside the range of the data, so we should not predict life expectancy from it.

(f) (i) $Y = 33.57 + (0.45 \times 40) = 51.57$ years.
    (ii) $Y = 33.57 + (0.45 \times 52) = 56.97$ years.
    (iii) $Y = 33.57 + (0.45 \times 90) = 74.07$ years.

CHAPTER 14

14.1 (a) See Table A2.4. It appears that a large proportion of boys did not plan their first intercourse, along with a smaller proportion of girls.

TABLE A2.4 Whether first intercourse was planned by respondent: table including totals

Was first intercourse planned by respondent?	Sex		
	Female	Male	Total
Yes	14	7	21
Somewhat/sort of	11	7	18
No	18	29	47
Total	43	43	86

Source: Ingham et al., 1996

(b) H_0: there is no association between gender and whether first intercourse is planned or not.

H_A: there is an association between gender and whether first intercourse is planned or not.

TABLE A2.5 Expected values for question 14.1 (b)

Was first intercourse planned by respondent?	Sex Female	Male	Total
Yes	10.5	10.5	21
Somewhat/sort of	9.0	9.0	18
No	23.5	23.5	47
Total	43	43	86

The expected values are shown in Table A2.5. The test statistic is calculated as follows:

O	E	$\dfrac{(O-E)^2}{E}$
14	10.5	1.17
11	9.0	0.44
18	23.5	1.29
7	10.5	1.17
7	9.0	0.44
29	23.5	1.29

$$\chi^2 = 5.80$$

There are two degrees of freedom and so, at the 5% level, $\chi^2_{2,\,0.05} = 5.9915$.

The test statistic 5.80 is slightly smaller than 5.9915, so it does not lie in the critical region. We must accept the null hypothesis and conclude that there is no significant association at the 5% level between gender and whether intercourse is planned or not.

14.2 (a) H_o: there is no association between highest educational qualification and number of children ever born.

H_A: there is an association between highest educational qualification and number of children ever born.

TABLE A2.6 Expected values for question 14.2 (a)

Highest educational qualification	Number of children born 0	1 or 2	3 or more	Total
A level equivalent or higher	82.81	365.96	221.23	670
Below A level or none	258.19	1141.04	689.77	2089
Total	341.00	1507.00	911.00	2759

The expected values are shown in Table A2.6 and the test statistic is calculated as follows:

O	E	$\dfrac{(O-E)^2}{E}$
116	82.81	13.30
225	258.19	4.27
364	365.96	0.01
1143	1141.04	0.00
190	221.23	4.41
721	689.77	1.41

$$\chi^2 = 23.40$$

There are two degrees of freedom, so the χ^2 critical value will be 5.9915. The test statistic is well above the critical value (23.40 > 5.9915) and so the null hypothesis can be rejected. There is an association between educational qualifications and the number of children ever born to women.

(b) If the test were carried out at the 1% level, the critical value would be 9.2103. The test statistic 23.40 is greater than this, so the null hypothesis would still be rejected. There is a significant association at the 1% level between educational qualifications and number of children ever born.

(c) The residuals are shown in Table A2.7. Three of the residuals are significant because they are greater than 2 or less than −2. We can conclude that women with A Level or higher qualifications are significantly more likely to have no children (because the residual is positive) and significantly less likely to have three or more children (because the residual is negative) than women with lower qualification levels. Women with qualifications below A level standard are significantly less likely to have no children than more highly qualified women.

TABLE A2.7 Residuals for question two 14.2 (c)

Highest educational qualification	Number of children born		
	0	**1 or 2**	**3 or more**
A level equivalent or higher	3.65	−0.10	−2.10
Below A level or none	−2.07	0.06	1.19

14.3 (a) The expected values are shown in Table A2.8. Two of the expected values are below 5; this is a problem if we want to carry out a χ^2 test.

TABLE A2.8 Expected values for question 14.3 (a)

Placement type	Sibling status		Total
	With siblings	Without siblings	
Foster care	51.83	129.17	181
Home on trial	4.87	12.13	17
Residential	3.15	7.85	11
Other	5.15	12.85	18
Total	65.00	162.00	227

(b) The expected values after collapsing the 'residential' and 'other' categories are shown in Table A2.9.

TABLE A2.9 Expected values for question 14.3 (b), after collapsing categories

Placement type	Sibling status		Total
	With siblings	Without siblings	
Foster care	51.83	129.17	181.00
Home on trial/residential	8.02	19.98	28
Other	5.15	12.85	18
Total	65.00	162.00	227

(c) H_0: there is no association between having a sibling or not and the type of residential placement.
H_A: there is an association between having a sibling or not and the type of residential placement.

The test statistic is calculated as follows:

O	E	$\frac{(O-E)^2}{E}$
53	51.83	0.03
8	8.02	0.00
4	5.15	0.26
128	129.17	0.01
20	19.98	0.00
14	12.85	0.10

$$\chi^2 = 0.40$$

There are two degrees of freedom, so the critical value for a test at the 5% level will be 5.9915. The test statistic is much smaller than the critical value, so the null hypothesis would be accepted. There is no association between having a sibling or not and the type of residential placement.

Appendix 3

BASIC MATHS CHECK

If you struggled with maths at school, or indeed if school itself is a very distant memory, this appendix is for you. You could either check through it at the start of the course to get your maths up to scratch, or use it as a reference guide if you get stuck on a specific topic later on.

This maths check covers three areas of mathematical knowledge that are assumed elsewhere in the book: proportions and percentages, negative numbers, and algebra.

PROPORTIONS AND PERCENTAGES

Proportions and percentages are very similar, the main difference being that a proportion can take any value from 0 to 1 inclusive, while a percentage usually takes a value from 0% to 100% (although percentages greater than 100% are possible).

To change a proportion into a percentage or vice versa, simply follow the rules below:

> Proportion → percentage: multiply by 100
>
> Percentage → proportion: divide by 100

For example:

- To turn the proportion 0.56 into a percentage, multiply by 100: $0.56 \times 100 = 56\%$.
- To turn the percentage 48.5% into a proportion, divide by 100: $48.5 \div 100 = 0.485$.

Notice that when you do this, the numbers stay the same and just the decimal point moves.

Usually, life is not this simple and you will have to start from scratch with some numbers. For example, you send a postal survey to 144 people, but only 108 of them respond. What proportion respond? Here, the total number of people is 144 and the number we are interested in, the number who responded, is 108. To find the proportion who responded, we divide 108 by the total 144 as follows:

$$\text{Proportion responding} = \frac{108}{144} = 0.75$$

The percentage responding will be the proportion multiplied by 100:

$$\text{Percentage responding} = \frac{108}{144} \times 100 = 75\%.$$

So to calculate a proportion or percentage from some data, the rules are:

$$\text{Proportion} = \frac{\text{number of interest}}{\text{total}}$$

$$\text{Percentage} = \frac{\text{number of interest}}{\text{total}} \times 100$$

Another example would be if you counted that 63 students out of the 94 studying sociology were female. The proportion and percentage of female students are calculated as follows. (Normally you would calculate either the proportion *or* the percentage, not both.)

$$\text{Proportion female} = \frac{63}{94} = 0.6702$$

$$\text{Percentage female} = \frac{63}{94} \times 100 = 67.02\%.$$

Watch out, in case you are not given the total. If a friend studying politics told you that there were 82 males and 44 females in his year group, you must first find the total number of students studying politics before calculating the proportion who are male or female:

$$\text{Total students} = 82 + 44 = 126$$

$$\text{Proportion male} = \frac{82}{126} = 0.6508$$

$$\text{Proportion female} = \frac{44}{126} = 0.3492.$$

Note that because all the students have been classified as either male or female, the two proportions add up to exactly 1.

NEGATIVE NUMBERS

Most people intuitively understand what a negative number such as –5 means. Difficulties with negative numbers usually occur when a calculation is involved, for example, when two negative numbers are multiplied together, or a negative number is subtracted from another number.

The rules to follow here are:

Two signs the same → makes a positive (+)

Two different signs → makes a negative (–)

Let's first apply these rules to adding and subtracting. In this case, what matters is whether the two signs together in the middle are the same or different.

When you have two pluses together in the middle, they combine to make a plus (two signs the same). For example:

$$+8 + (+2) = +10$$

This is normally written $8 + 2 = 10$ because we usually assume that numbers are positive (+) unless we are told otherwise.

When you have a plus and a minus together in the middle, the two signs are different so they combine to make a minus. For example:

Either $\quad 8 + (-2) = 8 - 2 = 6$
Or $\qquad 8 - (+2) = 8 - 2 = 6$

Two minuses together however make a plus because the signs are the same. For example:

$$8 - (-2) = 8 + 2 = 10$$

Similar rules apply to multiplying and dividing. This time the signs of the two numbers you are multiplying or dividing by are important. If both numbers are the same (both positive or both negative), the result will be positive. If one number is positive and the other negative, the result will be a negative number.

For example, multiplying:

$3 \times 3 = 9 \quad$ signs same
$-3 \times -3 = 9 \quad$ signs same
$-3 \times 3 = -9 \quad$ signs different
$3 \times -3 = -9 \quad$ signs different

For example, dividing:

$6 \div 3 = 2 \quad$ signs same
$-6 \div -3 = 2 \quad$ signs same
$-6 \div 3 = -2 \quad$ signs different
$6 \div -3 = -2 \quad$ signs different

ALGEBRA

We have deliberately not called this section 'Basic algebra' or 'Simple algebra' because you may feel initially that it is anything but simple! However, algebra is really all about following a set of rules, so providing you understand and follow the rules, you cannot go far wrong. There is nothing mysterious about it!

There are two main things you need to know: what order to do things in, and how to move something from one side of an equation to the other.

What order to do things in!

Equations are often full of +, −, × and ÷ signs, along with brackets. Where do you start?

The main thing to remember is to work out anything inside brackets first. For example:

$$(10 + 8) \div 2$$

Here you should work out the 10 + 8 in brackets first and then divide by 2 to get an answer of 9:

$$(10 + 8) \div 2 = 18 \div 2 = 9$$

However, if the same equation was written with the brackets in a different place, the answer would be different! In the following example, the 8 ÷ 2 in brackets must be calculated first, before adding onto the 10:

$$10 + (8 \div 2) = 10 + 4 = 14$$

Brackets can clearly make quite a big difference!

Sometimes there will not be any brackets in an equation, where perhaps there should be. In such cases, × and ÷ operations should always be carried out before + and − operations.

If our equation was written with no brackets, as follows, the 8 ÷ 2 should be calculated before adding the 10, because dividing has priority over adding:

$$10 + 8 \div 2 = 10 + 4 = 14$$

Moving things from one side of an equation to the other

The most common type of equation that you will meet will be something like the one following. The aim is to solve the equation by working out what the value of X is. To do this you need to get X on its own on one side of the equation and all the other numbers on the other side.

$$X + 2 = 5 \qquad X = ?$$

But how can we move something over to the other side?

The answer is to move it and change the +, −, × or ÷ to its opposite:

Opposites:	+ changes to −
	− changes to +
	× changes to ÷
	÷ changes to ×

To solve $X + 2 = 5$, the 2 needs to be moved to the other side of the = sign, to leave the X on its own. As the 2 is added to the left-hand side, it can be subtracted from the right-hand side to solve the equation:

$$X + 2 = 5 \rightarrow X = 5 - 2 \rightarrow X = 3$$

The following are some more examples of equations solved using this method:

$$X - 3 = 8 \rightarrow X = 8 + 3 \rightarrow X = 11$$

$$X \div 4 = 10 \rightarrow X = 10 \times 4 \rightarrow X = 40$$

$$X \times 2 = 30 \rightarrow X = 30 \div 2 \rightarrow X = 15$$

More complex equations may involve the use of brackets and negative numbers. The following examples show in detail how four equations are solved. The workings are given on the left, with explanations on the right.

EXAMPLE 1

$$\frac{X + 5}{10} = 2.5$$

To solve the equation, we must get X on its own

$X + 5 = 2.5 \times 10$ The whole left-hand side was divided by 10. The 10 has been moved over to the other side and is now multiplied (remember × is the opposite of ÷).

$X + 5 = 25$ The right-hand side is worked out.

$X = 25 - 5$ The + 5 is moved to the other side and becomes −5.

$X = 20$ The equation is solved!

EXAMPLE 2

$X - (2 \times 3) = 10$

$X - (6) = 10$ The section in brackets was worked out first.

$X = 10 + 6$ The 6 is subtracted from the left-hand side and so can be moved to the right-hand side and added.

$X = 16$ The equation is solved.

EXAMPLE 3

$\dfrac{X}{5} = 6 + (-2)$

$\dfrac{X}{5} = 4$ The right-hand side has been calculated. The + and − signs combine to make a −, and 6 − 2 = 4.

$X = 4 \times 5$ The left-hand side was divided by 5, so the 5 is moved to the right-hand side and is multiplied.

$X = 20$ The equation is solved.

EXAMPLE 4

$3X + 2 = 11$

$3X = 11 - 2$ To remove the +2 from the left-hand side it is subtracted from the right-hand side.

$3X = 9$ The right-hand side is worked out.

$X = 9 \div 3$ $3X$ means 3 times X. To get rid of the × 3, it must be moved to the other side and changed to ÷ 3.

$X = 3$ The equation is solved.

Hopefully this appendix will have given you some hints on coping with the maths involved with statistics. If these kinds of things are still causing you great problems, try looking at a GCSE maths textbook.

Appendix 4

MATHEMATICAL NOTATION EXPLAINED

This book has avoided using notation as much as possible. However you will need to understand what various notations mean when you see them elsewhere.

Believe it or not, mathematical jargon is designed to make life easier for you rather than harder! Using letters is much quicker than writing down lots of numbers, and fortunately there are only a few things you need to know about at this stage.

Often we use letters as shorthand for variables. For example we might be investigating population growth and infant mortality in eight countries. We could call the two variables X and Y for speed, so:

$$\text{Population growth} = X$$
$$\text{Infant mortality} = Y$$

Of the eight countries, the first is Tanzania and the second Kenya. In shorthand therefore:

$$\text{Population growth in Tanzania} = X_1$$
$$\text{Infant mortality in Kenya} = Y_2$$

So the observations will be called $X_1, X_2, \ldots, X_8$ and $Y_1, Y_2, \ldots, Y_8$.

However, this is still quite a long-winded way of writing things. To shorten what we need to write even further, we can use the letter i, where i means any of the countries. The observation for the ith country will be X_i. This is particularly useful when we are adding up a set of observations, for example to calculate a mean or standard deviation.

In Chapter 4 we met Σ, the Greek capital letter sigma, which means 'sum of'. In that chapter, we simply wrote ΣX to indicate 'sum of all the values of X'. However, in most texts you will read, it is written more accurately as follows. To indicate 'sum of values for population growth in the eight countries', we should write:

$$\sum_{i=1}^{8} X_i$$

You can see that X_i has been used as the proper way of writing 'any value of X', and the numbers above and below the Σ indicate 'observations 1 to 8'.

Similarly if we wanted to write 'sum of values for infant mortality for countries 1 to 4', it would be:

$$\sum_{i=1}^{4} Y_i$$

Check that you understand what you have just read by answering the following questions.

QUESTIONS: NOTATION

The following are the ages of four women when they were married for the first time:

Woman	Age	Notation
Pauline	32	X_1
Ramona	21	X_2
Amy	24	X_3
Katrina	27	X_4

What do the following notations (a)–(c) below mean? Work out what number they are equivalent to, using the data in the table.

(a) $\sum_{i=1}^{4} X_i$.

(b) $\left(\sum_{i=1}^{3} X_i \right)^2$.

(c) $\left(\sum_{i=1}^{2} X_i \right)^2 + \left(\sum_{i=3}^{4} X_i \right)^2$.

ANSWERS: NOTATION

(a) The sum of observations 1 to 4:

$$32 + 21 + 24 + 27 = 104$$

(b) The sum of observations 1 to 3, all squared. Note that everything inside the bracket is done first, before squaring:

$$(32 + 21 + 24)^2 = 77^2 = 5929$$

(c) Observations 1 plus 2, squared, added to observations 3 plus 4, squared. Again, the sections in brackets must be worked out first:

$$(32 + 21)^2 + (24 + 27)^2 = 53^2 + 51^2 = 2809 + 2601 = 5410$$

If you can cope with these questions, you should have no problems with understanding notation.

REFERENCES

Butler, David and Kavanagh, Dennis (1992) *The British General Election of 1992*. Macmillan.

CIPFA (1997) *Charges for Leisure Services Statistics 1997–98*. SIS Ref. 82.98, The Chartered Institute of Finance and Accountancy.

Cliffe, David with Berridge, David (1991) *Closing Children's Homes – an End to Residential Childcare?* National Children's Bureau.

Conradt, David P. (1996) *The German Polity*, 6th edn. Longman.

Central Statistical Office (1995) *Social Focus on Women*. Edited by Jenny Church and Carol Summerfield. HMSO.

Department of Health (1997) Personal Social Services, Local Authority Statistics: *Children Looked After by Local Authorities, Year Ending 31 March 1996, England*. Government Statistical Service.

Department of Social Security (1990) *Children Come First: the Government's Proposals on the Maintenance of Children*, vol. 2. HMSO.

Department of the Environment, Transport and the Regions (1997) *Transport Statistics Great Britain, 1997 Edition*. London: The Stationery Office.

Fisher, R.A. and Yates, F. (1974) *Statistical Tables for Biological, Agricultural and Medical Research*. Addison Wesley Longman.

Heath, Anthony, Curtice, John, Jowell, Roger, Evans, Geoff, Field, Julia and Witherspoon, Sharon (1991) *Understanding Political Change – the British Voter 1964–1987*. Pergamon.

Ingham, Roger, Jaramazovic, Emily, Stevens, Diane, Vanwesenbeeck, Ine and Van Zessen, Gertjan (1996) *Detailed Comparative Material from Each Site: Protocol Development for Comparative Studies on Social and Contextual Aspects of Heterosexual Conduct and the Risks of HIV Infection*. European Commission Biomed Concerted Action, BMHI-CT94-1338.

Mosteller, Frederick and Wallace, David, L. (1964) *Inference and Disputed Authorship: The Federalist*. Addison-Wesley.

OECD (1997) *Employment Outlook, July 1997*. OECD.

Office of Population Censuses and Surveys (1993) *1991 Census: Hampshire, Ward and Civil Parish Monitor*. Government Statistical Service.

Office of Population Censuses and Surveys and General Register Office Scotland (1993) *1991 Census: Sex, Age and Marital Status, Great Britain*. Government Statistical Service.

Office for National Statistics Social Survey Division, General Household Survey, 1990–1, 1991–2, 1992–3, 1993–4, 1994–5, 1995–6 (computer files). Colchester, Essex: The Data Archive (distributor). SN:2937, SN:2986, SN:3166, SN:3170, SN:3538, SN:3690.

Office for National Statistics (1996a) *Social Focus on Ethnic Minorities*. Edited by Jenny Church and Carol Summerfield. HMSO.

Office for National Statistics (1996b) On behalf of the HEA: *Health in England 1995 – What People Know, What People Think, What People Do*. Ann Bridgwood, Gill Malbon, Deborah Lader and Jil Matheson.

Office for National Statistics (1997a) *Living in Britain: Results from the 1995 General Household Survey*. Compiled by Olwen Rowlands, Nicola Singleton, Joanne Maher and Vanessa Higgins. London: The Stationery Office.

Office for National Statistics (1997b) *Young Teenagers and Alcohol in 1996. Volume 1: England*. Edited by Eileen Goddard. London: The Stationery Office.

Office for National Statistics (1997c) *Family Spending: A Report on the 1996–97 Family Expenditure Survey*. Government Statistical Service. London: The Stationery Office.

Office for National Statistics (1997d) *New Earnings Survey 1997, Part D, Analyses by Occupation*. London: The Stationery Office.

Office for National Statistics (1997e) *1995 Birth Statistics, England and Wales*. Series FM1 no. 24. London: The Stationery Office.

Office for National Statistics (1998a) *Living in Britain: Results from the 1996 General Household Survey*. Compiled by Margaret Thomas, Alison Walker, Amanda Wilmot and Nikki Bennett. London: The Stationery Office.

Office for National Statistics (1998b) *1991 Census, Key Statistics for Urban and Rural Areas: The South East*. Government Statistical Service.

Salt, John, Singleton, Ann and Hogarth, Jennifer (1994) *Europe's International Migrants*. HMSO.

Tittmar, H.G. (1976) 'Circadian alternations in condom retrieval', *Portsmouth Journal of Psychology*, no. 25: 12–16.

Trussell, James and Westoff, Charles F. (1980) 'Contraceptive practice and trends in coital frequency', *Family Planning Perspectives*, 12(5): 246–249.

UCAS (1995) *University Statistics 1993–94, Volume Two: First Destinations of University Graduates*. Universities' Statistical Record.

UNDP (1997) *Human Development Report 1997*. Oxford University Press.

Wellings, Kaye, Field, Julie, M. Johnson, Anne and Wadsworth, Jane (1994) *Sexual Behaviour in Britain – The National Survey of Sexual Attitudes and Lifestyles*. Penguin.

INDEX